# THE CONTEMPORARY RECEPTION OF CLASSICAL RHETORIC: APPROPRIATIONS OF ANCIENT DISCOURSE

**Kathleen E. Welch**
*Department of English*
*The University of Oklahoma*

Lawrence Erlbaum Associates, Publishers
1990    Hillsdale, New Jersey   Hove and London

Lawrence Erlbaum Associates, Inc., Publishers
365 Broadway
Hillsdale, New Jersey 07642

**Library of Congress Cataloging-in-Publication Data**

Welch, Kathleen E.
  The contemporary reception of classical rhetoric : appropriations
of ancient discourse / Kathleen E. Welch.
    p.  cm. — (Communication)
  Includes bibliographical references.
  ISBN 0-8058-0131-6
  1. Rhetoric.  2. Rhetoric, Ancient.  I. Title.  II. Series:
Communication (Hillsdale, N.J.)
  PN175.W38  1990
808′.009′045 — dc20                                        90-3137
                                                             CIP

Printed in the United States of America
10  9  8  7  6  5  4  3  2  1

*For my parents,*
*Mary Jane and James K. Welch*

# Contents

# Preface

This book presents a version of how classical rhetoric has been studied since 1965 when Edward P. J. Corbett published *Classical Rhetoric for the Modern Student* and suggestions for those appropriations that are the most productive for current rhetoric and composition studies. Many other interpretations exist and are important. In the version presented here, I hope to show that classical rhetoric as it developed in fifth and fourth century B.C. Greece remains powerful as a system for producing texts as well as for interpreting texts. I connect rhetoric and composition throughout the book because I believe that composition is a primary form of rhetoric and one that becomes more powerful when theories of rhetoric are shown to be central to composing.

I hope to contribute to the lively critical conversation that exists now in rhetoric and composition studies and to focus attention on the possibilities and the problems that classical rhetoric as a critical system offers us. Raising questions and suggesting explorations for tentative answers have been central motives in the writing of this book. I have not set out to write a field coverage survey of classical rhetoric but instead to focus on particular questions that can contribute to current constructions of rhetoric and composition studies. The teaching of writing and some of its assumptions are a central concern of the book. I use the word "reception" as interpretation in general rather than in the more particular sense of reception theory that has been a vital area of critical theory. I have tried to make concepts from classical rhetoric as accessible as possible. Consequently, I have deleted accent marks from Greek keywords to encourage wider use of the keywords as loan words. I hope to reach a wide audience in the disciplines of English and Speech Communication and to question some of the assumptions of language study in the last generation.

Earlier versions of some sections have appeared. A few pages of Chapter One appeared in *Rhetoric Review* in a different form. Parts of Chapter Two and a few pages of Chapter Three appeared in *Rhetoric Society Quarterly* in different versions. Chapter Four was published in different form in *Written Communication*.

I thank the Research Council of the University of Oklahoma for providing two summers of research and writing. Dean Kenneth L. Hoving and Dean E. C. Smith of the Graduate College and the Office of Research Administration have supported this project from the beginning, and I am very grateful for their help. My colleagues in rhetoric and composition at the University of Oklahoma English department— Michael C. Flanigan, David Mair, and James N. Comas—have provided ideas, support and a valuable intellectual context for this project. David Mair's careful and sensitive readings of early stages of the manuscript were invaluable. My husband Howard Bluestein has provided understanding and inspiration, and I thank him for his unwavering support. I also thank Donovan J. Ochs and John Frederick Reynolds for reading the completed manuscript and making many important suggestions. I also wish to acknowledge David Marc, Mary McClain, George Econo-mou, Rachel Fagan, and Melanie Wright.

Kathleen E. Welch

# COMMUNICATION

A series of volumes edited by:
**Dolf Zillmann** and **Jennings Bryant**

# PART I

A Critique
of Contemporary
Appropriations of
Classical Rhetoric

# 1

## The Heritage School
## of Classical Rhetoric
## in the United States

The claim that knowledge should be "value-free" is itself a value judgment.

—Terry Eagleton, *Literary Theory*

Each language articulates or organizes the world differently. Languages do not simply name existing categories; they articulate their own.

—Jonathan Culler, *Ferdinand de Saussure*

### THE TWENTIETH-CENTURY REAWAKENING
### OF THE ORAL SPELL

The reassertion of orality in the twentieth century in the form of the electronic media—a phenomenon that Eric A. Havelock describes as "the reawakening of the oral spell after a long silence"[1]—makes the study of the inclusive theories of classical rhetoric even more pressing than it was, say, in the early nineteenth century before the large changes in consciousness and culture brought about first by the telegraph, then by film, video, computers, and other electronic forms of discourse. Realizing the verbal relationships between the two realms allows us to understand all language and eventually all symbol systems—including the electronic ones—more effectively. Perhaps most significantly, clas-

---

[1]Havelock, *The Muse Learns to Write: Reflections on Orality and Literacy from Antiquity to the Present.* p. 31.

sical rhetoric provides a means for individual production of discourse in speaking, in print, and in electronic form.

A large part of the strange history of classical rhetoric—from the fifth century B.C. in Sicily to the late eighteenth century in England and the United States—has received wide-ranging treatment in George A. Kennedy's *Classical Rhetoric and Its Christian and Secular Tradition from Ancient to Modern Times,* a traditional book that presents a compelling version of classical rhetoric as it is formed and reformed in successive historical eras. Kennedy studies the various and sometimes extraordinary uses classical rhetoric has been put to, and his synthetic, traditional presentation answers and raises many questions about historical appropriations of ancient discourse. Kennedy's useful book offers important sources to writers and readers of rhetoric. His treatment, for example, of individual texts of classical rhetoric and his analysis of phenomena such as technical rhetoric are valuable presentations of rhetoric.

*The Contemporary Reception of Classical Rhetoric* does not aim to achieve this kind of comprehensive analysis. The concept of "coverage" has been put aside. Instead, the central inquiry into the appropriations of classical rhetoric will focus on a unique set of language and culture issues that have compelled many scholars to study classical rhetoric in the generation beginning in the mid-1960s.

An important preliminary question needs to be asked. Why should anyone bother to study classical rhetoric? What benefits can this very old material offer us? The presence of electronic forms of discourse, including computers and video forms, compels any writer in rhetoric and composition to ask if reasons for studying ancient rhetoric still exist. Does the writing of a group of people whose world and word views appear to have differed so radically from the communication forms of the twentieth century offer us real possibilities for the formation of contemporary rhetoric and composition theories? Does a collection of writing—some in the form of fragments—from fifth-century B.C. Greece to second-century A.D. Rome—actually have the capacity to provide useful material for the current theorizing of written and spoken discourse? If useful theories do emerge from our interpretation of this period—and this usefulness is not self-evident—then how do they relate to the teaching of writing as thinking? In this chapter I approach these questions partly by saying that our late-twentieth-century universes of discourse, to adapt James Moffett's phrase, maintain affinities with classical universes of discourse because of two primary characteristics: first, the adaptability of the systems of classical rhetoric; and second, the range that the classical theories of rhetoric and composition offer and in fact depend on. Classical rhetoric has never disappeared. Why will it not go away?

## DISTINCTIONS BETWEEN ENCODING AND DECODING
## IN RHETORIC AND COMPOSITION STUDIES

Classical rhetoric as a series of systems persists partly because it takes account of all the possible uses of written and spoken language. While at various historical times it emphasizes some kinds of speaking and writing over other ones (the declamation, for example, in Quintilian's second-century context as well as in the Second Sophistic; or the preliminary exercises that constitute the progymnasmata), classical rhetoric nonetheless self-consciously concerns itself with all the manifestations of discourse. The theoretical framework for producing and for analyzing discourse appears in all 700 years of the formation of classical rhetoric. The theories that evolved during these centuries are adaptable and extensive.

The adaptability of classical rhetoric to new language situations, including political, cultural, and linguistic change, provides it with much of its power as well as its longevity. Classical rhetoric can readily address any situation partly because it focuses not only on critical stances toward discourse that already exists, but because it presents elaborate theories for the production of discourse as well. The definitive productive function that finds its existence with the critical function distinguishes classical rhetoric from subsequent theories, which frequently tend to confine themselves to the analysis of discourse after it is expressed. The global, adaptable stance assumed in the classical development of rhetoric has never confined itself to ways of reading, or reception. Instead, it conditioned reception by emphasizing speaking and writing, or production. The nature of this inherently intertwined relationship provides a breadth of language possibilities that becomes impossible when only one kind of language use is emphasized. Aristotle, for example, confronts discourse as a productive art as well as an analytical art. While he focuses on the analysis of discourse in Book I of the *Rhetoric*, he does not exclude its applicability to the production of spoken or written texts. These two aspects of communication in language, of verbal expression, appear to be interconnected in Plato's *Phaedrus* as well; the process of Platonic dialectic itself involves the activity of forming discourse while at the same time criticizing that discourse in order to reach a higher level of understanding. The Sophists, including Isocrates and Gorgias, treated the production of discourse as well as its reception. As a group, the Sophists enjoyed great success in teaching people how to create discourse. Aristotle, Plato, and the Sophists did not privilege reading or hearing over writing or speaking. Their training, therefore, was necessarily more active than passive. It went beyond the given of a spoken or a written text to the arena of making the texts themselves; encoding and decoding were seen as mutually empowering activities.

## HISTORICIZING THE 1960S IN RHETORIC AND COMPOSITION STUDIES

One center of contemporary preoccupation with classical rhetoric can be located with Edward P. J. Corbett's *Classical Rhetoric for the Modern Student,* a book first published in 1965. The publication of the book signalled a crucial moment in the systematic study of classical rhetoric in the United States in the contemporary era. The book has been in print continuously (in second and third editions) and has supplemented its status as a writing textbook. It has become a central text for people working in the historicizing of rhetoric and composition. Corbett's book provides theories of analyzing discourse, of producing it, and of applying it to a variety of situations. In other words, it is traditionally Aristotelian. Corbett's book appeared originally in the context of energetic change in English studies, particularly in rhetoric and composition studies. It appeared during a time of intellectual and social ferment in language studies.[2] Two years before the publication of Corbett's book there appeared a book that set the tone of the charged atmosphere of revision in English studies. The innovative study intensified the contemporary preoccupation with rhetoric and composition. Richard Braddock, Richard Lloyd-Jones, and Lowell Schoer's *Research in Written Composition* appeared in 1963 and marked a historically crucial moment in the discipline of English in the United States.[3] These 1963 and 1965 books in rhetoric and composition studies contributed to a rehistoricizing of writing as thinking. These publishing events—as well as events such as the 1966 Dartmouth Anglo-American Conference on the Teaching of English—reveal an epistemological change in attitudes toward the production and reception of written discourse. The rehistoricizing and reinterpretation of classical rhetoric and composition represented by Corbett's book emerged as part of a movement of restructuring in the discipline of English, a movement the Braddock, Lloyd-

---

[2]For examples of additional constructions, see Victor J. Vitanza's "Critical Sub/Versions of the History of Philosophical Rhetoric"; Sharon Crowley's "The Current-Traditional Theory of Style: An Informal History"; and James Berlin's *Rhetoric and Reality: Writing Instruction in American Colleges, 1900–1985.*

[3]Both *Classical Rhetoric for the Modern Student* and *Research in Written Composition* have been cited continuously since their respective publications in 1965 and 1963.

Jones, and Schoer book was part of and helped to create. An intense critical conversation about the nature of producing written language rose to consciousness about 1963. That conversation continues. I hope that *The Contemporary Reception of Classical Rhetoric* enters the critical conversation about the production of written discourse as well as of oral discourse. Partly because of this aim, I do not intend to present a traditional history of rhetoric since 1965. The field-coverage model of many works of criticism (especially in the discipline of English) is beyond the scope of this book, and so I do not discuss that paradigm.

One kind of historicizing of United States rhetoric and composition studies appears in "The Revival of Rhetoric in America" by Robert L. Connors, Lisa S. Ede, and Andrea A. Lunsford. They state that *"Classical Rhetoric for the Modern Student* signalled the most vigorous use of classical rhetoric attempted in modern education" (p. 11). Arthur N. Applebee, in *Tradition and Reform in the Teaching of English,* also examines the classical tradition and its relationship to the discipline of English and chooses as one area of focus the upheaval in English studies occurring from 1963.[4]

The stance of *The Contemporary Reception of Classical Rhetoric* designates the contemporary resurgence of classical rhetoric with Corbett's synthesis of the theoretical, the productive, and the practical configurations of rhetoric in the 1965 book. The intellectual climate of mid-1960s language studies provided one context for the writing and the reception of this book, which has remained a powerful conceptualization of classical rhetoric. Certainly a large and important body of writing on classical rhetoric had been sustained throughout the century in Speech Communication, English, and, to lesser extents, in other disciplines. Corbett's work on classical rhetoric represented a decisive moment in North American rhetoric and composition studies (Connors, Lunsford, & Ede, p. 9). Obviously, Corbett was working in a vital and fluid context in the discipline of English. The 1965 book appeared at a particular moment of flux in language scholarship, in education, and in United States society. Corbett's work appeared in the larger context of rejuvenation in the study of writing. This renewal finds three of its most

---

[4]An alternative year for the designation of the beginning of contemporary work (a date that will always be arbitrary) in rhetoric and composition is the Anglo-American Seminar on the Teaching of English held at Dartmouth College in 1966. Applebee writes in *Tradition and Reform in the Teaching of English:* "Approximately fifty specialists in English and the teaching of English at the elementary, secondary, and college levels were brought together in an unusual attempt to gain a new perspective on their common problems. The ensuing clash of deeply rooted assumptions about the teaching of English was a cathartic experience for all involved, and sharply altered the professional emphasis of NCTE leaders" (p. 229).

succinct expressions in the Braddock, Lloyd-Jones, and Schoer 1963 book, in the Corbett 1965 book, and in the Dartmouth 1966 Anglo-American Seminar on the Teaching of English. I locate these three moments as synecdoches of a larger movement of change in the study of the English language. The books and the conference, all occurring in the brief span from 1963 to 1967, stand out as parts of a whole movement of change in the way that people in the United States chose to study their native tongue in that erupting historical period. The enormous changes in English studies since that time find one of their sources in the work of that period of the 1960s.

As Connors, Lunsford, and Ede point out, the power of classical rhetoric studies in the mid-1960s was best revealed by the fact that attacks were being made on the work (p. 11). These attacks have always accompanied classical rhetoric, particularly, as in the Connors, Lunsford, and Ede example, when it was having substantial effects on language studies. It appears to act as a lightning rod of criticism, an attractor of controversy and trouble. Its historical connection to trouble actually reveals another symptom of its adaptability.

John Schilb, in "The History of Rhetoric and the Rhetoric of History," critiques the historicizing of rhetoric performed by Connors, Ede, and Lunsford. He argues that they are "using particular textual strategies that they haven't stood back from and contemplated" (p. 25). His call for heightened self-consciousness in the historicizing of rhetoric and composition is an important call for change. In "Differences, Displacements, and Disruptions: Toward Revisionary Histories of Rhetoric," Schilb writes that "the new frequency of historical references by composition scholars is troublesome . . . because it suggests a confidence on their part in their ability to excavate and use the past that in most cases simply hasn't been earned" (p. 30). Both of these articles raise important questions about the ways we construct the past.

## TWO CONTEMPORARY STANCES TOWARD
## CLASSICAL RHETORIC

The contemporary reception cf classical rhetoric can be interpreted by two prominent and very different stances toward the primary texts and the contexts that range from fifth-century B.C. Greece to second-century A.D. Rome. My interpretive stance in making these categories rests on the assumption that coverage of all stances has always been impossible and that omniscient narration sustained by the authority of notes obscures interpretive problems. The two schools of interpretation that I choose to locate here present remarkably divergent analyses of the same group of classical texts and contexts. The first school can be conveniently called the Heritage School.

The Heritage School appears to interpret the concepts available in classical rhetoric as a series of writings that exist in a more or less objective world of artifacts, knowledge, and retrievable reality. This mode of interpretation, based on a world view that composes an external reality that is discrete from an internal reality of perception, represents a familiar stance and derives partly from the Cartesian dualism that creates ways of knowing for many people and whose familiarity has made it appear to be "normal" or "natural." This stance leads to an even more familiar view that any group of writings can be decoded as definite entities, as palpable objects that do not change. Their assumed unchanging nature makes them very susceptible to "logical" examination and to the idea that one true interpretation exists, that it can be found, and that it can be conveyed.

The following passage provides an example of this theoretical stance. Its conclusions maintain power through frequent citation and almost as frequent acceptance. The passage illustrates the treatment of the historical epoch of classical rhetoric and a selection of writings that emerged from the period:

> Because this [classical] rhetoric operated in an aural world it became the art or science of oral rather than of written discourse. Because its principal functions were to argue the relative merits of laws and policies, and to attack or defend from attack in the courtroom, it became primarily the art of persuasion . . . rhetoric was written with an eye to easy prescription and stressed the development of mechanical or "artificial" procedures and routines. Because speaking was regarded as a fine art as well as practical tool, rhetoric was given both aesthetic and pragmatic dimensions. (p. 50)

The quotation comes from Douglas Ehninger's "On Systems of Rhetoric," an article that provides an incisive and important discussion of three central epochs in historical rhetoric. The article synthesizes difficult material and is especially persuasive in its treatment of eighteenth-century rhetoric. In spite of the carefully argued post-classical interpretation, Ehninger, in his presentation of classical rhetoric, indicates the assumptions that have guided the Heritage School analysis of writing and cultures from the classical period. While Ehninger here explicitly treats central aspects of historical rhetoric, he refrains from providing his readers with the means of analyzing how he approaches "history." The passage indicates an assumption about history that appears to derive from Auguste Comte's theory of positivism. This kind of positivism assumes that a series of phenomena from the classical period was orally dominant (the mutually exclusive categories of the phrase "oral rather than of written discourse," p. 50) and that writing and its relationship to oral discourse need not be discussed as a substantive issue (his assumption "because this rhetoric was primarily aural"). The passage, perhaps most crucially for our purposes here, does not consider the nature of historicizing. The location of past epochs is presented as self evident and "natural;" positivistic assumptions about the nature of the reality of classical rhetoric are embedded in Ehninger's text. Consequently, as with all assumptions, the reader is taken along with the assumptions almost without knowing it. Readers are not allowed to participate in a dialectic of assumptions; rather, the results of the assumptions—in this case, an analysis of the reputed oral dominance of classical rhetoric—provide the writer-reader dialectic. Since the assumption is subtextual, it is difficult to disagree with Ehninger's points. He presents a palpable world of classical rhetoric; its "reality" is assumed on behalf of the reader.

The contemporary rhetoric and composition scholars in the Heritage School range from Douglas Ehninger in the 1968 "On Systems of Rhetoric" to Richard E. Young, Alton L. Becker, and Kenneth L. Pike in the 1970 *Rhetoric: Discovery and Change* ("The Classical Tradition", pp. 2–5). They cover the disciplines in the United States of Speech Communication and English and include scholars and teachers of various specialties.

In these and many other works, classical rhetoric appears to be valorized according to the interpretive bases of Comte's positivism and Descartes' rationalism: a definite world "out there" exists and is readily available for retrieval. The examples offered here cover the two disciplines which have most concerned themselves with rhetoric and composition since 1965: English and Speech Communication in the United States.

The Heritage School can itself be categorized in a variety of helpful ways. The way that I have chosen for the analysis here focuses on the interactive functions of translation, context, and culture. The first stance disregards the inevitable translation problems from Homeric and Attic Greek. The second stance depends on the use of formulas, usually numerical ones, as a structure for presenting classical rhetoric (for example, the division of speech genres into the threesome of epideictic, judicial, and legislative; or the division of individual orations into six parts). The third stance that helps to define the Heritage School lies in the consistent removal of contexts of classical rhetoricians and their ideas that have come down to us either in their writing (for example, Plato's writing) or in versions of their ideas presented by other writers (for example, versions of many Sophists' ideas in the writing of Plato and Aristole or Plato's version of Socrates). The issue of decontextualizing in the reception of classical rhetoric finds its life in the prior issues of disregarding translation problems and formulizing complex concepts. The decontextualizing of classical rhetoricians and the ideas that they developed, a phenomenon that depends on the first two issues of translation unconsciousness and the reliance on formulas, pervades much of the work in classical rhetoric studies since 1965, in spite of the work of the dialectical critics of rhetoric.

Working alongside the writers of the Heritage School have been the writers of another discernible school in the contemporary reception of classical rhetoric. For the descriptive convenience of my own rhetorical stance, we can call this diverse group the Dialectical School. These critical voices include writers such as Corbett, Walter J. Ong, Eric A. Havelock, Donovan J. Ochs, Richard Leo Enos, C. Jan Swearingen, Victor J. Vitanza, John Poulakos, and Susan C. Jarratt. These and other writers can be categorized by the way that they appropriate and confront the problems of translation, of the formulizing of knowledge, and of decontextualizing texts. Perhaps most importantly of all, the Dialectical Critics—who range from the traditional to the revolutionary—rely not on discovering a palpable rhetorical "reality" out there, but concentrate instead on contemporary epistemological constructions that in turn are capable of producing an interpretation of classical rhetoric. These critics' presentations of classical rhetoric all depend on knowledge as opposed to information or commodity, on synthesis as opposed to the isolation inherent in formalist criticism, and on the wide-ranging array of contemporary theory as opposed to rationalistic/positivistic historicizing.[5]

A reading of these two constructions of the various schools in the contemporary reception of classical rhetoric can reveal basic assumptions toward the currently useful or useless appropriations of ancient ways of thinking about discourse.


## TRANSLATION AS THE CREATION OF NEW KNOWLEDGE

A language is only as dead as its decoder. When moving from one language to any other language, the new realization (the translation)

---

[5]See Gary F. Waller's "A Powerful Silence: 'Theory' in the English Major" for a description of the historical ("kings-battles-and-parliaments" paradigm, p. 33) and formalist domination of English curricula versus the theory-dominant paradigm, the one that I am calling dialectical. Applebee locates the dominance of New Critical theory between 1943 and 1953 (p. 163).

should maintain complexity rather than kill it. As one epigraph of this chapter notes, modern linguistics has not regarded translation as dependent on a one-to-one correspondence, a substitution of a word or sentence from one language into another language. Rather, post-Saussurean linguistics has regarded each language as possessing unique categories of its own.[6] The writers of the Heritage School have systematically bypassed translation theory and instead have relied on the assumption that a one-to-one correspondence exists between one language and any other language. This rhetorical stance reflects what Saussure characterizes as a general public attitude toward language, that languages merely name: "There is first of all the superficial notion of the general public: people see nothing more than a name-giving system in language, thereby prohibiting any research into its true nature" (p. 16). Saussure's identification of a central translation problem holds special importance for interpretation in classical rhetoric. The area of keywords provides a crucial location where Saussure's translation/substitution problem exists for writers working with classical rhetoric. As the classicist W. K. C. Guthrie has pointed out especially effectively, keywords represent complexities of thought that cannot adequately be translated into other languages. The keyword problem is made worse by the predominance of many English translations—particularly of Aristotle and Cicero—that are so old that they do not speak to many users of contemporary English.[7]

Sensitivity to the fluidity that necessarily exists within one language and to the semantic problems inevitably raised by translation should be recognized as an underlying premise of the study of classical rhetoric. Anything less than this attention to language fluidity will lead to the familiar flattening of concepts and, finally, to boredom. The boredom for contemporary readers derives from the trivializing of language. Maintaining keyword complexity is not particularly difficult. Enos points out in Winifred Bryan Horner's *The Present State of Scholarship in Historical and Contemporary Rhetoric* that "A minimum knowledge of the Greek alphabet makes these early works uniquely valuable, since critical terms in Greek can be isolated easily and discussed in class" (p. 11). This kind of treatment of keywords leads to an engagement of reader and classical text that cannot come about through single-level translations that

---

[6]See Saussure's *Course in General Linguistics*, translated by Wade Baskin, for this fundamental change in language study. See especially pp. 1–5, "A Glance at the History of Linguistics," pp. 15–16, and pp. 23–27.

[7]Guthrie, *The Greek Philosophers*, pp. 1–21, "Greek Ways of Thinking." See also Francis MacDonald Cornford, trans., *The Republic of Plato* (cited by Guthrie).

depend on the erroneous concept of one-to-one correspondence of meaning.

The study of keywords that Guthrie and Enos suggest helps offset another interpretive problem troubling the study of classical rhetoric: the common dependence on translations that are two or three generations old. While, for example, Lane Cooper's 1932 translation and commentary of Aristotle's *Rhetoric,* as well as J. H. Freese's 1926 Loeb Classical Library version, represent literate and sensitive pieces of work, they do not conform to the idiolects of most readers now, particularly those of student readers. Look, for example, at the treatment of Aristotle's three "artistic proofs" in Book I of the *Rhetoric.* Cooper uses "artistic" (p. 8) and Freese uses "artificial" (p. 15). How clearly do these words speak to contemporary readers of English? Has not "artificial," for example, come to mean something inferior? Even "artistic," which appears to be more apparently neutral, does not tell readers very much. In other words, the term does not help us to make this material our own, to internalize it. The word "proof" poses even more difficulties in the post-empirical universe of discourse and must surely invite more interpretations of Aristotle as a "logic-chopping automaton" (Lunsford & Ede, p. 43). Would it not be more meaningful to late twentieth-century readers to translate *pistis* as "persuasion," given the meaning "proof" has acquired in the last two hundred years of empirical use? In addition, could we not try "interior" for "artistic?" We could then have the perhaps more meaningful phrase of "interior persuaders" for "artistic proofs." The way would then be set for interpreting *ethos,* *pathos,* and *logos* with more of the psychological complexity that, for example, Nan Johnson relies on in "Ethos and the Aims of Rhetoric," and that occurs in everyday discourse. We have in this case an example of periodic retranslation leading to an acknowledgment of the complexity of the discourse of ancient writers and of late twentieth-century readers. Such problems as the static translation of *ethos* as "ethical proof" could then disappear. The phenomenon of fifty and sixty year old English texts compels readers to compensate in at least two ways. After the translation from Greek into 1920s English, the contemporary reader must translate again into current English. The problem arises, of course, from stopping with the first translation. In either case, crucial energy is lost. While scholars who specialize in these issues may not find difficulties with phrases such as "artistic proof" and "inartistic proof," students and other readers new to the material do encounter difficulty and writers in other specialties may simply be put off. Rhetoric and composition specialists who are accustomed to the translation of *pistis* as proof may have interiorized this English translation, so that the word resonates well for them. However, people who are coming across the concept of *pistis* for the first time may cling to the empirical meanings of "proof." In the cases of both students and critics in related fields, the conveying of classical rhetoric concepts is unnecessarily hampered.

One way to interpret classical rhetoric texts lies in the appropriation of keywords. I adapt "keyword" from the work of scholars such as Guthrie and Francis Cornford from the discipline of the classics and Raymond Williams from the discipline of English. While Guthrie and Cornford use two words (key words or key-words) Williams relies on one word and in fact converts the word into the title of a 1976 book, *Keywords: A Vocabulary of Culture and Society.* If we rely on a combination of the Guthrie model and the Williams model, we will have devised an important interpretive strategy for the decoding of sometimes obscure classical rhetoric texts. In his influential translation and commentary of the *Republic,* Cornford writes: "since often a single Greek word can only be represented by two or three in English, the literal translator may easily find that the number of words he has used exceeds Plato's by 20 or 25 per cent" (p. vii). In this 1941 preface of a translation that has become a standard one in English, Cornford assesses the contemporary state of Platonic translation and finds difficulty with the Jowett translation and the Loeb translation. Cornford continues: "Some authors can be translated almost word for word. The reader may fairly claim to be told why this method cannot do justice to the matter and the manner of Plato's discourse. In brief, the answer is that in many places the effect in English is misleading, or tedious, or grotesque and silly, or pompous and verbose . . . Many key-words, such as 'music,' 'gymnastic,' 'virtue,' 'philosophy,' have shifted their meaning or acquired false association for English ears" (p. v–vi). Guthrie, in *The Sophists,* in 1969, cites Jowett as evidence for his own caution about the uncritical use of received translations.

Guthrie reveals his sensitivity to writerly and readerly contexts, translation, and connection in *The Greek Philosophers* and elsewhere:

> their effect is unconsciously felt rather than intellectually apprehended. Even in contemporary languages, beyond a few words for material objects, it is practically impossible to translate a word so as to give exactly the same impression to a foreigner. . . . When we have to rely on single-word English equivalents like "justice" or "virtue" without an acquaintance with the various usages of their Greek counterparts to different contexts, we not only lose a great deal of the content of the *Greek* words but import our own English associations which are often quite foreign to the intention of the Greek. (p. 4)

The interpretations of Guthrie, Cornford, and other dialectical critics contrast vividly with the translation assumptions of the Heritage School.

## CLASSICAL AND CONTEMPORARY CONTEXTS AND INTERPRETATIONS

A cogent and helpful example of the Heritage School rhetorical stances occurs in the *Bedford Bibliography for Teachers of Writing*, both in its first edition in 1984 and in the slightly revised form of the 1987 second edition. Patricia Bizzell and Bruce Herzberg write in the second edition, "Classical rhetoric assumes that ideas are fully formed and only then expressed in words. . . . The general assumption that thought precedes writing has had as much influence on writing instruction as has the classical heuristic itself" (1987, p. 1). This statement expresses concisely a primary stance of the Heritage School. This stance dichotomizes thought and discourse, severing the interaction of the two that Isocrates, Plato, Aristotle, and many other classical rhetoricians have established. In other words, the technology of writing, according to Bizzell and Herzberg's assumptions, did not affect thought. The bibliographical portion on classical rhetoric of both editions of the *Bedford Bibliography* (pp. 14-17, 2nd ed., pp. 11–12, 1st ed.) fully reflects the Heritage School's conceptualization of classical rhetoric. Both bibliographies reveal important aspects of the writers' language values. Leaving out all the schools of the Sophists and almost all of Plato and Aristotle, they go on to Roman rhetoric to include an early, derivative piece of Cicero, the *De Inventione (On Invention)*, a work from Cicero's youth that, when regarded without his other rhetorical pieces, becomes misrepresentative. It is interesting to note that *On Invention* was the only text of Cicero available to most of the medieval period and therefore was frequently cited during that period. The later discoveries of Cicero's more important writing made citations of *On Invention* less relevant than they had previously been. Nevertheless, citations of *On Invention* as substantive Ciceronian writing continue, representing an interesting medieval residue. The writers follow this path in the first edition; in the second edition, Bizzell and Herzberg add the pivotal *De Oratore (On the Character of the Orator)* and thereby improve their selection. Nevertheless, even with the improved selection they promote a view of Cicero's work that does not connect to his writing. They undermine his radical positions substantially because of the Heritage School assumptions.

They open the section "Classical Rhetoric: Stages of Composing, Functions of Discourse" in this way: "The modern rhetorical tradition begins with ancient Greek and Roman rhetoric, as expounded by Aristotle [p. 65], Cicero [pp. 66, 68], and others." Classical rhetoric here becomes decontextualized because translation issues have forced the inevitable turn to formulas, a construction that resembles the divorce between thought and discourse. A text such as the *Bedford Bibliography* assumes particular importance because of its powerful distribution network. Connected as it is to a prestigious publishing company, St. Martin's Press, the *Bibliography* reaches a huge number of rhetoric and composition instructors, many more than most scholarly journals reach. This extensive and impressive network provides the *Bibliography* with a large influence that most critical works on rhetoric do not share.[8] The fact that the *Bibliography* is distributed free increases its availability, particularly to apprentice teachers.[9] The awareness of this power is indicated by the publisher of Bedford Books of St. Martin's Press, Charles H. Christensen. In a "Publisher's Note" in the second edition, Christensen writes, "We are gratified by the response to the first edition. Not only has it proved a useful addition to the professional libraries of thousands of individual instructors but it has also found a place on the reading lists for many graduate courses on the teaching of writing" (p. i). Both the *Bibliography* and the previous example of Ehninger's "On Systems of Rhetoric" contain helpful analyses of some aspects of historical rhetoric by serious and incisive writers. However, this useful-ness is seriously undermined because of the repetition of outdated translations (severing "thought" and "discourse"), because of the use of formulizing of the keywords of classical rhetoric, and because of the unwarranted (in the post Ong/Havelock world) reliance on the unrela-

---

[8]This publication raises questions that are central to contemporary rhetoric and composition studies. What role do the textbook publishing companies (mostly parts of conglomerates now) play in the dissemination of scholarship and pedagogical practice in the United States? See my article "Ideology and Freshman Textbook Production: The Place of Theory in Writing Pedagogy" for an analysis of the largely unrecognized power of publishing companies that distribute writing textbooks. The center of power over the ways that writing and language are taught through the instruction for teachers and students that occurs in textbooks is a subject that needs further research. The financial and distribution strength enjoyed by many conglomerates (many formed during the 1980s) that now own publishing companies constitutes one of the most powerful sources for language instruc-tion in the United States. See also W. Ross Winterowd's "Composition Textbooks: Publisher-Author Relationships."

[9]Bizzell and Herzberg have responded to some of these critiques in *Rhetoric Review* (Vol. 8, No. 1). I believe that the distribution system of St. Martin's Press is so impressive and the marketing of a free booklet so attractive that in practice the *Bedford Bibliography* has more power than many texts on historical rhetoric that are out of print, very costly, or otherwise difficult to obtain.

tedness of speaking and writing in the ancient world. Bizzell and Herzberg replicate exactly the assumption we saw operating in the Ehninger excerpt, namely, that orality dominated or created classical rhetoric. The Heritage School remains consistently unaware of how we know of these texts in the first place: through writing. By the fourth century B.C., writing had become a center of intellectual concern and was substantially changing ways of thinking. These problems lead to the decontextualizing of crucial movements of thought in the seven hundred years of classical rhetoric. Classical rhetoric in the *Bedford Bibliography* becomes decontextualized because translation issues have compelled categorizations, or ways of thinking. The cordoning off of thinking and discourse occurs when keyword translations rely on a one-to-one correspondence, on the "false association for English ears" that Cornford noted (p.vi).

Important Greek keywords such as *pistis, ethos,* and *arete* shrivel for many late-twentieth-century readers when translators present them as, respectively, "proof," "ethical proof," and "virtue." These translations tend toward the "tedious" and the "pompous" that Cornford describes. Only residual ancient connections remain for the current reader. As a result, readerly resistance to ancient concerns grows in this situation. For example, an understanding of the perplexing brilliance of the Sophists requires that we realize with appropriate fullness that *arete*, a capacity that many Sophists proclaimed to be able to teach, does not and cannot mean (if people are actually going to *read*, i.e., dialectically engage) a contemporary English-speaker's idea of "virtue," a trait that frequently has a vague association with masculine achievement, feminine sexual suppression, or wholesomeness in its unattractive manifestation. The various meanings of *arete* include the characteristic of something fully realized, what one does best. The *arete* of a knife, in a standard example, resides in its ability to cut well, the achievement of its own best capacity. Relying on a late-twentieth-century meaning of "virtue" leads to a strange fictionalization of what the Sophists and Plato fought over. It relies on the one-for-one substitution that both Saussure and Cornford complained about. While various philosophical definitions have accumulated around "virtue" and provide the discipline of philosophy with important material, many speakers of English now regard "virtue" as an issue that is rather uninteresting or at least archaic. Of course, the history of "virtue" remains important. The Latin translation of *arete* as *virtus* partly connects virtue to virility/masculinity, as did some Greek connotations (see Liddell & Scott, pp. 100–101). This historical association provides richness for the word. Nevertheless, when *arete* is made to connote only "virtue" and excludes function, what a thing does best, in one of its various meanings, a communication breakdown has occurred. When there is no appropriate connotation—or belief—for a reader there can be no internalization or learning.

A further example in the argument against presenting keywords through translation-as-substitution can be found in the dialectical struggle of *nomos* and *physis* and the undulations of change they went through both separately and together from Homeric times, through the beginnings of rhetoric with Corax and Tisias, through the Sophists, and on through Plato and Aristotle. More than an etymological issue (although it is partly that), the flux and counterflux of *nomos* and *physis* in these four possible divisions of classical Greek history reveal the changes in values, in religious and moral beliefs, in the power people have over law, and their relationships among themselves in an everyday sense as well as in a legal sense. Consequently, to translate *nomos* and *physis* only as "law" and "nature" from Homer in the eighth to twelfth centuries B.C. to Sophocles' very different uses in the fifth century, through the Sophists and Plato and Aristotle in the fifth and fourth centuries, is simply to miss the issues that were taking place in the language/culture flux that rhetoric helped to create and in turn reflected. The fact that language creates as well as reflects cultures is a commonplace in critical theory now. "Rhetoric" and "dialectic" have always partaken of similar changes. These fluctuations provide one of the reasons that Aristotle opens his *Rhetoric* as he does, forcefully asserting what the two things are: rhetoric is the antistrophe of dialectic (Cooper, p. 1). Aristotle announces the relationship of these keywords immediately. Keywords have to be approached with the complexity (or an attempt at it) with which they were used and with the complexity any reader will bring to them. Dialectical readers know that a translation differs from the language being translated. Nevertheless, in spite of this problem, we can get at ancient worlds of language in a much better way if we recognize the resonance and power of keywords.

I do not wish necessarily to argue in favor of familiar treatments of intentionality. While motives, psychology, and various other constraints of writers can be used helpfully in the interpretation of texts and contexts, much contemporary theory has revealed that readerly constructions create texts as much as writers do. David Bleich, Stanley Fish, Wolfgang Iser, Norman Holland, and others have taught people new ways to think about decoding.[10] I do wish to argue here that contexts

---

[10]See, for example, Bleich, *Subjective Criticism*, and *Readings and Feelings: An Introduction to Subjective Criticism*; Fish, *Is There a Text in This Class?*; Iser, *The Act of Reading*; and Holland, *Five Readers Reading*.

and languages whose aliveness and structures of consciousness lie far away from contemporary experience require kinds of reading that depend on some awareness of the situations that gave rise to them. For example, the itinerant teaching of most of the Sophists, the ways they produced spoken and written discourse, their teaching philosophies, and so on constitute information that contributes to knowledge of one part of classical Greek rhetoric and composition. Writerly intentions and readerly intentions need to be considered together.

How are writers and teachers of rhetoric able to overcome the perplexing problem of the presentation of keywords through translation-as-substitution and the texts and contexts that they appear in? One answer lies in the use of multiple translations. Figure 1 indicates the radical changes among three standard translations of a passage from Aristotle's *Rhetoric*. Since the issue in this passage is *philein*, it presents especially compelling language issues: *philein* and its other forms do not signify only "love." The word may signify "like," the esteem of friendship, and other related but different human responses of a positive kind. The one-to-one substitution of "love" for *philein* deprives the latter of many of its meanings. In many passages, the English translation of "love" alone does not work for speakers of contemporary English. Readers who have studied ancient Greek are more likely to understand the layers of meaning in keywords. Few readers in the United States, however, any longer have this training. Consequently, alternative routes to understanding classical keywords and their textual and cultural contexts must be located. One strategy resides in comparing translations, as in the *philein* example in Figure 1. These comparisons of keyword translations provide readers with accretions of meaning and resist the translation as formula that Saussure described as the mere substitution of one word for another word. The comparisons promote, as Culler indicates in an epigraph of this chapter, the idea that each language creates its own categories. The creation of categories that exist in each language replaces substitution and recognizes the uniqueness of all languages. This crucial recognition enables the reader not only to see the interest that inheres in classical rhetoric but to see the attractiveness of all languages. Writers in the Heritage School appear to recognize the attractiveness only of some modern manifestations of language. Ancient discourse is relegated through the blandness of translation-by-substitution to a category that resembles antiques: more or less useless *objects* that can be appreciated by only a few privileged, trained connoisseurs.

Another premise of Heritage School interpretation/historicism is closely related to translation breakdown. This basis for interpretation

4. Let us now state who are the persons that men love or hate, and why, after we have defined love and loving. Let loving, then, be defined as wishing for anyone the things which we believe to be good for his sake but not for our own, and procuring them for him as far as lies in our power. A friend is one who loves and is loved in return, and those who think their relationship is of this character consider themselves friends. This being granted, it necessarily follows that he is a friend who shares our joy in good fortune and our sorrow in affliction, for our own sake and not for any other reason. For all men rejoice when what they desire comes to pass and are pained when the contrary happens, so that pain and pleasure are indications of their wish.

J. H. Freese (1926)

Let us now turn to Friendship and Enmity, and ask towards whom these feelings are entertained, and why. We will begin by defining friendship and friendly feeling. We may describe friendly feeling towards any one as wishing for him what you believe to be good things, not for your own sake but for his, and being inclined, so far as you can, to bring these things about. A friend is one who feels thus and excites these feelings in return: those who think they feel thus towards each other think themselves friends. This being assumed, it follows that your friend is the sort of man who shares your pleasure in what is good and your pain in what is unpleasant, for your sake and for no other reason. This pleasure and pain of his will be the token of his good wishes for you, since we all feel glad at getting what we wish for, and pained at getting what we do not. Those, then, are friends to whom the same things are good and evil; and those who are, moreover, friendly or unfriendly to the same people; for in that case they must have the same wishes, and thus by wishing for each other what they wish for themselves, they show themselves each other's friends.

Rhys Roberts (1924)

2.4. [LOVE (OR FRIENDSHIP) AND HATRED.] Let us now discuss what persons men love, and what persons they hate, and the causes of these emotions; but first let us define love [friendship] and the act of being friendly. Let loving [liking, being friendly] be defined as wishing for a person those things which you consider to be good—wishing them for his sake, not for your own—and tending so far as you can to effect them. And a friend is one who loves [likes], and is beloved [liked] in return; men deem themselves friends when they think that they stand in this mutual relation.

From these assumptions it follows that a friend is one who shares another's pleasure in good fortune, and his pain in what is painful, not for any ulterior motive, but simply for that other's sake. All men take pleasure in the realization of their own wishes, and are pained at the reverse; so it follows that our pains and pleasures are a sign of what we wish. [Your friend is your second self; the sign, proof, or test, of friendship—of identical wishes—is the identity of your pains and pleasures with his.] And they are friends who have come to regard the same things as good and the same things as evil, they who are friends of the same people, and they who are enemies of the same people; for between these there must needs be an identity of wishes [good, for example, to the common friend, harm to the common enemy]. And so one who wishes for another the very things he wishes for himself will, it appears, be that other person's friend.

Lane Cooper (1932)

FIG. 1 Comparative Translations of a Passage From Aristotle's *Rhetoric*, II. IV. 1–3

20

and dissemination is the use of the formula as a vehicle of thought. When Heritage School critics use reductive or even wrong translations of keywords and refrain from interpreting keywords in the light of multilayered meanings, they tend also to replace the material that is lost with formulas such as the three speech genres and the six parts of an oration. In other words, the unacknowledged (perhaps unconscious) dismissal of complex, classical rhetorical thinking occurs when formulas are presented as substantive material. In addition to the numerical formulas, the typical severing of thought and discourse provides a salient example of this Heritage School premise. These critics, in their particular version of historical rhetoric, formulize Aristotle's *Rhetoric* into a dichotomy of thought and discourse. According to Bizzell and Herzberg, Ehninger, and any other number of Heritage School critics, Aristotle conducted his own writing and speaking by devising his ideas through thought and then presented that thought fully formed. In this construction, thought and language are made to be separate entities. In addition, these critics suggest that Aristotle, in his capacity as a teacher, instructed his students and his readers and listeners that one completely generates material in the mind and then presents it. Some critics, for example, C. H. Knoblauch and Lil Brannon in *Rhetorical Traditions and the Teaching of Writing*, present this dichotomized Aristotle as the source of weakness in the contemporary study of thought and language as it exists in composition studies. This dichotomy leads many readers to dismiss Aristotle as benighted and not worth studying. The dismissal has as one of its roots the various historical reactions against Aristotle, phenomena that Richard McKeon discusses in "Rhetoric in the Middle Ages." As he points out, these responses, including the Renaissance reaction and the Romantic reaction against rhetoric, retained a great deal of Aristotle's thinking. In addition to retaining that which they believed to be expunging, the writers of the somewhat regular reactions against Aristotle borrowed his structures as well.

The use of formulas in the historicizing of rhetoric and composition in the last generation remains remarkable. Questions such as why so many people came to depend on constructions such as the three kinds of speech genres do not arise. The question of the function of, say, the five canons of rhetoric do not appear in Heritage School discussions. They are presented as synthetic, extensive facts. The most important question of why anyone would want to study rhetoric and composition is not discussed because the question is not asked. The unasked questions supply the interest in rhetoric and composition, the reason that anyone would want to study it and to apply it in everyday discourse. Translation-as-substitution and formulized concepts appear to derive from classical rhetoric texts themselves. But so much material is left out in this presentation of classical rhetoric that the dialectical energy of the field dissipates. Formulas make information accessible. However, they assume a passive decoder. Integrated knowledge, as Ong, Jerome Bruner, Michael Polanyi, Bleich, Fish, Iser, and other writers have demonstrated, depends on an active decoder. Dialectical reading finds its life in activity.

The presentation of information as fact is important in the reception of classical rhetoric. Its material is far away from modern readers. The information in the familiar formulas of the three genres of oratory, the five canons of rhetoric, the six parts of an oration, and so on appears to have no intellectual grounding when the concepts are decontextualized from ancient contexts and from contemporary concerns. The formulas appear to be value-free; their presentation joins a discourse community that believes that a great deal of language is value-free, especially culturally defined important language such as that used by scientists. But no language of any kind has the capacity to be value-free, as the Eagleton epigraph reminds us. Informative discourse carries with it the implicit assertion that its substance is free of value, interpretation, or the subjectivity that partially defines all human beings. Information appears to skip the exchange of dialectical language. In fact, information soothes all of us partly because it asks for no pact of interaction and because it carries with it the calm weight of authority. Its movement remains in one direction. Information does not constitute unidirectional thinking, regardless of unidirectional, informative listmakers such as E. D. Hirsch in *Cultural Literacy: What Every American Needs to Know* or in the instruments of standardized competence tests. Information presented in conjunction with questioning, exposition, authorial presence, or argument can be converted into thought. Nevertheless, its mere presentation can never substitute for thinking. Classical rhetoric as information is as accessible as other kinds of information. In this form it appeals to some readers and writers because of its accessibility. The often cryptic texts of this period of intense language theorizing are especially vulnerable to critics who choose to convert the material into information. Aristotle's compilations of lecture notes are notorious for their critical characteristics. As Ellen Quandahl points out in "Aristotle's *Rhetoric*: Reinterpreting Invention," "the *Rhetoric* is difficult to read, full of discrepancies, gaps, and repetitions" (p. 128). It is little wonder that readers have tended to formulize the text so that they and other readers can understand it. Nevertheless, the very advantages of accessibility-through-formulizing also bring with them readerly resistance. Formulas become boring rather quickly. Classical rhetoric as a series of formulas becomes dull as quickly as formulas in other areas do.

## THE LURE OF THE INFORMATIONAL

A more complex motive lies behind the lure of the informational in the contemporary reception of classical rhetoric. Formulas constitute a kind of information that relates closely to the ways that language manifests itself in primary orality, a historical stance developed by Ong and Have-lock, Milman Parry, Albert B. Lord, Jess B. Bessinger, and other writers. The early appropriators of ancient Greek rhetoric, for example, the anon-ymous writer of the *Rhetorica Ad Herennium,* wrote more closely to the psychological constraints and possibilities of primary orality. In this era that precedes writing dominance, the transmission and retrieval of vital cultural knowledge, as well as of information, was conveyed through speaking. As Ong states, particularly in *Orality and Literacy* and *The Presence of the Word,* this manner of communication leads to the formation of a particular kind of consciousness. The transmission of knowledge was conveyed through devices such as formulas so that they could be re-membered and transmitted. The nature of memory made this way of thinking and communicating especially effective. The presence and per-haps the power of the numerical formulas that dominate much of the contemporary reception of classical rhetoric probably originate in the world of primary orality. When these formulas are transformed into the written word, however, their simplicity, the very attribute that makes them effective in primary orality, makes them appear simple or stilted. They often appear to be naive. This change derives from their abbreviated quality, from their coding as parts that stand in for wholes to be sup-plemented orally, and, most significantly, in the structure of conscious-ness that they reflect. In written discourse, the supplementation by the encoder does not occur. Rather, a shift in responsibility occurs so that the decoder is required to supplement the shortened material. At some point after print culture asserted its hegemony in cultural consciousness, some-time in the European Renaissance, the residually oral formulas lost their original metonymic power and appeared to be trivial. This triviality accounted for many of the criteria in reactions against rhetoric. If we recognize the oral nature of these formulas we can understand why they have failed so many readers. In addition, we can understand more fully the symbiotic relationship between thought and the forms that discourse assumes in various historical epochs. Rather than causing problems in the interpretation of classical rhetoric, their occurrence provides historical interest as an example of residual primary orality. However, an aware-ness of the remaining primary orality appears not to be indicated in the writing of Heritage School critics. There resides in its place a forgetfulness of the increasing power of literacy from the fifth century B.C. onward.

The formulas' persistence as a means of interpretation continues to orient much of the writing not only on classical rhetoric but the dissemination of new thought in language study. Formulaic, informational language interpretation can be found elsewhere in language study (for example, in the formulas of what Richard Ohmann calls literary chronology, or traditional literary history in *English in America*). So there is an intriguing theoretical basis in the continuation of the power of formulas. They are lodged deeply, as Ong and Havelock explain, in human history and consciousness. The formulas have lost what Ong calls the dynamism of the spoken word; they now appear trivial. It becomes impossible to determine the usefulness, the pleasure, and the vitality of classical rhetoric. One asks, after James Britton, in another context, "What's the Use?"

## FORMALIST READERS AND CLASSICAL RHETORIC

An interpretation issue that derives from ancient reading and writing conditions provides a further basis for turning to formulas for the decoding of classical rhetoric both as a system and as a series of texts. The primary writings of classical rhetoric are resistant to formalist criticism. The methods of New Criticism—examining a piece of writing according to internal tension, tone and texture, and interior unity, to name three characteristics—do not because of their definition of writing offer substantive help with writing that is often in fragmentary form (the presocratic thinkers, for instance, or the remaining writing of many of the Sophists).[11] Nor do these methods account for the connection of written presocratic texts to the spoken word. Aristotle's lecture notes strike a balance between an oral world that was becoming increasingly literate. His written texts appear to be unorganized because they are repetitive, sometimes contradictory, and frequently tentative, traits that are expected in speaking but that become negative in writing. The lecture notes that comprise Aristotle's *Rhetoric*, for instance, possess the oral qualities of repetitiveness, contradiction, and tentativeness.

---

[11]See *The Presocratic Philosophers: A Critical History with a Selection of Texts*, by G.S. Kirk, J.E. Raven, and M. Schofield, 2nd ed., for a detailed examination of the fragments available from some of the earliest parts of Greek literacy. See Jonathan Barnes, *Early Greek Philosophy*, for an alternative selection of presocratic writing. Barnes presents the fragments in context. For example, Thales' fragments are presented in the writing of Simplicius, Herodotus, Aristotle, Proclus, and Diogenes Laertius. This presentation helps to account for the various agendas of the writers who cited the presocratics. See Guthrie, *The Sophists*, and Mario Untersteiner, *The Sophists*. For a synthesis of both groups see Kathleen Freeman, *Ancilla to the Pre-Socratic Philosophers*.

Readers trained in the methods of the New Criticism—the majority of readers who went to school in the United States from about the late 1940s until the present—naturally resist the dissonance that repetition, contradiction, and an absence of internal unity bring to the formalist-trained sensibility. Applebee writes that the New Critics "simultaneously excluded from the area of primary concern questions of history, biography, or ethics; their special task was to explore the structure (and hence meaning) and the success (and hence worth) of a given piece of literature, with the success itself being judged on the basis of structural principles" (p. 162). A sophistic fragment, a written speech of Isocrates or Cicero, a compilation of lecture notes by Aristotle, a dialogue of Plato, all provide the new-critically trained reader with an unsolvable puzzle and therefore one that is not worthy of study, or of explication. As has been pointed out, particularly among critical theorists of the last twenty years, many texts were excluded, for example, biography, autobiography, many forms of the essay, scientific writing, and a host of other kinds of writing. Surely the rigor that the New Critical hegemony brought to the study of reading has to be applauded. It drove out the random, romantic model of teaching reading and it overcame the dominance of philology and its exclusivity. But a large price was paid for the welcome change. In addition to the exclusion of almost all forms of nonfictional prose (a genre whose very name indicates a negative attitude) the texts of classical rhetoric were not condemned but radically ignored by generations of very influential theorists of reading. In the discipline of the classics, rhetoric texts were avoided with the same tenacity. The contemporary resurgence of interest in the many forms of nonfictional prose has provided some of the power of the new historicizing of classical rhetoric. Contexts, cultures, and consciousness are primary in the analyses of all the forms of nonfictional prose.

Dialectical critics such as Ong, Enos, and Swearingen resist the lure of transforming classical rhetoric into accessible information. These interpreters maintain the inherent complexities of classical rhetoric as systems and as texts while at the same time making those complexities available to contemporary readers with various agendas. They follow, as do other dialectical writers, Plato's own conception of the difficulty of people and their discourse. At *Phaedrus* 264, Plato has Socrates equate discourse with the body: "every discourse, like a living creature, should be so put together that it has its own body and lacks neither head nor feet, middle nor extremities, all composed in such a way that they suit both each other and the whole" (p. 53). With this organic metaphor, Plato acknowledges, as he does throughout his work (work which comes to us in the form of writing), the difficulty of interpreting people and their written and spoken discourse. We can understand the historical reasons for using the informational power of the formulas. Nonetheless, their two-dimensionality must be recognized as a constraint of residual primary orality. Plato's rendering of language and reality appears to be flattened by rhetoric critics who promote the two-dimensional.

In the essay "On Distinctions between Classical and Contemporary Rhetoric," Andrea A. Lunsford and Lisa S. Ede look dispassionately at historical problems in classical rhetoric, evaluate them, and conclude forcefully that much of Aristotle's work has been reduced to the unrecognizable. They assert, as do other dialectical critics, that much of the secondary work on Aristotle depends on "misunderstandings that can occur when commentators ignore the fundamental connections among Aristotle's writings" (p. 41). Later in the same essay, in citing Grimaldi's interconnections among Aristotle's works, Lunsford and Ede write, "The rational man of Aristotle's rhetoric is not a logic-chopping automaton, but a language-using animal who unites reason and emotion in discourse with others. Aristotle, (and indeed, Plato and Isocrates as well) studied the power of the mind to gain meaning from the world and to share that meaning with others" (p. 43).

The Aristotle as "logic-chopping automaton" that Lunsford and Ede have named represents the formulaic use that a significant number of rhetorical writers rely on in their presentations of classical rhetoric. The explication of Aristotle as automaton reveals the formulaic view of rhetoric that emerges eventually in many versions of historical rhetoric. This version relies on reducing the intertwining theories that make up classical rhetoric and replacing them with simple categories. The formulas, rules, dicta, and lists that comprise Heritage School presentations of classical rhetoric quite simply deprive classical rhetoric of its attractiveness. If texts and issues in classical rhetoric remain unconnected to Greek and/or Roman cultures, speech, writing, and ideologies, then "the forms of power and performance" (Eagleton, *Literary Theory*, p. 205) in classical rhetoric tend to disappear. Even more seriously, this kind of reductivism deprives readers of the connections between contemporary language theory and historical language theory.

## CULTURE AND CLASSICAL RHETORIC: THE RHETORICAL UNCONSCIOUS

To borrow from Fredric Jameson, we can perhaps claim that the Heritage School lives with a rhetorical unconscious. Jameson claims that all interpretations of texts are political and social. To deny this basic issue, Jameson demonstrates in *The Political Unconscious*, is to bypass the significance of texts. Jameson explains his task by stating: "I have tried to maintain an essentially historicist perspective, in which our readings of the past are vitally dependent on our experience of the present" (p. 11). Heritage School criticism and traditional formalist literary criticism share positivistic assumptions about locating a reality "out there." Each interpretive stance also tends to disregard the political and the social. These realms are categorized into irrelevant areas for aesthetic contemplation. While traditional formalist literary criticism has regarded the literary work as an object, traditional rhetorical studies, even as exemplified by the Heritage School, have been unable to deny the political. Rhetoric is inherently a social, communicative act. While the latter critics disregard current politics as a vital issue in all of historical rhetoric, they cannot—because of virtually all of the definitions of rhetoric—regard any rhetorical act or situation as nonsocial. Traditional literary criticism turns to versions of art-for-art's sake aestheticism at various historical moments, as a glance at a critical anthology such as Hazard Adams' *Critical Theory Since Plato* quickly reveals. Rhetorical history remains exempt from this reductionism because of the communicative/persuasive qualities that make rhetoric what it is. No matter how thoroughly politics and society are denied, no writer can make rhetoric asocial or apolitical. Just as denial of the political leads to "the windless closure of the formalisms" (Jameson, p. 42), so denial of cultural and political forces leads to a simplified and, finally, trivializing, construction of classical rhetoric. The Heritage School denies rhetoric of one of its definitive characteristics.

A rhetorical formula, as well as a mistranslation of keywords, cannot exist without the act of decontextualizing. The denial of context leads directly to the problem examined earlier with the appropriations made of the keyword *arete*. If a reader of Aristotle does not know that he is discussing *arete* as a scientific investigator, as a thinker who goes about looking for the functions of things, then the reader would not know that *arete* for Aristotle, if not exactly for the Sophists or for Plato, indicated, among other things, function. The argument for making context primary in the study of classical cultures is made by McKeon in the anthology *Introduction to Aristotle*. Aristotle's "works are not easily accessible, and, when they are accessible, the place of any one work in the complex system of his philosophy is not discernible from reading it alone. The significance of what Aristotle says in development or support of a theory is usually clarified by the theories expounded in related sciences" (p. vii). When McKeon wrote this piece in the nineteen-forties, he focused on the convolutions of Aristotle's writing, not just at what his commentators claimed that he said. In other words, he sought to separate the text from the traditions. The point is to illuminate classical languages and cultures and to make connections. The complaints made by McKeon, Lunsford and Ede, Enos, Grimaldi, and others center on unconscious decontextualizing.

The decontextualizing of texts and issues in classical rhetoric derives from a primary symptom of the rhetorical unconscious: the merging of 700 years of rhetorical theory into one idea, so that Corax and Tisias in the fifth century B.C. are made equivalent to Quintilian in the first century A.D. The making of a monolith such as this one requires bypassing the epistemologies of various rhetoricians and therefore ignoring the systems of their thought and obscuring crucial cultural distinctions. In other words, decontextualizing necessarily obscures the thought of classical rhetoricians.

Ong, in *Orality and Literacy*, takes account of contextuality by establishing the fluidity and therefore the vitality of classical rhetoric. He moves in many directions to convey dialectics of mind, language, and consciousness. By relying on this strategy, he interiorizes the work of Plato and others and presents for us the deeply held conflicts Plato struggled with, conflicts which are available to any reader who does not believe explicit or implicit ideas such as the divorce between thought and discourse that I discussed earlier. The change in consciousness that comes about in the change from speaking dominance to writing dominance (argued throughout *Orality and Literacy*) affects all the work in classical as well as in contemporary rhetoric. The interiorization that Ong reveals represents the kind of response that makes interpretation of classical rhetoric a vital source of cultural knowledge. It consistently and consciously incorporates current language theory. Interpretation of this kind leads to more studies grounded in theorizing rather than in two-dimensional, finite categorizing. Ong, like Aristotle, shows us that categories must be a result of prior thought, synthesis, and psychological acuity and must lead away from themselves. Relying unconsciously on a monolith—that classical rhetoric is one entity over 700 years—creates false categories.

The problems of interpretation isolated in this chapter—translation, formula, and context—pervade much of the reception of classical rhetoric. One critical stance to assume in response to these interpretive hurdles lies in multiple translations of keywords, a reading strategy that provides *contexts* with texts and must dispense with formulas. A nagging problem of classical rhetoric studies since the early 1960s has been that Heritage School presentations have not located the *kairos*—the means of persuading their decoders of the opportune moments to enact the persuasion—of the validity of classical rhetoric. That validity inheres in the everyday uses of language, not in a heavenly realm of linguistic perfection.

Dialectical reception of classical rhetoric connects ancient discourse to contemporary, lived language. In other words, dialectical criticism "creates" classical rhetoric. The formula and the monolith cannot withstand this treatment.

Because of the problems of translations, of converting language theory into formulas, and making the writing of the Sophists, Plato, Aristotle, Cicero, and other rhetoricians equivalent to one another, classical rhetoric is frequently, forcefully, and passionately regarded as a danger, as a way of approaching language that damages student writing (Knoblauch and Brannon's call for classical rhetoric to be "frontally assaulted," p. 79, for example). This reception of classical rhetoric resembles the reception of many of the theories that comprise critical theory: both classical rhetoric and contemporary critical theory are regarded frequently as dangerous entities, almost as imperialist forces intent on conquering the territory of the humanities. Terry Eagleton's *Literary Theory: An Introduction* discusses some of this negative response. But far from damaging the study of language, culture, and art, classical rhetoric provided a culture of language, of writing as well as reading, that enabled a different version of the "humanities" to exist. James L. Kinneavy has written in "Restoring the Humanities" that "It is a bald historical fact that the humanities were born in a rhetorical manger" (p. 20). This birthing has a lot to teach us about subsequent appropriations of the "humanities", as does the difficult metaphor of restoration.

Classical rhetoric comprises the most complete system that has ever been devised for the production of and the analysis of all the forms of discourse. Its breadth relies on its vital connection to the everyday uses of language as well as to more "artistic" kinds of language, such as a play by Aeschylus or of an oration against Catiline by Cicero. The theories formulated by the Sophists, Plato, Aristotle, Cicero, Quintilian, and others of the classical period take account of language written, language spoken, and the means available for persuasion regarding any subject possible. The sustained interest in "practical" language, in language as it occurs among individuals, as Plato puts it in *Phaedrus,* provided for the beginning of the systematic treatment of rhetoric in early Greece in the fifth century B.C., remained the dynamic center for the next 700 years, and impelled the texts and contexts of classical rhetoric in post-classical epochs. There is no rhetoric without the ordinariness and dailiness of language.

The Heritage School treatment of classical rhetoric resists this extensiveness and segregates language into formulas. Nowhere in these treatments is there an indication that the formula lives on as part of residual primary orality, a time before writing when formulas enabled people to transmit cultural knowledge and values. The residual orality provides great historical interest and reveals the continuation of primary orality during the most advanced stage of literacy. However, when this oral connection goes unrecognized, its presence in forms antagonistic to the written word such as the formula undermines advances in rhetoric and other kinds of language studies. In other words, the forms of consciousness brought about by advanced literacy clash with the residual codes of primary orality.

Many of the strongest critics of the study of classical rhetoric appear to have reached their interpretations based on the precepts of the Heritage School. In Chapter Two I analyze in depth one of these influential receptions, *Rhetorical Traditions and the Teaching of Writing*. In that chapter a second type of response to the Heritage School is examined, the presentation of early American receptions of classical rhetoric in *Writing Instruction in Nineteenth-Century American Colleges*. This 1984 book by James Berlin distinguishes itself for the purposes set forth here because Berlin is a dialectical critic who assumes the familiar stances of the Heritage School on classical rhetoric. These two categories of contemporary response—part of the surging interest in rhetoric and composition studies of all kinds in the last generation—illustrate the pervasive power of the familiar Heritage School dissemination. These critics deserve praise for responding to the Heritage School as they have. Given the foundations of hardened translation, the series of numerical and closed formulas, and a decontextualized monolith spanning seven hundred years, these post-Heritage School critics are responding sensibly and with restraint.


## ELITISM, NOSTALGIA, AND CLASSICAL RHETORIC

All writers, whether of the Heritage School, of the Dialectical School, or of any other stance, need to take account of past systems of rhetorical knowledge and application and production. Writers who oppose classical rhetoric tend to discount historicism generally. That is, they tend not to be self-conscious about how people go about making histories; they tend, like Ehninger and Bizzell and Herzberg, to assume a palpable, rationalistic "reality" out there, a world that awaits discovery, rather than a world that they themselves in large part construct.

The Heritage School responds in part to two central issues that cling—especially in the United States—to classical studies of any kind. They are the phenomena of nostalgia and elitism. Interpretation through nostalgia is not unusual in any kind of discourse study.

Glossing over difficulties of writers' lives and denying ideology remain common components of much twentieth-century literary criticism as well as of rhetoric and composition, particularly in the Male Masters mode of English studies, in which a canon of essentially white male writers is presented as the substance, the truth, of a national literature. Bleich has analyzed the reverential response to what is taken to be unquestioned reality in *Subjective Criticism*. "Literary pedagogy had enacted this viewpoint by proceeding on the axiom that 'literature is a reflection of people, and in it we can see human problems and concerns that we are going through ourselves.' ". . . . [This] "extraordinary generality, rooted as it is in centuries of habitual religious thinking, directs our attention away from the physical details of our actual reading experience or speaking experience, and toward the need to develop behaviors compliant with received moral authority" (p. 7). In the case of classical rhetoric studies, as in the case of traditionalist literary studies, there has frequently been a tendency to long for the return to a nonexistent past. The interpretation of classical texts from the nostalgic point of view tends to flatten texts and contexts through a denial that differs from the kind discussed earlier. The nostalgic stance takes these writers farther away from late twentieth-century readers than they already are. They present readers with a hierarchical structure of language theories that cannot be challenged, and, most importantly, they trade in intellection or emotional engagement for religious faith. In turn, responders to the nostalgic interpreters are put off—and rightly so—by this unquestioning stance. Faith is no doubt the reason that Knoblauch and Brannon, in one of the best points they make in their challenging and engaging book, use as a subtitle "That Old-Time Religion" (pp. 22–50). While most people would not deny the place of faith in life (although the Marx and Engels critique here is apt; mystification obscures many political and cultural troubles), asking faith to act as an interpreter of the rhetorical activities of writing and reading is, at best, inappropriate, and, at worst, damaging. The often-maligned formalists of the New Criticism earlier in the twentieth century worked to displace nostalgic critical stances with intellectually rigorous criticism. (See, for example, John Crowe Ransom's "Criticism as Pure Speculation" and Allen Tate's "Literature as Knowledge"). Nostalgic criticism presents at least two immediate obstacles for people working in rhetoric: (1) depending on faith in inappropriate ways suppresses thought and inquiry and the possibilities and power of persuasion; and (2) creating an unchangeable hierarchy of privileged texts depends on argument from very questionable authority. One modern reception of Aristotle's *Rhetoric* acts as a useful example of both these problems:

when the *Rhetoric* is treated as an Arnoldian touchstone,[12] a great work against which all other great works can be usefully judged, then this important rhetorical tract becomes a source of faith rather than of intellectual inquiry or basis of belief. In the second instance, the creation of a hierarchy of texts, the *Rhetoric* is placed at the top of the hierarchy. This placement goes so far as to make the *Rhetoric* the beginning of classical rhetoric, rather than a product of and response to at least a century and a half of intense rhetorical inquiry, pedagogy, and writing that began systematically with Corax and Tisias in the fifth century B.C. The classical texts at the top of the hierarchy cannot really be challenged and so cannot be interacted with. In this context, Aristotle's *Rhetoric* comes to resemble a sacred text more than a document on rhetoric.

An issue related to nostalgic criticism in the history of rhetoric and of English studies is the phenomenon of elitism. The disappearance of the widespread study of Greek and Roman writing in the United States is due in large part to its association with elitism. This issue, in fact, made the discipline of the classics lose sight of its function (its *arete*). A tradition of genteel education and culture conveyed in subtle and not so subtle ways the elitist stance of some classical studies. Most damaging was the interpretation of classical writing as inherently superior. Their usefulness in the universe of discourse was lost sight of in the United States, if not in England (Applebee pp. 1–14, 26). While the virtual disappearance of classical studies in the United States goes beyond the scope of this book, its life and dwindling in relation to rhetoric and composition studies need more investigation. A commonplace in rhetoric and composition studies holds that the discipline of English has been well on its way to imitating the decline of Latin and Greek studies in the United States. Bleich's chapter "Language, Literacy, and Criticism" in *Subjective Criticism* discusses this problem from the point of view of reader response theory. Nostalgia and elitism, along with decontextualizing, face us as problems in the disciplines of English and Speech Communication, and in secondary and primary general education as well. While one may say that the clash between the reductivists of the Heritage School and the inquirists of the Dialectical School acts as a productive clash creating new ways of thinking, a more pessimistic,

---

[12]See Matthew Arnold's "The Study of Poetry" for a discussion of the idea of touchstones in literary discourse. Arnold posits the idea that there are standards of highest achievement in literature against which all other literary works can be judged. This idea, which remains entrenched in education at all levels, has been seriously challenged in the last twenty years of literary theory.

and probably more realistic, view would argue that no dialectic can exist between these two camps because the epistemologies of the two sides are radically opposed. We are dealing with many historicists in the Heritage School who do not—in print, at least—look at their central assumptions. These assumptions are presented as part of nature (*physis*) and definite. This kind of thinking leads to the making of automatons. Automatons, which live apart from any knowable order of life for actual, breathing readers, appeal only to those who have already been persuaded of the Heritage point of view.

The Heritage School tends to kill the inherent pleasure and vitality of rhetorical and compositional work, just as it kills the pleasure of reading works of literary discourse. The language death that results does not persuade anyone to study the material of, say, Isocrates, Demosthenes, Plato, Aristotle, and other writers. Scholars and students will not respond to dead rhetoric because automatons cannot speak to us. We cannot engage in dialectic with them.

All critics of language need to maintain some awareness of their epistemological underpinnings and therefore the values that they bring to a text. As Jameson writes, "no interpretation can be effectively disqualified on its own terms by a simple enumeration of inaccuracies or omissions, or by a list of unanswered questions. Interpretation is not an isolated act, but takes place within a Homeric battlefield, on which a host of interpretive options are either openly or implicitly in conflict" (p. 13). The issues raised in this chapter include the "interpretive options" not only of the contemporary reception of classical rhetoric but of the ways that language study in general in the United States promotes certain values and epistemologies over other ones. Giving up the unconsciousness that pervades United States pedagogy requires every scholar and teacher—including the Dialectical ones—to indicate awareness of his or her value system.

# 2

Presentations of Heritage
School Classical Rhetoric:
"Logic" and False
Oppositions of Ancient and
Modern Language Issues

The "interpretive options" that Jameson refers to in *The Political Unconscious*, and the value systems that each option necessarily brings with it,
form the center of rhetoric and composition studies in the United States,
as they form the center of other fields of study. The field of rhetoric and
composition—along with the field of critical theory—has perhaps dis-
played the greatest awareness of the unavoidable presence of value
systems in language. A crucial self consciousness has pervaded the field
of rhetoric and composition studies and has enabled researchers to
advance knowledge and pedagogy in English and Speech Communication, if not always in other disciplines. These self-conscious, system-
conscious writers compose what I have called the Dialectical School of
rhetoric and composition studies. Their primary shared characteristic—
in the midst of their great diversity—as revealed in their writing, consists
of some access to the epistemologies and the intellectual contexts that
enable them to have ideas about rhetoric and composition studies in the
first place. This attribute is shared by people working in critical (or
postmodern) theory across many disciplines, from English to architec-
ture to legal studies to sociology. This self-aware attitude of dialectical

critics is difficult to maintain, partly because no one can have full access to the value system that she or he operates with. In addition, we all tend to find particular belief systems "natural" and "normal."

The familiarity of one's belief systems—far from being just a blinding mechanism—enables one to carry on with day to day activities. Classical rhetoric, in Plato's sense of "a universal art . . . having to do with all matters, great as well as small, good and bad alike"[1] and in Aristotle's sense of "discovering in the particular case, what are the available means of persuasion,"[2] covers as its domain all the language use that we employ in our everyday activities, from writing an inventory to reading a poem. The apparently utilitarian (or what some people regard as harmless) language uses that enable and constitute everyday activity comprise one region of rhetoric. The structures—psychological, philosophical, and linguistic—that underlie these everyday uses also constitute a region of classical rhetoric. Dialectical critics of classical rhetoric tend to address the psychological, philosophical, and linguistic issues that partly constitute classical rhetoric. These considerations distinguish Dialectical School interpretations from Heritage School interpretations, even as other characteristics obscure their differences.

While Heritage School interpretations do prove useful, they tend—in the interpretive field in which I am writing—to rely on a conception of historical reality that offers the steadiness of, say, an anchor. The reality that is assumed to exist, the anchor that provides stability, remains unacknowledged; it is forgotten about. The stability is treated as unchangeable and unchanging. In the previous chapter, I discussed this familiar rhetorical stance as one version of positivism, with a substantial and rich intellectual history of its own. Positivism works well in the conventional hard sciences and social sciences. It works well for what Aristotle called definite knowledge. Positivism works far less well for what he called contingent reality, or the world of probability. Rhetoric exists within and in turn helps to create the realm of probability. The apparent (or posited) definiteness of a scientific theory cannot work for a rhetorical theory.

Probability resists the definite. One can predict discourse situations, but one cannot be certain about them in advance of their happening. This issue is why rhetorical training rests on being able to meet a language issue that arises in a given context. With no preparation, a rhetorically trained person—of the kind evoked by Plato, Isocrates, Aristotle, Cicero, and Quintilian, to name five classical writers—can meet the requirements of a given communication situation. In other

---

[1]See *Phaedrus*, Jowett translation, p. 503.
[2]See *Rhetoric*, Cooper translation, p. 7.

words, probability has been accounted for. It can be predicted (the future evaluated) but it can be definite only in hindsight (the past evaluated). The temporal distinction of definite discourse situations that are more definite because they have already happened (for example, a speech by Cicero that has been written) and discourse situations that might happen (for example, a plan to speak in a particular way at the Forum) provides a primary difference between the production (the encoding, or the writing or speaking) of a text and the reception (the decoding, or the reading of or listening to) a text.

Four primary language issues stand out as characteristics of Heritage School positivism in the contemporary reception of classical rhetoric: (1) the use of formulas in lists, rules, and dicta (or prescriptions); (2) the severing of thought and discourse, thereby making each process appear to be discrete; (3) decontextualizing concepts by using formalist literary techniques of isolation when they are inappropriate for the material, the writer, the reader, or the context; and (4) relying on Saussure's identification of translation-as-substitution (p. 16), a move that results in what Cornford, Guthrie, and others have called mistranslations.

These four characteristics of positivism contributed to the complex conversion of Aristotle's theories of logic (that is, the systematic use of reasoning and argument) into "automaton" logic.[3] The historicizing of logic, obviously an important aspect of the history of what is usually called western thought, intertwines with the historicizing of rhetoric but it is not the point of this chapter or book.[4] Rather, a version of thought frequently called "logic," but in fact not connected to traditional logic, provides the focus of concern here.


## FAMILIAR LOGIC AND TRADITIONAL LOGIC


The "logic" analyzed in this chapter refers to the common idea of logic as exaggerated reason, hyperationalism, and a procedural way of thinking that not only excludes emotion but in fact looks down on it. I refer to this version as familiar logic. For many people in the late twentieth and twenty-first centuries familiar logic resides at the top of a hierarchy, coldly and sometimes rigidly casting its eye over what its

---

[3]I adapt "automaton logic" from Lunsford and Ede's "Aristotle as logic-chopping automaton." In "On Distinctions between Classical and Modern Rhetoric," p. 43.

[4]See Jean Dietz Moss, "Prolegomenon: The Revival of Practical Reasoning" for a cogent, traditional historical survey of practical reasoning, pp 1–21; Wilbur Samuel Howell, *Logic and Rhetoric in England, 1500–1700*; McKeon, "Rhetoric in the Middle Ages;" and Ong, *Ramus, Method, and the Decay of Dialogue*.

practitioners regard as unrigorous ways of thinking. This familiar logic is the kind that produces "logic-chopping automatons."

Another of the many kinds of logic, a version that I call traditional logic, goes hand in hand with positivism in many histories of western ideas. In a *Times Literary Supplement* article, Martha Nussbaum articulates the role of traditional logical interpretation and its relationship to Plato in the United States and England: "interpreters stressed the need for close attention to logical structure, discovering tacit premises and in general mapping Plato's arguments in a lucid and perspicuous way" (p. 850). Nussbaum describes some of the ways that traditional logic has been appropriated by the discipline of Anglo-American philosophy:

> Analytic interpreters, eager to make Plato emerge as philosophically respectable according to their own standards of respectability, found Plato's use of the dialogue form, of characters, of myth and literary language, to be an embarrassment. Brought up on the Lockean dogma that the literary use of language is always a vice in argument aimed at truth, they kept silent about Plato's indiscretions and got on with the business of analysing the portions of his text that most obviously lent themselves to analysis. (p. 850)

Various revisions of the traditional logical stances have widened the inquiries into texts and contexts that are available to us from ancient eras. Nonetheless, the scholarly privileging of "logical structure" remains firmly entrenched in the twentieth century, not only in its obvious home in the discipline of philosophy in the United States and England, but in rhetoric and composition studies in the disciplines of English and Speech Communication as well. Because of the inevitable (and frequently unrecognized) movement of academic ideas to the general public, traditional logic has exerted great influence on everyday discourse, such as in the commonplace phrases of the dismissive "You are being illogical," or the analytical "You are shifting the grounds of our argument," or, one of the commonest epithets of all, "You are irrational." The discourse of the natural sciences and the social sciences tends to bypass these obvious, familiar-logical statements (partly because people in those fields tend not to personalize overtly by such structures as the first person singular) and instead relies on the more sophisticated — and less detectable — structure of logic that controls thought. Rhetoric and composition — classical or otherwise — appear to be inappropriate in scientific disciplines. The rhetorical is treated as the extraneous, as the decorative, much as the discipline of English is frequently treated.

Nonetheless, many writers in both classical and contemporary rhetoric and composition theory regard the scholarly discourses of philosophy, the natural sciences, and the social sciences as part of rhetoric. James L. Kinneavy, in *A Theory of Discourse: The Aims of Discourse*, places these kinds of writing primarily in the realm of reference discourse while partaking in secondary ways of the three other categories of discourse he sets up, expressive, persuasive, and literary. The theories of rhetoric and composition fit these fields as readily as they fit any other kind of discourse. While the language of positivism is conventionally written and read as if it is exempt from issues such as rhetorical stance, *ethos*, *kairos*, and other aspects inherent in language, the scholarship of the last generation has shown us that it is not exempt; language enables scientific thought as much as it enables poetry.

The Heritage School of classical rhetoric is positivistic in its assumptions and imitative of the natural and social sciences in its rhetorical stance. It assumes a definite, knowable reality "out there," it ignores the flux and counterflux of language that enables it to exist in the first place, and it presents methods of presenting the "truth" of that knowable reality. When Douglas Ehninger and Patricia Bizzell and Bruce Herzberg, in the separate examples I cited in Chapter One, present classical rhetoric as an orally-dominant, monolithic world in which thought and discourse are separated, they are writing in one rhetorical stance of the sciences, natural and social. They are able to come to the conclusions they do only because of the positivistic world view that their discourse appears to inhabit. In each of the Chapter One examples of Heritage School discourse, the interpretive fluidity of classical rhetoric is not addressed; rather, the nature of classical rhetoric is assumed and then promoted without apparent consciousness of the rhetorical issues that allow them to present their discourse. For example, the oral dominance that these writers present as a hallmark of classical rhetoric is portrayed as a fact with the certainty with which we think of electrons swirling in orbit within an atom. The problem with this kind of positivistic thinking is that it works well for the present scientific moment with electrons, but it does not help us understand the nature of written or spoken discourse. In other words, positivistic thinking, in the guise of either traditional or familiar logic, does not help us understand the manipulation that inheres in all language use (spoken, written, and electronic). Both kinds of logic leave too much unsaid, too much presumed. These ways of thinking tend to discount language manipulation as impressionistic, personal, harmless, and irrelevant. The Heritage School of classical rhetoric occupies the secure territory of positivism, asserting a reality that is never questioned. The problem with this rhetorical stance is that language use is not definite.

In the contemporary reception of classical rhetoric, the Dialectical School has in its many and various manifestations reevaluated the familiar Heritage School cordoning off of logic as a rational, positivistic language issue. Rather than privileging traditional logic or the more common familiar logic, many writers in the Dialectical School have repositioned traditional logic as one aspect of language use. C. Jan Swearingen, for example, writes in "The Rhetor as Eiron: Plato's Defense of Dialogue": "Plato's critique of sophistic rhetoric remains a viable critique of rhetoric and . . . was in no way superceded by Aristotle's carefully elaborate partitioning of rhetoric, poetics, logic, and ethics" (p. 290). Issues such as language manipulation, culture and context, and the demands of a particular language moment characterize the contemporary reception of classical rhetoric according to the widely varying rhetorical stances of the Dialectical School. The definiteness of positivism does not take interpretation very far into these issues.

Heritage School reliance on familiar logic has done much to make classical rhetoric unimportant and ultimately boring for many people. This chapter offers two explications of a "logic"-dominant (familiar logic) classical rhetoric, one from the Heritage School, and one from the Dialectical School. I intend to show that Heritage School reception of classical rhetoric, here in the form of familiar logic, appears in the work of rhetoric and composition critics of diverse stances.

The first example is the 1984 *Rhetorical Traditions and the Teaching of Writing* by C. H. Knoblauch and Lil Brannon. The second example is the 1984 *Writing Instruction in Nineteenth-Century American Colleges* by James A. Berlin. The first book analyzes the relationship between contemporary writing pedagogy and two rhetorical traditions. The second book analyzes the historicizing of a Dialectical School critic whose presentation of classical rhetoric in the United States relies on Heritage School views for segments of the history. The classical rhetoric portions of Berlin's 1984 book distinguish themselves from the rest of his presentation because they are discrete, even segregated, from most of his presentation of rhetoric's history in the United States. Moreover, Berlin's highly original presentation of Emersonian rhetoric can be read as an explication of Platonic rhetoric, in spite of Berlin's insistence that Plato is in various ways not interested in rhetoric.

## ONE DIVISION OF ANCIENT AND MODERN LANGUAGE CONSTRUCTIONS

The provocative and energetic *Rhetorical Traditions and the Teaching of Writing* relies on the opposition between "classical rhetoric" and "modern rhetoric" and in doing so raises some of the central interpretive issues for anyone working in contemporary rhetoric and composition studies. Since the nature of rhetoric—classical, modern, contemporary, or of any historical era—relates to the textual constraints of groups of writings and their contexts, I examine some of the central issues of Knoblauch and Brannon's writing strategies. That is, I examine their own rhetorical stance by analyzing some of their composition strategies. I intend to do a symptomatic reading of the language that the writers choose in their collaboration and to see how their language choices indicate basic values concerning rhetoric and composition as it is practiced and theorized in the last part of the twentieth century. Because any writer's rhetoric—a writer's language—reveals part of her or his construction of reality, it is helpful in our exploration of Knoblauch and Brannon's presentations to examine their language to see how their language constructions create the book.

Three primary language constructions distinguish themselves from the writing collaboration that produced the book: (1) the dichotomizing of what they call the mechanical and the organic; (2) the uses of assertions and evidence, or the reliance on what I have characterized earlier in this chapter as familiar logic; and (3) the removal of Plato from any relationship with rhetoric except an oppositional one.

Perhaps the most noticeable formal strategy they choose is their use of the dichotomy of the mechanical versus the organic. In this construction of rhetorical history, classical rhetoric is presented as mechanical, while modern rhetoric, beginning in the seventeenth century, is presented as organic. Like Coleridge and other Romantics, Knoblauch and Brannon prefer to construct a world that is nurturing and sustaining when it is organic and that is anti-human and deadening when it is mechanistic. Also like the English Romantic poets, they wish to valorize the organic world by contrasting it with the nonliving mechanical world. These familiar metaphors for ways of conceiving of the world have been with us for so long that we are immediately able to understand what Knoblauch and Brannon mean to express.

At the same time, we all live in a critical climate in which organic metaphors appear not to work as effectively as they once did. They have created the center of one critical stance for almost two hundred years. In a critical climate in which the so-called logocentric universe has been challenged by deconstruction (see, for example, Barbara Johnson's explanation of Derrida in *Dissemination*, pp. viii–x) and surface language intentions have been explored by psychoanalytical interpretations, do organic metaphors remain adequate? Knoblauch and Brannon write:

> In general, classical rhetoric tended to define a mechanistic, skill-based model of composition, using preconceptions about the shapes of completed texts as the basis for describing writers' activities. For instance, texts

are supposed to have introductions anad conclusions; therefore, introducing and concluding were regarded as skills to be learned separately and then combined to produce acceptable writing. Modern rhetoric, by contrast, tries to define the process of composing, not the shapes of texts, assuming that the process is organic, not a series of discrete parts. (p. 80)

Thus Knoblauch and Brannon arrange the last 2500 years of discourse theory: white versus black, modern rhetoric versus classical rhetoric. After establishing this dichotomy, Knoblauch and Brannon do not move away from this position. They cannot move away, because it forms the conceptual basis of their book. They do perform a brief metacommentary on their use of this dichotomy in a note. Beyond this allusion to Coleridge, however, they do little to discuss some of the implications this rhetorical stance forces them into.

Perhaps the issue to probe in this construction is this one: are we working with a dead metaphor here? Are the mechanics of the clock and the vitality of the plant (its "process") the best controlling metaphors for Knoblauch and Brannon's very interesting argument? Secondly, are the polar opposites that create these paradigms the most effective organizing principle for the universe of written discourse that Knoblauch and Brannon are examining? This conceptual point is crucial because the writers base all their subsequent arguments around these metaphors.

Knoblauch and Brannon assert that the study of classical rhetoric reinforces a mechanistic (bad), outdated universe of discourse, the nonthinking teaching of writing that many rhetoric and composition scholars struggle against. They promote instead the abandonment of classical rhetoric in favor of what they call "modern rhetorical theory" (the organic mode). One premise of this book maintains that the two approaches are mutually exclusive. Because of this apparently insurmountable mutual exclusion, they promote the abandonment of classical rhetoric in favor of a modern rhetoric that begins in the seventeenth century. They believe that classical rhetoric may be worth studying, as Milton is worth studying, for general "enrichment," but they believe that its mechanistic reality has given us nonphilosophical, theory-unconscious contemporary writing pedagogy.

While many issues present themselves here, I confine myself to Knoblauch and Brannon's own construction of the history of rhetoric. It appears that they themselves may have joined the world of the mechanistic because of the way that they have chosen to historicize rhetoric. By opposing classical and modern rhetoric, by creating a world of dark and a world of light, they have placed themselves in the ranks of the mechanistic. Consider their repeated prescriptions for the eradication of nonphilosophical, skill-based contemporary writing pedagogy:

remove classical rhetoric from instruction. They promote the curing of the ills of contemporary writing pedagogy—and there are many—with the decisive removal of classical rhetoric. However, the writers—and many who share their rhetorical stance—appear not to see that their often-repeated prescription is itself mechanistic. Their intentions and their execution do not overlap on this "classical" and "modern" opposition, the issue that is the foundation of their book. Their own use of the mechanistic allows them to discern a world of problems—labeled here as "classical rhetoric"—and a world of energizing possibility— labeled "modern rhetoric." But it is their own dichotomized conception of the history of rhetoric that allows them to create the concrete categories that provide the basis for their book and enable them to substitute one category of rhetoric for the other. They appear to do exactly what they accuse classical rhetoric of doing: they mechanize language.

A second structural device now becomes clear. The assertions of familiar logic come to act as evidence. Many of these assertions are offered in the form of large generalizations. In every chapter of the book, but especially in the first three chapters (pp. 11–76), assertions are made and then later regarded as evidence that eventually function as arguments that have been documented. Thus repeatedly in this book the assertion metamorphoses into evidence and eventually into fact. This writing strategy is not easy to analyze. One location of their writing strategy occurs in an important note on Michel Foucault. In a note for Chapter One, "Philosophy in the Writing Class," Knoblauch and Brannon write:

> The irreparable epistemological disjunction between ancient and contemporary thought is fundamental to our argument because it accounts, in our judgment, for the infertility of classical rhetorical concepts in modern discourse theory as well as in the modern classroom. The work of Michel Foucault is especially important to our position, in particular, *The Archaeology of Knowledge* (New York: Harper and Row, 1972) and *The Order of Things: An Archaeology of the Human Sciences* (New York: Pantheon Books, 1970). Foucault describes the epistemological shift with great subtlety, and the excitement of his arguments repays attentive reading despite their complex form. (p. 20)

This note stands in the text as persuasive evidence in the way that many scholarly notes do. It is based on the traditional logical structure that informs almost all academic writing. However, a problem arises immediately when one takes a closer look at the use of this kind of evidence. The Foucault statement is so broad that it cannot usefully support any statement. Knoblauch and Brannon cover two very difficult books by Foucault and tell us that they are hard to read but well worth the trouble. This information and recommendation do not provide evidence. Foucault is, indeed, crucial to contemporary rhetoric and composition studies; however, they undermine their important connection when they characterize Foucault's work as dealing with the singular "epistemological shift," rather than with the series of epistemological issues that he treats. If we are to respond to Foucault's important work, we need to be shown some examples of how to do that. The note cited here does not do that. It may entice us, but it does not persuade us by helping us to interiorize any of Foucault's work.

This use of Foucault indicates a primary writing strategy and rhetorical stance of Knoblauch and Brannon. They treat scholars on their "side" in the same way that they treat scholars on the other "side," as the Foucault references illustrate. They rely not only on their considerable knowledge and scholarly ability but also on generalizations and assertions that later reappear as documented fact. Their crucial point about the sterility and boredom of much contemporary writing pedagogy is largely lost for many readers. The important part of their work is hidden. They have, in fact, joined the Heritage School even as they have "frontally assaulted" it (p. 79). They have, it appears, made themselves lose their important insight from the very beginning of their book. The Foucault insertion states clearly and wisely that Foucault should be part of contemporary composition. However, even though I agree with this claim, I do not see here the persuasive material to make that claim, and certainly not any material that supports their major contention that classical rhetoric is dangerous.

Less structurally significant, but more rhetorically engaging, is the strategy of transferring one of the primary figures of classical rhetoric — Plato — from the "side" of classical rhetoric to their own organic "side." They select part of his work — his attack against sophistic rhetoric — to attack another part of his work — philosophical rhetoric — as it is manifested in the relationship of rhetoric and dialectic, one of the main topics of *Phaedrus*. Plato's elaborate work on theoretical rhetoric is not selected for this book-length treatment of historical rhetoric. The writers choose the Plato who compared *sophistic* rhetoric to cooking in *Gorgias*, not the Plato who merged the complexities of language and *eros* in *Phaedrus* and elevated rhetoric to a place close to dialectic. Their use of Plato exactly illustrates Lunsford and Ede's point about the fragmentation of the texts of classical rhetoric (pp. 41–43).

Knoblauch and Brannon's predetermined conclusions that derive from their dichotomized version of historical rhetoric lead them necessarily into persuasion breakdown in their presentation of evidence.

They set up an angle and they apply their "evidence" to fit that angle, a strategy that all encoders use and that might work here if they considered some alternative possibilities and showed us why those possibilities do not fit. Instead, they make assertions repeatedly rather than provide persuasion consistently. Familiar logic holds sway on every page of the book.

The removal of Plato from classical rhetoric also illustrates one of the book's major problems, and one of the major problems in contemporary rhetoric and composition studies. Knoblauch and Brannon decontextualize classical rhetoric. They do this by carefully plucking Aristotle's concepts out of their larger contexts, in exactly the manner William M. A. Grimaldi has shown us creates large interpretation problems (*Commentary*, pp. 349–356). They compound this problem by relying almost completely on secondary sources for their work in classical rhetoric, which they (their citations of George Kennedy's work are good examples) also take out of context. Decontextualizing becomes an important basis for Knoblauch and Brannon's argument. Look, for example, at their treatment of the complexities of *topoi* and of *logos*: these concepts are reduced to single-level, skill-oriented descriptions of nonthinking operations.

Their reliance on decontextualization is promoted by their acceptance of fifty-year-old translations that were examined in Chapter One. The bypassing of the clusters of meaning embedded in every keyword (such as *logos*) is, of course, another hallmark of the Heritage School. Only by using translation-as-substitution can the seven hundred years of classical rhetoric be reduced to a monolith. Gorgias' *logos* and Aristotle's *logos* are strangely equated. The translation issues are difficult to trace because of the absence of an index, but a reading of the chapter "Ancient Rhetoric in Modern Classrooms: That Old-Time Religion" reveals that keywords are taken for granted, that they are unexamined, and that translation-as-substitution replaces the complexities of keywords. Since, as Saussure indicates, languages articulate their own categories (Culler, p. 13), a book on language benefits especially from considering this primary linguistic fact. The writers need at least to indicate that they realize that the problem exists, even if they do not treat it at length.

The undulations of change that a keyword such as *logos* undergoes do not fit the mechanistic world view of *Rhetorical Traditions and the Teaching of Writing*. The conceptual bases of the book do not work. The factual errors create a series of difficulties. If they had reconsidered and rearranged their material (*contra* their reduction of the classical canon of *taxis*, or *dispositio*) they could have pressed more convincingly their important, timely case against current nonphilosophical writing pedagogy.

In spite of these difficulties, researchers in rhetoric and composition are fortunate to have Knoblauch and Brannon's book. The work offers an excellent illustration of some of the major problems in the contemporary reception of classical rhetoric: (1) the making of a monolith of seven hundred years of language history, a strategy that denies the language flux that is always a primary issue; (2) the attendant decontextualizing of writers and their concerns, as well as of readers and their concerns; and (3) the selection of secondary sources that themselves form the tradition of the Heritage School of rhetoric and composition criticism.

The problematic historicizing of rhetoric that Knoblauch and Brannon engage in—their use, for instance, of military metaphors (p. 79)—is typical of the tension that rhetoric has always been involved in.

## RHETORIC AND COMPOSITION ARE FACULTIES AS WELL AS SUBSTANTIVE CATEGORIES

Since rhetoric and composition are both a faculty and a form, and not only a substantive category, they are very susceptible to peculiar constructions. The productive clash between sophistic rhetoric and philosophical rhetoric that Plato sets up for us in the form of dialogue/dialectic/rhetoric is one of our earliest examples of this phenomenon. The movement of the clash is analyzed by George Kimball Plochmann and Franklin E. Robinson in *A Friendly Companion to Plato's Gorgias*. They write:

> demonstration and inquiry are two sides of the same coin in the *Gorgias*, . . . what seems to have been convincingly demonstrated later on turns out to have been a phase in an on-going inquiry of broader dimensions . . . (p. 321)

Plochmann and Robinson explain why *Gorgias* requires interpretation that takes account of these many changes within the text:

> What looked on first inspection to be a solid set of answers finally discloses itself to have been a propaedeutic, not less important for that reason, but now an incentive for further examinations of the same or closely related topics. In the *Gorgias*, at least, a principle and a tentative hypothesis are identical, viewed from two aspects. (p. 321)

Knoblauch and Brannon present exactly the kind of interpretation that Plochmann and Robinson argue against.

A clash that Knoblauch and Brannon do identify reveals a very real problem in contemporary rhetoric: writing instruction often reifies students and then their discourse, writing teachers frequently cling with religious zeal to the idea that theory has nothing to do with their work, and a gridlocked, positivistic attitude toward written discourse often prevails and limits the possibilities of "forming/thinking/writing" that Ann E. Berthoff has named for us.

However, Knoblauch and Brannon do not historicize this pedagogical problem. Rather than seeing a struggle or a dialectical clash in the development and definition of rhetoric and composition, Knoblauch and Brannon surgically remove Plato from the part of classical rhetoric he helped to create, a problem explored in more detail and as part of a trend in Chapter Four. So the dialectical energy of Plato's concerns with rhetoric and access to basic reality simply disappear. Knoblauch and Brannon seem to borrow Plato's arguments but in fact they distort them by eliminating most of his essential ideas of rhetoric. The main injustice that they do to Plato's work is the one they do to all of classical rhetoric: they decontextualize him and his writing. The surgical removal of his ideas from their milieu does not allow Plato's ideas to function very engagingly. This mode of interpretation—the equivalent of making Plato commit verbal suicide—prepares the way for all their subsequent discussion of classical rhetoric.

The mechanistic nature of their own book might indicate to Knoblauch and Brannon that the urge to categorize is inherent in the dialectical clash of knowledge and person. They artfully arrange their dichotomies (their "sides") so that this strategy is obscured. Knoblauch and Brannon are artful because they not only remove Plato from rhetoric, they present Plato as if he were on the organic "side."

More artful than this maneuver is their persistent and unexamined construction (their fiction) of the monolith of classical rhetoric. Monoliths are easier to handle than multiplicities. Their monolith/reality partly depends on this collapse. They melt down hundreds of years of what George Steiner has called the Heraclitean flux of language into a sheet of impenetrable metal. One must question their conceptual bases before the meltdown because afterwards there is nothing to work with except their construction.

If we think of the history of rhetoric as a series of dialectical tensions, we can see Plato's struggle with rhetoric as one stage in this continuing struggle rhetoric has with itself. Plato embodies the always present dialectical tension of rhetoric in his apparently straightforward connection of rhetoric to cooking in *Gorgias*. He captures, as do Knoblauch and Brannon, a rhetoric that is rule-centered, technocratic, and dependent on tricks—essentially a mode of discourse that has so tightly bound itself in rules that it has strangled knowledge and thinking. However, Plato does not stop with sophistic rhetoric and technical rhetoric. He uses his explications of these two kinds of rhetoric to persuade us, in *writing*, that philosophical rhetoric is too important to be abandoned.

The Platonic struggle—rhetoric as a series of tricks versus rhetoric as a promoter of knowledge (technical rhetoric and philosophical rhetoric)—is not clearly seen unless one considers more of Plato's works than *Gorgias*. Knoblauch and Brannon do not cite the Plato of *Phaedrus* when they bring Plato over to their stance in the argument. The issue before Knoblauch and Brannon should be this: there are at least two kinds of rhetoric, technical rhetoric and philosophical rhetoric. Plato discusses both of them and enacts both of them. Knoblauch and Brannon choose only one to treat, Plato's attack on technical rhetoric, because it fits so well into their mechanistic/romantic historicizing of rhetoric. They ignore Plato's complex investigation of rhetoric, its possibilities for knowledge, that we see complexly and artistically presented in *Phaedrus*. In other words, Knoblauch and Brannon interrupt Plato's own dialectic. This monotheoretical approach to rhetoric typifies all of Knoblauch and Brannon's strategies in the book. They deprive rhetoric and composition of its own dialectical history and replace it with one issue: classical rhetoric is mechanistic (technical). Selecting only one part of Plato's writing on rhetoric weakens Knoblauch and Brannon's writing *ethos*.

The issues that appear to separate classical rhetoric from modern rhetoric have been explicitly changed by Lunsford and Ede, Swearingen, and Grimaldi. In fact, the charts that Lunsford and Ede offer in their essay "On Distinctions between Classical and Modern Rhetoric" (pp. 40, 65), refute Knoblauch and Brannon's thesis. While Lunsford and Ede's seminal article was probably not available to Knoblauch and Brannon during the writing of *Rhetorical Traditions and the Teaching of Writing*, Grimaldi's connections between classical and modern rhetoric were available, as was the work of Richard McKeon on the same subject (for example, "Rhetoric in the Middle Ages," pp. 1–32). One of Grimaldi's most important points is that the emphasis on Aristotle's formal logic (Lunsford and Ede's "logic-chopping automaton") has led many critics to ignore Aristotle's emphasis on what we would now call psychological issues. In fact, the psychological contact between human beings rests on the same principles that Plato teaches us with his work on *daimon* and his symbiotic analysis of rhetoric and dialectic (for example, in *Symposium* and in *Phaedrus*). In the same way, Aristotle's interior persuaders (usually translated as "artistic proofs") have the power for modern rhetoric that they had in classical rhetoric. While different historical periods have their own emphases, as Susanne K. Langer shows in *Philosophy in a New Key*, there is always a commonality, or at least a residue, of a former period's preoccupation. There is even a recursiveness of ideas. For example, the Platonic Socrates' analysis of the *daimon* in *Phaedrus* and *Symposium* is as meaningful to us now because of post-Freudian psychology as it was in fourth-century B.C. Athens. Anton Ehrenzweig explores the possibilities of undifferentiated creativity in a way that echoes Plato in *Phaedrus*, particularly in the last section. Aristotle's work on *ethos* in the *Rhetoric* recurs in Kenneth Burke's emphasis on mystery and hierarchy in *A Rhetoric of Motives*. While Knoblauch and Brannon are entirely correct in reminding us that many important language and thought issues have occurred since Quintilian's time and that much of this thought is absent from writing pedagogy, they are wrong in seeing two discrete universes of discourse, one ancient and one modern. The problems are not that clearly cut.

Knoblauch and Brannon are right in passionately inveighing against much current writing instruction. They opposed what Kennedy calls technical rhetoric in *Classical Rhetoric and Its Christian and Secular Tradition from Ancient to Modern Times:* the handbook-based, rule-bound boredom that proliferated in fourth-century B.C. Athens as it proliferates (for many of the same reasons) in the twentieth-century United States. Knoblauch and Brannon oppose rule-based, nonphilosophical writing instruction because it is counterproductive to thought. They begin from a strong position: we suffer deficiencies whose assumptions need to be addressed more seriously. But Knoblauch and Brannon weaken their larger case in their construction of classical rhetoric. They historicize this period as a monolithic unit of seven hundred years. In rightly opposing the nostalgia that characterizes so much of the contemporary reception of classical rhetoric, they convert primary classical writing into inert texts. They reify classical rhetoric almost out of existence. Knoblauch and Brannon's own use of translation-as-substitution, their inattention to keyword formation, and the disregard of current idiolects, match exactly the essential strategies of the Heritage School.

Knoblauch and Brannon's presentation of classical rhetoric—from the first chapter to the last note—is itself monolithic: their classical rhetoric begins with a hyperlogical Aristotle, ignores Gorgias, Isocrates, and other rhetoricians, regards Plato as a nonrhetorician, and glides smoothly to Rome without a hint of temporal, geographical, cultural, ideological, or linguistic change. Classical rhetoric for these recent additions to the Heritage School is a very long, impenetrable sheet of rock. It is forbidding, inhuman, and dangerous. It is so fraught with difficulty in this interpretation that the primary response of Knoblauch and Brannon is that classical rhetoric must be "frontally assaulted" (p. 79), an image worthy of many a Greek and Roman writer.

Lunsford and Ede, Swearingen, Grimaldi, Corbett, Ochs, Ong,

Havelock, Enos, and others (only one of whom—Corbett—I can find referred to in this book) construct classical rhetoric in alternative ways. Their approaches defy prescription, translation-as-substitution, and formulizing because they depend on consulting primary texts in late twentieth-century idiolects, on attending to the complex resonance of keywords, and on attending to the interrelationship of language and culture that is the collective of ideas called classical rhetoric. These writers understand and engage the clash of dialectics that defines classical rhetoric. These exploratory critics, who differ substantially among themselves in their theoretical bases and interpretive lenses, enact a presentation of rhetoric that invites newness rather than the closed fist of positivist definiteness. The critical conversation in classical rhetoric studies produced since 1965 does not exist in *Rhetorical Traditions and the Teaching of Writing*, a premier example of positivism gone astray in the historicizing of rhetoric and composition.


## INTERPRETATION AND THE RHETORICAL UNCONSCIOUS


Crucial interpretive challenges in classical rhetoric and composition studies were widely available not only to Knoblauch and Brannon but to Bizzell and Herzberg as well. Some of these alternative interpretations could have led these four scholars to re-examine some of their assumptions. A sense of something missing pervades both these presentations of historical rhetoric, a sense of the missing that goes far beyond the usual reading between the lines of a Gricean analysis of texts. The palpable sense of the missing lies in the fact that their critical assumptions are not overtly or covertly examined. While I do not advocate a "field-coverage model" (Vitanza in " 'Notes' Towards Historiographies of Rhetorics") of surveying the best and worst of all that has been said and thought about classical rhetoric (an adaptation of the Arnoldian agenda), I do advocate that critics display some self-consciousness. Victor J. Vitanza makes this point in " 'Notes' Towards Historiographies of Rhetorics; or, Rhetorics of the Histories of Rhetorics: Traditional, Revisionary, and Sub/Versive." The unconsciousness of Knoblauch and Brannon's book is connected to the silence on the dialectical stances of many contemporary writers on classical rhetoric and composition. Knoblauch and Brannon become their own worst enemies in this regard. They damage their collective *ethos* by appearing to be unaware of fascinating and large bodies of critical dialogue in their chosen fields of discussion. They forfeit what Aristotle called the most important interior persuader, *ethos*, (*Rhetoric*, Cooper, p. 1) by writing as if they do not know about the last generation of critical dialogue on classical rhetoric. Their rhetorical stance is perplexing.

The writing strategy of rhetorical unconsciousness that Knoblauch and Brannon choose is unfortunate for another reason as well; specifically, their analysis of nonphilosophical, theory-unconscious writing instruction remains compelling. This instruction, which writing instructors witness every day, plods on with the energy of its own unexamined repetition and the weightiness of its definitive passivity; it weakens much of the contemporary research in rhetoric and composition and of language study generally, as the hundreds of writing textbooks in print so boringly testify. But instead of identifying the problems of the Heritage School, they have heaped validation on it. They have made it stronger than it ever was. Their "frontal assault" (p. 79) aims at the wrong "target." Their victory, to continue their military imagery, becomes all the more impressive. By not engaging any part of this generation's most compelling writing on classical rhetoric and composition, Knoblauch and Brannon are able to sweep over not only the seven hundred years of classical rhetoric but to continue making peculiar constructions of the rest of rhetorical history. This kind of historicism needs some investigation.

In boldly setting themselves against technical, dry rhetoric, they have given away the strongest element in the means of persuasion available to them. They have lost Plato's rhetoric and dialectic, the form of rhetoric that is the most inclusive of human symbolic action and that has changed little since the fourth century B.C., regardless of Foucault's changes in *episteme*. They have lost the psychologically astute, prescholasticized Aristotle of the *Rhetoric*, where the interaction of the interior persuaders teaches us more about encoder presentation than I.A. Richards' mechanical rhetoric and other Heritage School works ever have. They have lost the representation of Greek rhetoric written and spoken by Cicero and enacted for us in his letters as he stood in a unique moment in the history of orality and literacy.[5] They have lost the definitive work of Marshall McLuhan, Ong, Havelock, I.J. Gelb, and Lucien Febvre and Henri-Jean Martin on the shifts in consciousness and language brought about by technology and consciousness change. So compelling, in fact, is the work of McLuhan et al. that any extended work on classical rhetoric must surely take account of it, even if these writers' ideas are refuted in the critical conversation. All the dialectical writers I name here are committed in some form to a more conscious rhetoric, to the material that "comes before method and makes it

---

[5]See Tony M. Lentz's *Orality and Literacy in Hellenic Greece,* especially the chapter "Orality and Literacy in Basic Education," pp. 46–70.

pertinent, directed, and organized," to quote Knoblauch and Brannon's own agenda (p. 1). Knoblauch and Brannon have, because of their initial stance of joining the Heritage School, given up their very strongest supporters. These writers too are against a "narrowly denotative" (Knoblauch & Brannon, p. 96) classical rhetoric. But unlike Knoblauch and Brannon, these scholars have interpreted other histories and other kinds of consciousness in classical rhetoric.

## CLASSICAL RHETORIC AS A NOETIC FIELD IN UNITED STATES PEDAGOGY

In *Writing Instruction in Nineteenth-Century American Colleges,* Berlin demonstrates that rhetoric is always a social construction and that it arises from a noetic field, in the sense that Ong has established in *Rhetoric, Romance, and Technology.* For Berlin a noetic field is "a closed system defining what can, and cannot, be known; the nature of the knower; the nature of the relationship between the knower, the known, and the audience; and the nature of language. Rhetoric is thus ultimately implicated in all a society attempts. It is at the center of a culture's activities" (p. 2). The rhetorical stance that Berlin announces in the opening of this book assumes importance because it leads to his fusion of the public and the personal in rhetoric through the writing of Ralph Waldo Emerson. This fusion reinvigorates the concept of the romantic in English-speaking cultures, rescuing it from the emotional, self-dominated conception of the "romantic" that has constituted one version of it for many years. Most importantly, Berlin ties public and personal rhetoric to the language that has been taught in United States schools, thereby explicitly acknowledging the primary way that schools create culture. To explicate the noetic fields that rhetorics necessarily occupy, Berlin identifies three dominant nineteenth-century rhetorics in the United States: classical rhetoric, psychological-epistemological rhetoric, and romantic rhetoric. Each of these rhetorics inhabited a different noetic field.

Berlin's presentation of classical rhetoric stands out from the originality of the rest of his book because it follows so clearly the lines of Heritage School presentations of classical rhetoric. In fact, Berlin conforms closely to four of the primary characteristics I have identified in the Heritage School.

First, Berlin historicizes classical rhetoric by beginning systematic rhetoric with Aristotle in the fourth century B.C. rather than with Corax and Tisias in the fifth century B.C., the various schools of the Sophists, including Isocrates, and Plato. In other words, the swirl of rhetorical activity of the fifth century B.C. is left out in a way that suggests that it never existed or was not important. Berlin begins rhetorical history with Aristotle and then portrays its seven hundred years as Aristotelian in a very logical sense. Other rhetorical voices are not heard in this presentation. The Heritage School monolith is consequently established.

The second Heritage School presentation that Berlin relies on is the dominance of "logic" in classical rhetoric, a position that tends to accompany the first issue of the monolith. Familiar logic pervades this presentation. Berlin writes,

> Classical rhetoric defines the real as rational. The universe is governed by the rules of reason, and the human mind is so constructed that, at its best, it is governed by the same rules. Knowledge is therefore found through the formulization of these rules of reason—in Aristotelian logic. This logic is deductive, requiring the application of generalizations to particular situations—in other words, the use of the syllogism. Induction is included in the system, but it is not as important as deduction because truth must always be derived through a set of prior, nonempirical principles, found through the rules of deductive logic, that will explain the significance of the particular (p. 4).

Berlin furthers his logic-dominant interpretation of classical rhetoric by firmly placing Aristotle in the Heritage School: "In Aristotle, then, we discover a noetic field in which the world is made up of a finite set of truths, logically arranged and discovered through logical principles" (p. 5). Classical rhetoric once again becomes a version of Aristotle as logic chopper and therefore rather easily dispensed with.

The third aspect of Heritage School classical rhetoric that appears here is the severing of thought and discourse: "Since his [Aristotle's] rhetoric is deductive, the search for the available means of persuasion amounts to exploring what one knows, and then applying it to the situation under consideration" (p. 5). The language/thought opposition, so common in Heritage School presentations, is taken to an extreme by Berlin: "Language for Aristotle is little more than a simple sign system, with thought and word enjoying a separate existence, to be brought together only for purposes of communication. Rational truths exist apart from the means used to express them" (p. 6). The familiar logic and the splitting of thought and discourse enable each other to exist in this construction, as they did in the previous examples of *Rhetorical Traditions and the Teaching of Writing* and *The Bedford Bibliography*. A similar split occurs in Berlin's presentation of clasical rhetoric when he overlooks the growing power of literacy in the classical period and instead privileges orality. Berlin writes, "Aristotle's rhetoric is preeminently oral and politically conservative. It is oral, at least in part, because it is designed for speaking situations involving small groups" (p. 6). As we saw earlier in this chapter with *Rhetorical Traditions and the Teaching of Writing*, the rhetorical stance of suppressing in interpretive discourse the power of literacy in ancient Greece goes far beyond the problem of making an error or omitting an important aspect. The suppression changes the intellectual configuration of ancient Greece. The work on orality-literacy-secondary orality written by Ong, Havelock, Lentz, Bessinger, Parry, Lord, Enos, and others can no longer, as we have seen previously, be ignored. Berlin's innovative use of noetic fields as they apply to United States pedagogy and social constructions breaks down in his explanation of classical rhetoric because he has misrepresented the noetic fields of that period by deleting literacy from his interpretation. Consequently, the rest of his interpretation of this version of nineteenth-century United States rhetoric does not work.

Berlin relies heavily on Marjorie Grene's 1963 *A Portrait of Aristotle*, an interpretation that rests firmly in the philosophical, logical mold that Nussbaum has characterized as one prominent version of philosophical research in the United States and England. In joining this discourse community for the classical rhetoric portions of the book, Berlin prevents himself from considering the orality-literacy hypothesis, the multilayered meanings of keywords and the problems of translation, the implications of quickly severing thought and discourse, and the results of emphasizing the familiar logic that accompanies so much of the commentary on Aristotle and his writing.

Fortunately, Berlin's presentation of classical rhetoric does not substantively affect his radical interpretations of other aspects of rhetoric, constructions that apply to all eras of rhetoric and not just to the nineteenth century in the United States. Berlin is particularly astute in his analysis of the revolt of people in the United States against "aristocratic universities" (p. 18). The elitism that clings to classical studies and the nostalgia for a nonexistent golden past have made classical studies of all kinds—not just classical rhetoric studies—appear to be useless or even dangerous, as we saw in Chapter One. The elitism of United States aristocrats periodically undergoes expunging, and Berlin accounts for these changes well. They are connected to the noetic fields he organizes his book with, and they reveal a great deal about recurrent surges of unhappiness with public education that form a substantial part of the history of United States pedagogy, ideology, and culture.

The purging of aristocratic dominance in United States educational systems in general, and rhetoric and composition studies in particular, has had no greater power than in nineteenth-century transcendental-ism. Berlin, in his most persuasive section of the presentation of United States rhetorics, makes Emerson's writing and speaking the center of this most powerful period (pp. 42–57). Berlin retrieves the romantic stance from the overly personal, overly isolated stance that many scholars in the discipline of English—both in composition and in literary studies—have valorized in their research and in their curricula. The Male Masters mode of United States literary studies (all male, all white, and frequently preoccupied with male relationships to United States land and geography) and the Romantics of composition studies (the student writer in isolation, exploring his or her feelings as the "reality" of living) are reconstructed by Berlin in his sensitive explication of Emerson's writing and rhetoric, particularly in the two often-ignored essays on eloquence. Instead of the standard composition and literary models of the romantic writer, Berlin finds a union (a "fusion") between the public person and the individual person in Emerson's rhetoric. Berlin finds this union through his use of the noetic field that gives rise to Emersonian rhetoric. This noetic field, Berlin's new understanding of the romantic, does not privilege the public person over the private person, "commu-nication" over "expression." He avoids these oppositions so common in the history of rhetoric and composition studies by showing Emerson's creation of a third category, the fused state of public and private, the transcendence of these two categories. Berlin writes: "Emerson can be seen as anticipating modern epistemology, arguing for reality as the product of the interaction of the perceiver and that which is perceived" (p. 47). This accurate and compelling description of Emerson's rhetoric can provide one basis for the contemporary reconstructions of historical rhetoric and composition studies. It mends at least two kinds of factions: (1) it connects the often artificially separated regions of rhetoric and composition, allowing scholars who make substantial distinctions be-tween rhetoric on the one hand and composition on the other to have a theory that emphasizes their similarities; and (2) it shows a way to overcome the familiar and unhelpful rifts between rhetoric and compo-sition studies and literary studies. Both these splits have created language curricula in the United States that are skill-oriented rather than thinking-oriented, that are instrumentalist, in Gadamer's sense of a handy tool, and that reside in curricula as ultimate truth. "Content" in both these versions of language education rules all. If Berlin's presen-tation of Emersonian romantic rhetoric can be adapted to curricula in the disciplines of English and Speech Communication, then he will have done more than rehistoricize nineteenth-century rhetoric and composi-tion studies; he will have helped to radicalize language curricula that are frequently distinguished by their ability to make a fascinating subject utterly boring and apparently useless, a condition frequently seen in freshman writing courses.

## BERLIN, EMERSON, AND PLATONIC RHETORIC

While reinterpreting Emerson in a synthetic way, in a manner that shows the epistemological underpinnings that rhetoric and composition studies share with literature studies, Berlin also inadvertently explicates Plato's rhetoric. Berlin states that Plato is not helpful in rhetoric:

> Those who see Emerson as advocating a rhetoric of self-expression place him—either consciously or unconsciously—within the Platonic tradition that denies the possibility of a rhetoric of public discourse. . . . For Plato, truth is not based on sensory experience. It is discovered through an internal apprehension, a private vision of a realm that transcends the material. (pp. 43–44)

This interpretation disregards Plato's commitment to the sensual realm. Plato's philosophy does not deny the sensual realm; rather, it takes full account of the sensual, palpable world. The strict dualism that characterizes much Platonic criticism frequently ignores one of the levels that makes a dualism in the first place: the world of the here and now. Perhaps because Plato's invocation of the Forms—so poetic, so ethereal—is often inviting and sometimes confusing, readers tend to discount the sensible world.

However perplexing Plato's forms may be, they do maintain a relationship with the sensible world. To discount the sensible world, then, is to leave out a significant portion of Plato's thinking. This idea, explored more fully in Chapter Four, takes on great importance in any era's reception of classical rhetoric. Dismissing Plato because he is not concerned with the palpable world, and then dismissing Aristotle because he is too committed to logic, and then ignoring the Sophists altogether leads to the conclusion that classical rhetoric is not only boring but possibly dangerous. Berlin has joined this particular discourse community for part of the 1984 book.

In spite of the stance that denies Plato's consistent accounting for and even commitment to the sensual realm, Berlin does recognize the rhetorical complexity of Plato's rhetoric:

> For Plato, the rhetorical experience encourages speaker and listener to break out of their ordinary perceptual set, to become free of the bondage

to the material world and past error. Rhetoric is subversive, a disruption of ordinary experience, requiring new ways of perceiving in order to overcome long-held conventions and opinions. (p. 44)

Berlin's recognition of the subversion of the ordinary, of the taken-for-granted, represents an important departure from the conventional stance that holds that Plato rejected rhetoric. Berlin's inclusion of Plato in a radical appropriation of rhetorics and their noetic fields is important and reinforces Berlin's larger argument that rhetoric, culture, and pedagogy are parts of the same thing, not isolated spheres acting independently of one another.

Ultimately, however, Berlin separates Plato and his intellectual heir Emerson:

> Despite his admiration for Plato, Emerson's philosophical idealism is not Platonic. His position is indeed closer to such moderns as Ernst Cassirer and Susanne Langer. Emerson starts with the difficult question of the relation between subject and object. Common Sense Realism takes the object, the material realm, as the ground of the real. Aristotle finds the real in the rational, while Plato looks to the supersensory, the absolute, for ultimate reality. Emerson departs from all as he locates the real in the fusion of the sensual and ideal. Reality is a human construction, joining the world of ideas to the material object in an act of creative perception. The sensory realm by itself is lifeless matter. The ideal by itself is meaningless abstraction. Knowledge is possible only in the interaction of the two. (p. 46)

The "moderns" identified here resemble the "modern epistemology" that Berlin refers to throughout this book. Knoblauch and Brannon rely on the same large and undifferentiated category for many of their interpretations. When Berlin writes that "Emerson can be seen as anticipating modern epistemology" (p. 47) one is led to assume that modern epistemology refers to late nineteenth and twentieth-century ideas. When, in other instances, he refers to "post-Kantian epistemology," one is led to assume that Berlin is referring to late-eighteenth, nineteenth, and twentieth-century eras. Since the phrases "modern epistemology" and "post-Kantian epistemology" (p. 49) appear to be used interchangeably, the reader remains unsure of the eras Berlin means to indicate. In addition, the meaning of either phrase is left unexplained.

Berlin comes close to aligning Plato's and Emerson's thinking when he adapts Richard M. Weaver's interpretation of Plato on public discourse and applies it to Emerson:

> Despite the harsh criticism Plato levels at rhetoric, Weaver explains, he offers the possibility of a rhetoric of public affairs in the *Phaedrus*. Weaver

sums up this revised position: "We now see the true rhetorician as a noble lover of good, who works through dialectic and through poetic or analogic association. However he is compelled to modulate by the peculiar features of an occasion, this is his method." These elements are the distinguishing features of Emerson's rhetoric as well—the rhetor as lover of truth, dialectic, and analogist who is responsive to his auditors. The important difference is that Emerson erects his system on a post-Kantian epistemology and a democratic egalitarianism. (p. 49)

Berlin's description of Emerson's rhetoric accords with the interpretations of many readers of Plato. When Berlin states that Emersonian "rhetoric must be committed to truth, it must be persuasive, and it must consider the particular audience" (p. 50), he is Platonic. By placing Emerson in "post-Kantian epistemology," Berlin makes many rhetorical ideas unavailable to Plato. Nonetheless, by reading Emerson through Weaver's version of Plato, Berlin obliquely acquiesces to Plato's role as a rhetorical theorist. In Berlin's construction, Plato is also "post-Kantian," as we see in the following summary of Emerson's rhetoric:

> Emerson's rhetoric, not restricted to securing a desired effect on the audience, was attempting to restore the search for truth to the composing act. Truth, moreover, is organic, is a holistic product growing out of the entire rhetorical situation—reality, speaker, listener, and language. All are involved in discovery and each changes in response to each. These are not static entities to be considered through mechanical calculation. (p. 57)

These words describe the rhetoric of *Phaedrus* as much as they describe the rhetoric of Emerson's essays.

In the 1987 *Rhetoric and Reality: Writing Instruction in American Colleges, 1900–1985,* Berlin assumes this stance toward Plato's rhetoric in his analysis of subjective theories of rhetoric (pp. 11–12). While his discussion of this kind of rhetoric is particularly trenchant, offering a detailed interpretation of the private writing that dominates many writing classes (p. 12), the Platonic bases for subjective rhetorics remain a problem for the reasons set forth above in the appropriation of classical rhetoric in *Writing Instruction in Nineteenth-Century American Colleges.* In separate sections on classical rhetoric, Berlin categorizes the field as transactional, which "discovers reality in the interaction of the features of the rhetorical process itself—in the material reality, writer, audience, and language. . . . The distinguishing feature of the version of classical rhetoric that appeared during the sixties and seventies was its commitment to rationality" (p. 155). Berlin then presents the Heritage School interpretation of classical rhetoric, with a clause given to the alternative presentations of Lunsford and Ede and of Grimaldi.

As in the case of the earlier book, Berlin's presentation of Heritage School classical rhetoric is isolated from the rest of his arguments so that the nonpersuasiveness of his appropriation of classical rhetoric does not substantively affect his very important analyses of other twentieth-century rhetorics. Nonetheless, a more complex interpretation of classical rhetoric in the United States would have strengthened both his books.

## CLASSICAL RHETORIC AND CONTEMPORARY WRITING PEDAGOGY

In the two book-length examples examined in this chapter, an intriguing split occurs. For both *Rhetorical Traditions and the Teaching of Writing* and *Writing Instruction in Nineteenth-Century American Colleges*, the ancient world of rhetoric represents the "logical" in a pejorative sense; the modern world of rhetoric represents high intelligence and general advancement. In addition, the writers of these books remove the only writer they like in classical rhetoric—Plato—from the field completely. In the same way, they remove all the Greek rhetoricians from Corax and Tisias onward. Why? Because these deleted writers are not "logical."

While Knoblauch and Brannon are committed to an individualistic, private vision of writing pedagogy, Berlin takes a larger view and sees the social construction of rhetorical reality that operates in the classroom as well as in politics and in culture. His recognition of noetic fields that are always operating—excluding some things and including others—makes his appropriation of historical rhetoric far more believable. Knoblauch and Brannon, who present a great deal of helpful material on pedagogy, all in the romantic compositionist stance, advocate a privatistic, eventually atomistic, kind of writing instruction. Their project is nurturing, individualized, and unconscious of the individual writer's role in culture, rhetoric, or ideology.

## REMOVING AUTOMATONS FROM CLASSICAL RHETORIC

Is it possible to construct the history of classical rhetoric since 1965 so that automatons are transcended? In other words, can we re-present a classical rhetoric that is not inherently inferior, outdated, or elitist? In addition, can the "modern" rhetorical era—whether it begins in the seventeenth, eighteenth, or nineteenth centuries, be viewed as an accumulation of all preceding historical periods, or as a continuing dialectic or sparring conversation? Can we recognize that we inevitably must read Gorgias and the rest through the lenses of such movements as modernism and post-modernism?

Affirmative answers to this question occur in numerous places. Two prominent examples occur in the work of Donovan J. Ochs in Speech Communication and Edward P.J. Corbett in English, who offer alternative interpretations of one kind of logical structure in classical rhetoric.

In "Cicero's *Topica:* A Process View of Invention," Ochs shows that Cicero's use of the *loci* in the mature *Topics* provides an elastic and adaptable means of developing logical thinking:

> the *Topica* presents a methodology for inventing matter and form for an oration that is considerably less mechanical than that offered in the *De Inventione*. . . . Cicero, most probably, did not view the topical system as a mechanical method. Instead, he seems to understand its active, dynamic character, but fails to address, clearly and concisely, its rhetorical nature. (p. 117)

Ochs' construction of Cicero as a thought-based theorist rather than a skill-based practitioner provides essential interpretation in any reappropriation of classical rhetoric. He shows how Cicero's theory can be appropriated by skill-based interpreters (the early *On Invention*, long the only Cicero available to western scholars, does read like a prescriptive, rule-centered textbook of the kind that Plato and Aristotle complained and that contemporary critics have also lamented). Ochs shows how other works of Cicero, in this case the *Topics*, offer thought-based writing theory. By interpreting Cicero's writing in context, by taking account of keywords such as *topoi*, and by resisting a formalist literary analysis that would exclude many of Cicero's writings, Ochs is able to present a Cicero who thinks in discourse rather than a Heritage School Cicero who carves rules of oratory into stone.

The kind of interpretation that Ochs provides appears also in Corbett's "The *Topoi* Revisited," in which a history of the *topoi* is presented:

> The topics are, to use W. Rhys Roberts's term, "lines of argument," and their classification is based on the characteristic ways in which the human mind reasons or thinks. For me, the notion that the topics represent the natural way in which the human mind reasons or thinks keeps the topics from being some kind of artificial gimmick that the ancient rhetoricians invented to facilitate the thinking process—a kind of "thinking by numbers." Just as the syllogism represented Aristotle's systemization of how the human mind reasons deductively, the topics represented Aristotle's codification of the various ways in which the human mind probes a subject

to discover something significant or cogent that can be said about that subject. (p. 47)

This reconstruction of the *topoi* and the placement of them in a larger historical context makes the *topoi* useful for both researchers and teachers of discourse. Ancient rhetoricians in these two contemporary appropriations of classical rhetoric are not automatons chopping but persons thinking.

## RELATIONSHIPS BETWEEN AUTOMATONS AND CONTEMPORARY ROMANTICS

The romantic movements in rhetoric and composition studies find two of their primary incarnations in Knoblauch and Brannon's book and in Berlin's books. The two kinds of romanticism differ significantly. Knoblauch and Brannon's version is revealed in chapters such as "Modern Rhetoric in the Classroom: Making Meaning Matter" and "Responding to Texts: Facilitating Revision in the Writing Workshop." These chapters treat writing pedagogy as a celebration of the writing student's self, an exploration of individual interiority that will enable the students to become more effective users of language and better people. Self knowledge in the sense of discovering areas of the writer's psyche, or personality, or previously not fully formed attitudes constitutes the quest for "meaning" in this kind of romanticism. Knoblauch and Brannon as well as romantics such as William Coles, Ken Macrorie, and many others have produced an impressive body of writing on this rhetorical stance in the teaching of writing. They have helped to move writing instruction away from the current-traditional paradigm that emphasizes artificial modes (exposition, description, narration, argument, many versions of process, and so on) and microscopic skill enhancement (error correction, traditional paragraph formation, and so on). This movement has made rhetoric and composition studies much more effective in many ways.

Frank J. D'Angelo, in *A Conceptual Theory of Rhetoric*, calls this approach "the new romanticism," a "new emphasis on writing which is relatively free of control and direction" (p. 159). D'Angelo writes: "These new approaches emphasize feeling rather than intellect, exploration and discovery rather than preconceived ideas, the imagination, creativity, free association, fantasy, play, dreams, the unconscious, nonintellectual sensing, the stream-of-consciousness, and the self" (p. 159). D'Angelo's own appropriation of new romanticism is tied to research in psychology, whereas Knoblauch and Brannon's approach does not treat the fields that make up cognitive and depth (post-Freudian) psychology.

The difficulty with the personal romantic approach—the kind not informed by psychological theory—is that it frequently leads student writers—and probably their teachers as well—to believe that writing and thinking are activities that exist separately from larger worlds. In other words, the privatization that is encouraged, the inward journey that students are encouraged to take, is not connected to other worlds the students inhabit. It is not enough to call these other worlds the public sphere, as this branch of composition romanticists has done. Rather, all writing—from a grocery list to a manifesto—transcends both private and public selves by partaking of systems that all speakers of the language share.

Proponents of this stance contend that students can learn to write with the teacher who acts as a facilitator but that the teacher cannot teach (p. 102). They discuss writing teachers as people who "promote growth" and who are "facilitators of growth" (p. 102). Personal writing and revision strategies unconnected to the theories that give rise to them are privileged in this kind of romantic classroom. This kind of romanticism is frequently and perhaps unfairly associated with anti-intellectualism because "natural" abilities are said to enable the students to become effective writers. Knoblauch and Brannon are explicit about the importance of keeping writing theory away from students: "what they [writing teachers] know about modern rhetoric only informs their teaching; it doesn't constitute class business" (p. 102).

Berlin's kind of romanticism is much closer to D'Angelo's theories of the romantic in writing. Berlin sees romantic rhetoric as a fusion of the interior of the writer and the exterior worlds that the writer inhabits. Berlin's interpretation of Emerson's transcendental romanticism is understandable from this point of view. Berlin, like Emerson, wants to transcend the private self and the public self through a fusion that makes each sphere more meaningful. For Berlin, the individual writer is unavoidably a part of a noetic field that is shared by others. In this rhetorical stance, Berlin is like a classical rhetorician, whereas Knoblauch and Brannon are part of the emphasis on the individual not necessarily constrained by public discourse purposes. Berlin understands, as Isocrates, Plato, and Aristotle did, the connections between and the sameness of private language and public arenas; and, like Quintilian, he understands the language training that the child should receive in order to combine personal capabilities and public performance. In other words, Berlin's romantic rhetoric enables all kinds of discourse to be generated and decoded. In his second book, *Rhetoric and Reality*, Berlin offers a persuasive synthesis of theories of the romantic and how they might fit curricula. In his treatment of subjective theories of rhetoric, Berlin identifies romantic positions as subjective, as opposed to objective (the positivist stance of a knowable and definable reality) and to transactional rhetoric (classical, cognitive, and epistemic).


## SOME CHARACTERISTICS OF AN INTEGRATION OF ROMANTIC COMPOSITION AND CLASSICAL RHETORIC

Any integration or resonant exchange of contemporary writing theory and classical rhetoric must take account of the power of familiar logic and the ways that traditional logic, or Moss's concept of practical reasoning, can be researched and taught without lapsing into familiar logic. One easy route to this integration would be a return to the texts and contexts of classical rhetorical practical reasoning. This would require an updating of texts, as was discussed in Chapter One. While Plato's writing has received careful and updated translations (see, for example, Yale University Press's *Dialogues of Plato*, translated and annotated by R.E. Allen), Aristotle's more problematic series of lecture notes that treat his theories of rhetoric have not enjoyed the same contemporary care. Cicero and Quintilian's rhetorical work need to be translated for late twentieth-century ears, minds, and psyches, but, as we saw in Chapter One, we still are using generations-old English texts for them. Richard Leo Enos has begun to remedy this problem by providing his own substantial translations of Cicero in *The Literate Mode of Cicero's Legal Rhetoric*. As we see in the Enos example, the accessibility of classical rhetoric texts depends on avoiding the problem Saussure complained about with translation-as-substitution. The recognition of and attention to keywords that Enos, Corbett, Ochs, and others display need to be extended. The Glossary in Winifred Bryan Horner's *Rhetoric in the Classical Tradition* (pp. 440–451) follows this agenda effectively by incorporating central concepts of classical rhetoric into the ordinary and extraordinary discourse of college writing students.

Traditional philosophical presentation of rhetoric as a primarily logical activity has not proven useful in contemporary rhetoric and composition studies, as this chapter partly seeks to show. Neither has the popular familiar logic in which logic is regarded as a sphere of evil. Rediscovering and discovering the possibilities of *logos* will enable contemporary studies in classical rhetoric to make connections among the other interior persuaders (*ethos* and *pathos*) and will provide, as Moss writes, "methods of stimulating and ordering thought about matters of common concern—that might inform our teaching of writing today" (p. 1). Moss continues her analysis by responding to the scholars committed to familiar logic:

Thus this negative evaluation of classical rhetoric is based upon a rhetoric shorn of the reasoning dynamic contained in the *topoi,* and expressed artfully in enthymeme and example, the conceptions of appropriateness and timeliness of *kairos,* and the necessity of framing discourse in regard to its end or *telos.* (p. 4)

The project that Moss establishes takes full account of keywords, translation difficulties, and the fact that classical rhetoric is not a monolith but a series of partly competing theories, some of which were prescriptive or appropriated as prescriptions and some of which were not.

Identifying what is referred to by a post-Kantian epistemology (or, alternatively, modern rhetoric) is important. Finding common ground between the ideas of modern rhetoric and ancient rhetoric has assumed great importance in the last decade of rhetoric and composition research because the two eras have been placed, as we have seen in this chapter, in opposition to each other. That purported opposition has created a great deal of strange intellectual heat.

While no one may be able to reconcile the old division of the ancient versus the modern that has been with us for a long time, we can at least learn to recognize its current manifestation in many of the contemporary appropriations of classical rhetoric.

## COMPOSITION AND LITERARY ROMANTICISM

A primary characteristic of literary romanticism has been the virtual worship of particular literary texts. Usually, these texts find their way into a canon of great books, works that have been declared in some fashion as central, crucial, and inexpendable. Arguments over canonicity have become regular features of some parts of the discipline of English in recent years, as well as in other disciplines. In spite of the expansion of the canon to include, for example, black writers, female writers, and so on, the concept of canon formation itself has received great resistance among English teachers, as Gary F. Waller's analysis of English department curricula in the journal *Profession* has demonstrated.

The center of many canons—and the resistance to changing it beyond the tokenizing of various groups—appears to be a belief in the mystic power of certain texts. In other words, many texts in English department curricula are regarded implicitly as sacred. Canon formation, of course, originally referred to groups of sacred texts. Some texts were included, some were excluded. The criteria for inclusion and exclusion fade from memories, just as issues of inclusion and exclusion blur in

Berlin's concept of noetic fields. The atmospherics of greatness set in, and the reasons for making a canon in the first place disappear from the memories of those who cling to it. A demystification of canonical literary texts could promote integrations or dialectics of both kinds of romantic composition and classical rhetoric. Integrations and dialectics would constitute an important contemporary reception of classical rhetoric. The desacrilization of texts and their writers in the field of literary studies would have a number of salutary effects. Two of these effects would be (1) a change in the perceived and insurmountable intellectual distance between novice (frequently student) writers and readers; and (2) more emphasis given to the writing processes of professional writers both in language curricula and in literary criticism.

Teachers who have presented students with sacred writing in the form, say, of Aristotle's writings, or Shakespeare's plays, or Abraham Lincoln's speeches, realize the difficulty that inheres in getting students to cross the chasm between the writers' greatness and their own perceived lowliness. This hierarchical construction, one that is very old in literary studies, sets up many problems, the most prominent one of which is student flight from the texts, their writers, and their cultures. Plato complained, as Havelock extensively demonstrates in *Preface to Plato*, that Homer's poems were eventually sacrilized in the education of children. Homer's poems were used in a variety of ways—including use as sacred texts—in educational systems in the fourth century B.C., and Plato protested, particularly in the *Republic*, against them. Sacrilized texts do not necessarily promote thinking. While they might promote thinking in religious studies (for example, in Bible studies or in Koran studies), in secular contexts they are just as likely to promote unthinking hero worship. The novice writers and readers who flee from canonical texts can be lost to critical writing and reading forever. An educational institution that promotes this flight has lost sight of its responsibility.

The stages of development that a text undergoes by any writer contains the instruction that is essential for a novice or student writer. In other words, the finished product of, say, a short story by Flannery O'Connor such as "A Good Man Is Hard to Find," can speak to writers (and not only readers) only if pre-finished product drafts, ideas, and/or problems are included in a writerly analysis. Nearly all writing text-books—books which proliferate in the United States and that appear to be a growth industry—treat the last stage of writing, the published version of a text, and therefore isolate the text from the factors that enabled it to come into being. While a new generation of textbooks does treat not only drafts of pre-last draft pieces but also the drafting done by selected student writers, the overwhelming number of textbooks token-ize these aspects in favor of the current-traditional paradigm of face-lifted versions of it (the vogue for "process" texts is a prominent example of the latter phenomenon).

In both these examples, the novice or student writer/reader is regarded as a problem, not as a resource. It is to the credit of composition romanticists such as Knoblauch/Brannon, Macrorie, Coles, and others that they privilege the student writer over literary texts or any other kinds of texts. These romanticists are so energetic in their desire to encourage student writing that they tend to forget, as I discussed above, the rest of the world, the rest of the noetic fields, that exist and that enable the "private" realm to exist.

Sacred texts belong to religions, not to departments of English and Speech Communication. Desacrilizing educational texts can enable students, teachers, and researchers to make connections to the powerful discourse of everyday life, of lived experience, and to see how language in all its various manifestations shapes the flux of interiority and exteriority that creates existence or perceptions of existence.

## LANGUAGE THAT PURPORTS TO BE VALUE FREE

The various kinds of romantic interpretations of rhetoric and composition and of literature present scholars and teachers with a wide array of choices. One choice is implicitly to present some language use as value free. Commonly, scientific language is presented unconsciously by many teachers as value free and objective. This positivist, Heritage School stance is an option, and it is a dangerous one. It robs students of the opportunity to see the power of language to help structure what we commonly call reality. In addition, the students are led to resist seeing foreign languages as creating their own categories and instead to see mere substitution systems. Students are prevented from gaining more power over their own lives by becoming more expert at their own written discourse and spoken discourse. No doubt, large populations in a particular culture are more easily manipulated by governments, by the encoders of the machines (and attendant psychological structures) of secondary orality, and by other institutions that largely create who we are in the late twentieth century. This objectivist stance deprives language—whether ordinary language or extraordinary language—of its ability to make people interact with others and themselves more effectively.

To assume the rhetorical stance that much language use is neutral and value free possesses many similarities with the rhetorical stance that claims implicitly that the history of rhetoric is out there and need only be retrieved. The implications of Heritage School language neutrality go far beyond the professional books and journals of groups of scholars and teachers. These implications determine to a great extent how students living in United States culture are taught to think. A great deal is at stake.

The Heritage School scholars of classical rhetoric write as if language is value free and can be neutral when so constructed. The Heritage School has many theories but appears not to be aware of them. Most prominent in this construction of language reality are the skill-based teachers who behave as if drills on issues such as invention, or revision, or peer group editing, can teach students how to think. By themselves, these exercises cannot teach students how to think in more sophisticated ways. Students must be led to understand that all thought is theory based, not that thought can be packaged in the form of a skill with exercises to heighten the skill.

Skill-based language instruction tends to validate "logic," whether familiar or traditional, at every turn. Language, like memory and psychology, is not logical. The skills that so concern many people working now in rhetoric and composition exclude theory either consciously or unconsciously. Perhaps most importantly, skill-based instruction is boring. It robs students of the fascination that inheres in their native tongue.

# PART II

## Rehistoricizing Classical Rhetoric

# 3

---

# Interpretive Options
# in the Historicizing
# of Classical Rhetoric

Narratives of history of many kinds—rhetorical, military, diplomatic, literary, and so on—continue to be produced with apparently omniscient writers presenting objective realities. This kind of history writing presents material in more or less chronological ways, with the attendant cause and effect arguments that chronological structures imply. This kind of writing constitutes much of popular writing and much of academic writing. Best-seller lists indicate the public desire for this version of narrative. Course reading lists indicate the academic desire— in disciplines such as English, history, music, philosophy—for this kind of narrative. The omniscience and apparent objectivity of the narrator in many fields of study teach us many things as they soothe us with the always-implicit idea that truth or at least objective knowledge resides in the pages of the chronicle. The structure of the discourse itself—part of its *logos*—is not questioned by the writer; rather, the structure is taken for granted as true, self-apparent, and not open to examination.

Alternatives to the writer-reader contract that posits a definite reality whose construction need not be examined are presented in Victor J. Vitanza's 1987 " 'Notes' Towards Historiographies of Rhetorics; or, Rhetorics of the Histories of Rhetorics: Traditional, Revisionary, and Sub/Versive." The article synthesizes much of the current work in positivist historicizing as well as in new historicizing. His repeated emphasis on the importance of self consciousness in the writing of

71

rhetorical histories is part of a larger movement in rhetoric and composition studies to question what appears to be "objective reality" in the presentation of histories as well as in pedagogical assumptions.

The three areas of history writing in rhetoric presented by Vitanza appear in the subtitle. The article presents a large body of material about the nature of historicizing and categorizes it in the three large categories of traditional, revisionary, and sub/versive, with subcategories in the first two areas providing further distinctions. This synthesis comes at a pivotal moment in the historicizing of rhetoric and composition. It shows us how far we have come in the contemporary era (for our purposes here, since 1965) in rhetoric and composition studies and the interpretive options that are available.

Vitanza's approach has the benefits of surveying a large body of work, of juxtaposing different paradigms for history writing, and of promoting critical self-awareness among historians of rhetoric and composition as well as among historians in other fields. A problem that derives from the structure of traditional, revisionary, and sub/versive histories of rhetoric is its apparent linearity. Vitanza, who is carefully explicit about favoring some forms of revisionary historicizing as well as sub/versive historicizing, moves from a negative reception (of the traditional historians of rhetoric) to a positive reception (of the sub/versive historians of rhetoric who respond in various ways to the Nietzsche/Freud/Marx precursors Vitanza shows). Many subtextual and textual references indicate that historians at the beginning of the scale are not aware of their own interpretive stances. This interpretation coincides in many ways with my own interpretation of the Heritage School. The apparently unexamined positivism, the reliance on a felt naturalness, and the maintenance of a supposedly "ideology-free" authorial presence make this kind of historicizing of rhetoric a problem for anyone reading it.

Nonetheless, some of the work that Vitanza categorizes as traditional and/or often benighted is not bound to Heritage School prescriptions but is bound instead to historical practices of "objectivity" and omniscience that nearly all readers will recognize or even be comfortable with. Much of the work of people in Vitanza's category of traditional historians of rhetoric (for example, George Kennedy, James J. Murphy, and others) does in fact offer historians of all stripes and stances a great deal of important material to work with. For example, Kennedy's presentation of the changes that classical rhetoric goes through from the classical period to the eighteenth century is traditional in its authorial, apparently objective interpretive stance. But this means of communication offers a wealth of ideas and possibilities for historicists of any stance, from the traditionalists to the sub/versives and back again. In other words, Kennedy's writing can be appropriated for diverse purposes. For example, Kennedy offers conceptual definitions of classical rhetoric over many centuries of western thought and so provides all rhetoric and composition critics with interpretations to reappropriate, subvert, or agree with. Similarly, James J. Murphy's *A Synoptic History of Classical Rhetoric* provides a series of essays that present classical rhetoric in ways that enable readers to know one version of the canon, to locate useful and sophisticated interpretations within that canon, and to extend their understanding of classical rhetoric. In other words, Murphy's book enables passive readers to become active interpreters. At every point in *A Synoptic History of Classical Rhetoric*, decoders are prodded on to other texts. It synthesizes traditional rhetorical issues as well as moves readers away from itself. Both Kennedy's and Murphy's work may be "traditional" in Vitanza's sense, that is, apparently unaware of an objectivist stance, but that stance leads to material that revisionary and sub/versive or any other kind of critic can appropriate.

Traditional critics such as W.K.C. Guthrie and Francis Cornford do not appear to use material from the sub/versive stance informed by Vitanza's conceptualization of Nietzsche/Freud/Marx, but the results of the interpretive stances of works such as Guthrie's *The Sophists* and Cornford's presentation of Plato's *Republic* remain important to anyone working in virtually any version of historical rhetoric and composition studies. These interpretations gain or lose validity in large part according to how they are appropriated.

## ALTERNATIVE INTERPRETIVE OPTIONS FOR HISTORICIZING RHETORIC AND COMPOSITION: THE ISSUE OF KEYWORDS

Vitanza's analysis (which he consistently presents as tentative) points to possibilities for change in historicizing rhetoric and composition. My own tentative suggestions for ways to rehistoricize rhetoric and composition include recasting the interpretation and promulgation of keywords from classical rhetoric. Keywords provide one location for radical change in the contemporary reception of classical rhetoric. In addition, they enable interpreters of diverse theoretical stances to partake of those changes. The use of keywords—central Greek and Latin word/concepts that contain clusters of interrelated connotations—offers critics and students multiplicities of meanings for complex Greek and Roman concepts. Both critical and pedagogical discourse benefit from this practice because keywords maintain ambiguity; in other words, keywords themselves contain dialectics.

Heritage School interpretations of keywords such as *arete, physis,* and *logos* ignore the elasticity and flux of these concepts. An awareness of keywords' ambiguity and multiplicities of meaning allows interpreters to take account of two primary kinds of response: (1) the ancient writer's contexts; and (2) the reader's contexts (in this inquiry, the contemporary reader's context). Discounting or ignoring these two kinds of contexts leads quite easily to the making of classical rhetoric into a monolith, a static kind of historicizing that presents the field as changeless over 700 years and that we investigated in Part I.

The keyword *arete* presents an opportunity for the expansion in interpretations of keywords. The concept of *arete* remains central to any interpretation of most of the Sophists and to Plato and Aristotle's reception of the Sophists. The most familiar rendering of *arete* as "virtue" presents a good example of the interpretive problems we face in appropriating classical rhetoric for contemporary purposes. Nearly all late twentieth-century connotations of virtue leave out the ordinariness of the keyword *arete*. Since its ordinariness provides much of the power of *arete*, this particular translation-as-substitution supplies readers with more problems than interpretive options.

A different version of the keyword problem can be illustrated by the keyword *kairos,* the opportune moment, or the time one may make one's point believed and a concept paramount in rhetoric. This keyword suffers a problem that differs from the problems of *arete*. Whereas *arete* as "virtue" is very common, *kairos* as anything at all tends to be rare.

I rely on the term "keywords," as discussed in Chapter One, because of its use among classical scholars such as Guthrie and Cornford and because of the contemporary connotations that Raymond Williams has given the word.

Appropriators of keywords who remain completely unaware of their escalating or de-escalating meanings over the seven hundred years of classical rhetoric and the similar fluctuations among post-classical readers, tend to base their single-level translations (their translations-as-substitutions) on the idea of classical rhetoric as a monolith. If, alternatively, classical rhetoric is seen as a series of dialectics, the keywords must be invoked in all their complexity rather than in all their univocality.

Any discussion of keywords must rely on giving up the familiar Heritage School idea that classical Greek rhetoric remains the same from Homer to Theophrastus. The primarily oral Homeric period, then the fifth-century B.C. milieus that produced many new kinds of writing, and then the fourth and third century B.C. contexts that brought about much philosophical and rhetorical work comprise three possible divisions that differ significantly from one another. *Physis*, for example, rendered frequently since the third century B.C. as "nature" and less frequently as "essence," means some things for the presocratic philosophers and other things for Plato. As a fluctuating concept, this word has its own history for classical rhetoric and composition studies. Of course, the idea of *physis* and its transformations are regarded as crucial for Greek philosophy and finally help define one basis of Greek thought as it appears in the texts that we have. The subject of the inquiry here lies not in traditional philosophical interpretations of *physis* but in the sometimes parallel and more often competing rhetorical interpretations. Any dictionary of philosophy, such as Dagobert Runes' *Dictionary of Philosophy*, provides a version of appropriations of keywords such as *physis* in the long history of the discipline of philosophy.

My own appropriation of keywords seeks to follow not traditional philosophical discussions but the writing of Williams and of Burke: to maintain ambiguity and complexity and resonance. This work does not fit into the agendas of most traditional work in the discipline of philosophy and is not intended to join those discussions. In the Introduction to *Keywords: A Vocabulary of Culture and Society*, Williams discusses the means of communication that groups develop:

> When we come to say "we just don't speak the same language" we mean something more general, that we have different immediate values or different kinds of valuation, or that we are aware, often intangibly, of different formations and distributions of energy and interest. In such a case, each group is speaking its native language, but its uses are significantly different, and especially when strong feelings or important ideas are in question. No single group is "wrong" by any linguistic criterion, though a temporarily dominant group may try to enforce its own uses as "correct." (p. 11)

Williams' "different formations and distributions of energy and interest" create the center of concern in my appropriation of keywords: different disciplines distribute verbal energy in different ways. The way here centers on the historicizing of rhetoric and composition studies as they have worked in the disciplines of English and Speech Communication rather than on standard traditions in the discipline of philosophy.

Keywords in rhetoric and composition acquire resonance primarily in relation to their use and to other parts of language. *Physis*, for example, takes on new and related meaning, and undergoes modification that appears to be buried in the culture that uses the concept; that is, the nuance of the word is so apparent to the people writing and speaking it that it does not require explanation. *Physis*, like *arete* and *kairos*, needs to be seen in its fluidity, with its relational meanings. The scant Homeric use of *physis* in the eighth to twelfth centuries is not like the frequent fifth-century Sophoclean uses, and that is not like later Platonic uses. *Physis* is an example of a keyword important to rhetoric and composition, a keyword that went through many subtle changes and that depended on context and relational meanings. Its fluctuating meanings remain important in rhetoric and composition issues. Readers undergo change as well and so the conditions of reception account for many of the fluctuations in the nature of keywords.

The interpretive difficulty with *physis* does not begin with its single appearance in the Homeric poems (an appearance used as evidence for later interpretations) but with its use by the cosmologists in the sixth century B.C. What written material do we have to work with when we take account of the changes the keyword *physis* went through? We have the Homeric reference, infrequent uses in the extant fragments of the cosmologists, the works in which the fragments are embedded (they are to be found in quotations beginning with Plato in the fourth century B.C. up until Simplicius in the six century A.D.),[1] literary use of the word, and accounts of ancient historians who wrote about early cosmologists. Each of these written sources presents interpretive problems. In the case of the cosmologists, however, we have the added and fascinating difficulty that all their work is embedded in the writings of other people. Their work comes to us not from the agendas of the thinkers themselves but as part of the conveyor's agenda. Because of this textual issue, Jonathan Barnes, in *Early Greek Philosophy*, chooses to present the extant writing of the cosmologists and other presocratic thinkers in the immediate verbal contexts of the writers who appropriated them. Barnes writes:

> In addition to later references and reports, we still possess some actual fragments of the original works of the Presocratics. The word "fragment" perhaps suggests a small scrap of paper, torn out of a Presocratic book and surviving by some fluke of time. That suggestion is inappropriate here, where the word "fragment" is used in a more generous sense: it refers to passages from the Presocratics' own writings—words, phrases, sentences, paragraphs—which have been preserved as *quotations* in the writings of later authors. These "fragments" constitute our most precious testimony to the views of the Presocratics. (pp. 25–26, Barnes' emphasis)

A difficult period in the historicizing of the keyword *physis* occurs in the Ionian cosmologists Thales, Anaximenes, and Anaximander. The di-

---

[1]See Kirk, Raven, and Schofield, *The Presocratic Philosophers: A Critical History with a Selection of Texts* and Harold Cherniss, *Aristotle's Criticism of Presocratic Philosophy.*

vergent yet always related appropriations of *physis* illustrate a continuing problem in rhetoric and composition studies.

One difficulty in interpreting the available written evidence lies in textual confusion that stems from the conspicuous (to the nonclassical reader) absence of clear meaning or intention of *physis* in the cosmologists' fragments and, indeed, the few occurrences of the word on which we can base a contextual analysis. Because there is not direct evidence of the cosmologists' attitudes, one turns to other sources, which include passages in Plato and Aristotle, in historians such as Theophrastus, and in the early doxographers. The method, while essential, is filled with considerable difficulty and even more fascination. These obstacles derive mainly from the problems that arise in reading Plato and Aristotle themselves: the ambiguity of the two writers in individual uses of *physis,* the shifts of meaning of the word that come from changes in use and context, and, most importantly, their roles as interpreters of the thought that preceded them. The last point holds particular importance because the motives of the quoters necessarily inform or even create the cosmologists' purported meaning. The rhetorical stances of the writerly roles of Plato, Aristotle, Theophrastus, and other recorder/interpreters (the historians) of presocratic philosophy provide some of the major ways the cosmologists' views are interpreted.

Given the difficulties present in deciphering just what subsequent commentators meant, readers can turn to alternative sources of the term for some more ideas about the appropriations of *physis.* Literary sources provide helpful evidence. The Homeric poet(s), Pindar, Aeschylus, and Sophocles provide important and widely varying versions. The privileging of literary sources as evidence has dominated many schools of interpretation. Richard Leo Enos has challenged the exclusion inherent in privileging literary sources by showing that epigraphical sources provide samples of ancient writing that can teach us much about ancient Greek ways of thinking.[2] Twentieth-century philologists such as John Burnet, A.O. Lovejoy, and J.L. Myres have written cogent arguments delineating what the cosmologists meant by *physis.* They appropriate Plato's and Aristotle's references (or quotations, as Barnes puts it) to the cosmologists and then the literary references.

The school of interpretation populated by writers such as Lovejoy, Burnet, Myres, and J.W. Beardslee constitutes an influential group of philologists and philosophers who have conditioned reception of classical rhetoric and, in fact, all classical studies, to an enormous degree. The philologists were one group of scholars to whom New Critics such

---

[2]Enos, "The Art of Rhetoric at the Amphiareion of Oropos: A Study of Epigraphical Evidence as Written Communication" in *Written Communication.*

as John Crowe Ransom and Allen Tate reacted. Gerald Graff, in *Professing Literature: An Institutional History*, characterizes the split as "scholars versus critics" in two chapters. The philologists, who defined themselves by specialized linguistic training, relied on exclusive knowledge. That is, their mastery of languages and technical linguistic issues led to their possessing (in the full sense of that word) special knowledge that most people could not have. New Criticism, as Graff points out, enabled anyone to be a critic. Training in understanding poetry, fiction, or drama could be accomplished in a relatively brief period of time. Training to become a philologist took many years and required special institutions. Philology, of course, remains as a stronghold in the discipline of English in the area of medieval studies. The staunch opposition of some medievalists in English departments to rhetoric and composition studies as well as to poststructuralist theories recalls the opposition that Graff describes in his "scholars versus critics" chapters.

Keyword discussions can easily become philological nitpicking. When Lovejoy contends that *physis* meant primal substance, the matter from which every other substance derives, and Myres contends that *physis* meant process, or becoming, for the cosmologists, we can see that from one point of view the implications are great for interpreting the work of the cosmologists. The first interpretation treats a world outside (the where-did-it-come-from approach), while the second interpretation treats a process that includes human beings. So this interpretive problem that derives from an examination of the keyword *physis* can lead to the very foundation of the thought of Thales, Anaximander, and the others (for example, their various conceptions of infinity, religious belief, how the world came to be, and the central issue of the relationship of the exterior world to the interior world of the person). On the other hand, the discussion can devolve into quarrels over microscopic problems that finally do not make any difference because they do not relate to any larger worlds.

Interpretation of the cosmologists foregrounds the fabrication that always takes place in reading. The reader of the cosmologists' quotations embedded in other writers' texts must supply, must fabricate, more self-consciously than the reader of more fully formed texts does. So little is written down that a great deal must be read in. The important issue is that the reader is more aware of supplying material than she or he is when reading other more developed texts. The absence of direct evidence and the interesting interpretations of subsequent commentators demand that the reader notice how ideas are conveyed. Because of the scantiness of the *writing* that remains of the cosmologists, interpreters are practically forced into recognizing that readers have to supply a great deal of material. So the study of the cosmologists in rhetoric and composition has the additional advantage of foregrounding acts of interpretation that are frequently taken for granted.

The interpretive difficulty of the concept of *physis* provides an example of the fluidity that keywords can offer us instead of the more familiar definiteness. Reductive, static criticism cuts off many possibilities.

## PROMOTING RHETORICAL AND HISTORICAL CONSCIOUSNESS IN LANGUAGE PEDAGOGY

Every pedagogy of every subject has a theoretical basis. All the subspecialties of rhetoric and composition studies have theoretical bases, which is to say that a system of interrelated concerns cohere with principles guiding a particular realm of inquiry. Freewriting derives from romantic composition theory. Revising strategies derive from aesthetic theories of art production. Diagramming sentences derives from the same theory that parsing Latin depends on, the mechanistic drilling of rote memorization that goes back to Roman education. Just as no language use is value free, so is no pedagogy free of theory or theories. Recognizing the links—the dependence—of writing pedagogy to rhetoric and composition theory constitutes the most important issue facing teachers at any level of education. The dominance of positivism, of which the Heritage School is one symptom, remains entrenched in United States educational systems. An aggressive resistance to examining theoretical bases and the value systems that necessarily inform them limits many kinds of intellectual inquiry in education. The objective paradigm analyzed by Bleich in *Subjective Criticism* creates the primary way many—perhaps most—people think. The major promoters of this phenomenon continue to be practically all of our educational institutions. These organizations appear to find their life force in the unexamined objectivist rhetorical stance that most of them tacitly assume.

In rhetoric and composition pedagogy, this stance has especially serious consequences, because writing is so patently nonobjectivist, so resistant to quantification of any kind. One strategy for transcending the limitations of objectivist thinking lies in promoting rhetorical and historical consciousness. We can categorize the kinds of rhetorical and historical consciousness now available to us. Three locations for consciousness that I have chosen to isolate in rhetoric and composition studies are: (1) the instructor possibility; (2) the reversal of the privileging of "skills;" and (3) the textbook possibility.

## RHETORICAL AND HISTORICAL CONSCIOUSNESS
## AMONG WRITING INSTRUCTORS

The discipline of English, where most written instruction has been emphasized, has undergone great changes since about 1965; the discipline of Speech Communication, where oral discourse instruction has been emphasized, has undergone great changes in the same period. The general education revision that is currently being enacted at colleges and universities across the United States offers the kairotic moment for revivifying (or vivifying, according to Graff and others) language instruction of every kind. The burning issue that faces us in this national pedagogical revision is: will we continue to work with a positivist paradigm that appears almost to drive itself or will we treat language training and training in all other fields as ways of thinking? Will we teach only *what* or will we teach *how* we come to know any *what?*

The current formal training of writing instructors in many universities provides instruction in the theoretical bases of writing. The universities cited by Gary Tate and David W. Chapman in their *Rhetoric Review* analysis of graduate programs in rhetoric and composition in the United States provide versions of training for writing instructors that tend to be theory-based or at least to include much theory. An awareness of the theoretical substrata that underlie all pedagogical practices pervades these programs. Theoretical awareness in these training camps is increased by the postmodern theories—Freudian, deconstructionist, feminist, Marxist, and so on—that thrive in many of the same English departments as well as in other departments. The bubbling up of theoretical systems of rhetoric and composition and of other areas in these programs provides intellectual excitement as well as rigor. The most effective training programs in the teaching of writing occur in programs where the writing instructors are apprentices pursuing advanced degrees. In this situation, all parties benefit. Because these apprentice instructors move through their programs (or become ineligible to teach after a set number of years), the part-time freshman writing instructors do not form a ghetto of teachers with no professional future.

Although the strengths of instructional training provide hope and models for change, they are not enough in the late twentieth and twenty-first centuries. Adequate formal training in writing instruction at the college level does not yet exist in enough places. The diminished status and the undertraining of part-time writing instructors continue to dominate the teaching of writing in many places.

One of the reasons that formal training in writing pedagogy remains weak lies in an economic construction. The teaching of writing remains labor intensive; it costs a great deal of money to provide smallish writing classes. This constraint results in, according to reports by the National Council of Teachers of English as well as by other organizations, the employment of large groups of apprentice teachers, part-time teachers, or nontenure-track professors. These people of widely divergent training and background are employed in a way that strikingly resembles the factory-line production of goods. The factory is the writing program at, say, a large university. The product of the factory is the freshman writing student. The worker in the factory is the part-time writing instructor or, in many cases, the disenfranchised, nontenure-track teacher who holds a Ph.D. but does not hold job security, adequate intellectual stimulation, or power outside the walls of the classroom. These three of the many components of the factory writing system (I will not go into here the absent owners of the factory or the economic system that creates them) reinforce one another in the rhetorical unconscious. They perpetuate themselves through cordoning off the many aspects of writing into a series of skill-based activities that, because of their isolation from the parts that make them interesting, become crushingly boring. In the following pages I examine briefly three components of this system: the factory writing program, the freshman student product, and the instructor worker.

Writing programs function economically to provide power and money for departments of English, where most writing programs are institutionally located. Both the power and the money generated by the almost-universally required freshman writing course remain crucial sources for the well-being of these departments. Since United States culture (mass, high, middle, midcult, and other designations) has tacitly declared literary discourse to be a peripheral, even decorative or effeminate issue, English departments have to look elsewhere for autonomy. They look to the place that United States culture has declared important: writing in the form of student composing. The factory writing program typically, therefore, collects per capita money from units higher in the institutional hierarchy, such as deans' and provosts' offices, and in addition collects the power of numbers guaranteed by required freshman writing courses. The large numbers of freshman students generate both the money and the power that derive from large numbers. English departments are able, then, to maintain the dollars and the power to offer courses from the sophomore to the Ph.D. level, courses that are not required, that are not declared to be culturally important, courses where a great deal of experimentation and innovation can take place. This system, described by Richard Ohmann in

*English in America* and by numerous writers in rhetoric and composition studies, has many advantages. Important work in language study can be well subsidized in this way; exciting new theories can be the focus.

The primary difference between literary instruction and writing instruction is that the former frequently is seen as genteel and the latter as proletarian. Their distinction is very similar to a class issue. Literary instruction remains firmly a part of the romantic point of view that sees "art" as ennobling, liberating, and that is, in a favorite word of people who espouse this attitude, "enriching." The revelatory terms of the literary romantic stance are not merely "enrichment," but "heritage," "tradition," "the arts," and Culture with a capital "C." These ubiquitous terms mask a conscious or unconscious elitist attitude that accords status to people who employ the codes of "the arts," even as the general culture sees their work as utterly peripheral. Literary studies in English departments focus on many of these codes.

The problem with the factory writing program and the English departments that live off their labor is that the opportunity for innovation and experiment (the subsidy) provided for the sophomore to Ph.D. level classes is frequently not exploited. Rather, the same courses that a professor took in graduate school become the courses she or he continues to teach as a professor. In other words, little change has taken place. The literary status quo remains. Reading sample catalogues of English departments throughout the country is a chilling experience; it indicates an amazing sameness of field-coverage, the familiar genre courses, and what Ohmann calls literary chronology. The current excitement, the profound intellectual energy, in the discipline of English has been ghettoized in rigorously unrequired courses in rhetoric and composition, in various theory courses, and in other nontraditional ways of studying language and literature. The recent preliminary report of the Association of Departments of English on catalog descriptions of English courses bears this out. Graff makes this point in the section "Tradition Versus Theory" in *Professing Literature*. When the exciting new courses are not required by any department, much less English departments themselves, their potential power for radical change and challenge in language instruction dissipates. Many factory writing programs have subverted this, but many cannot get out of the system. Ghettoes work to placate minimally a group of people and to keep them away from the dominant group at the same time.

The product of the factory writing system is the student writer. While course requirements were lifted in virtually every field in the late 1960s and the 1970s, freshman writing persisted in most institutions as one of the few courses required of all students. The reasons why freshman writing was exempt from the pressures of an elective-dominant system probably have to do with the conditions of late literacy, in the Ong-Havelock sense of the term. There is an almost universal belief that the ability to write "well" is central, not peripheral, decorative, or genteel, to citizens of the United States. Measuring any writer's ability requires quantification of a nonquantifiable activity, so there is continuing argument/discussion about writing achievement. Some instruments are able to reveal various kinds of limited information about student progress in writing instruction. However, measuring student writing progress remains challenging and will probably always be fraught with difficulty. In spite of the difficulty of measurement, United States culture continues to call out for writing instruction. This cultural recognition is characterized by being nongenteel, nonelitist, and very practical. It is practical in the sense that people intuit that the ability to write well brings important things: the ability to think, the ability to communicate with others, the opportunity to have more personal empowerment. These motives may not be accessible to people who intuit the power of writing, but it remains a force in their thinking, so much so that writing instruction is in fact given a great deal of power. Even though we cannot measure very well the progress a student makes in a writing course, the culture demands that we not only continue teaching writing but that we expand it. The freshman student product of the factory system remains attractive to people of very different stripes, even though the product is difficult to measure.

The third issue in the English department factory system that I am discussing here is the instructor-worker who is employed in the factory of the writing program. The exploitation of these workers is well documented but not changed by enough departments. The system operates so that underpaid and underprivileged language workers—many with Ph.D.'s—labor on the assembly line of producing student writers. The first thing to keep in mind about these workers is that they respond to oppressive systems in the way that some workers in manufacturing industries do: they subvert the system. Subversion can occur in a variety of ways. Many of these workers—probably most—find their own rewards and teach very effectively, something that requires enormous effort when one considers the heavy course loads they are required to teach. Other instructor workers, however, teach according to how much they are paid: they do very little. They reason that they are paid poorly to do a particular job, and so the job must not be worth very much. It is difficult to assign blame to people who adopt this attitude. Like workers in a factory who are forced into an adversarial relationship with "the company," instructor workers assume a stance of opposition to those who employ and exploit them. That opposition often takes the form of demanding very little work from the student products because it requires too much work in return. Perhaps they subvert by dispensing many grades of "A" (a subversive mode that found popularity in the late 1960s and into the 1970s in the form of grade inflation). Many subvert the factory system by maintaining intellectually rigorous courses that defy familiar English-department homilies, as Bleich calls them. These instructor workers provide a source of great power for the discipline of English in spite of the oppressive conditions that constrict them and therefore their students.

The instructor workers who recognize on some level the factory-like nature of their work often resort to what I have categorized as the second issue in rhetorical and historical consciousness, the privileging of "skill" over thinking, epistemology, and communicative expressiveness.

## THE PRIVILEGING OF SKILL
## IN WRITING INSTRUCTION

When writing instructors do not have sufficient training in language theory, they teach what is familiar to them; they teach language skills. Their unconscious composition theory expresses itself forcefully in the form of skill instruction, or isolated units of teaching that are meant to exercise cordoned off aspects of writing. This model resembles principles of physical training: instead of exercising muscle groups in a particular sequence, skill-bound writing instruction exercises discrete parts of writing. Both methods are intended to make the writer and the physical trainee better people. Although the method of exercising isolated muscle groups works well in maintaining physical well-being, the method does not translate effectively to writing instruction. On the contrary, training through exercising isolated writing procedures makes student writers less effective writers. Why? Because boredom overtakes any intellectual interest that the student may bring to the writing class or that may have been generated in the class itself. One definition of boredom is that it indicates that one's needs are not being met. When student writers are required to drill on topic sentences, paragraph formation, and error correction, their intellectual need for language is not being met. One pervasive response to the course in freshman writing is a crushing boredom. I believe that this boredom begins with the writing instructor. In the case of the instructor workers and privileged professors who teach writing, boredom in writing instruction tends to derive from teaching theory-unconscious skill workouts. This unconscious theory is based on a positivisitic/scientific epistemology that dictates that writing is a skill like carpentry or plumbing. The discrete units of training are the sentence, the paragraph, and the theme. The inherent wonderment of language, particularly the language of one's native tongue, and the dynamic nature of language perform-ance (written or spoken), are disregarded in this familiar system of pedagogy. This version of language is very boring to teach and, it follows, it is very boring to learn.

Many writers have identified the problems with what I am calling skill-based instruction. Two prominent ones are Plato in *Phaedrus* and elsewhere and Michael Polanyi in the essays "Knowing and Being" and "Sense-Giving and Sense-Reading" in *Knowing and Being*. Plato dis-cusses the organic nature of any discourse and the dynamic integration of its parts while Polanyi discusses the centrality of reintegration of any skill into the larger whole. Polanyi, in "Knowing and Being," writes:

> common experience shows that no skill can be acquired by learning its constituent motions separately. Moreover, here too isolation modifies the particulars: their dynamic quality is lost. Indeed, the identification of the constituent motions of a skill tends to paralyse its performance. Only by turning our attention away from the particulars and towards their joint purpose, can we restore to the isolated motions the qualities required for achieving their purpose. (p. 126)

In a related way, Polanyi writes in "Sense-Giving and Sense-Reading":

> to switch our attention to a subsidiary particular deprives it of its meaning. Such action admittedly does make us more fully conscious of such a particular, but its loss of meaning is due not to this but to the accompa-nying loss of its subsidiary functions. (p. 197)

Polanyi's observations have particular application to the teaching of writing. One of the major problems of the concept of skill-based writing instruction is that it suggests quantifiability. If you can write a topic sentence, then you can show that sentence as proof that you have acquired the skill. The pedagogy that follows from this structure is to generate in one's own writing and to locate in published professional writing topic sentences of paragraphs. When no topic sentence can be found, as often is the case in writing, the topic sentence is said to be implicit. So no matter what, a topic sentence is said to exist and is exploited and put in command in this kind of writing classroom. "Skill" is nearly pejorative in connotation. It is regarded, in our elitist world, as something proletarians have to make a living with. The connection to the proletarianization of freshman writing becomes clear. In the genteel world of language and literature training, maintaining distance from the gritty form of the language proletariat assumes great importance. Staying away from skills is one symptom of the desire for distance.

Those instructor workers and other teachers who accept the invitation to teach writing as a skill-bound activity can be said to be promoting anti-intellectualism. They also damage language training by making it boring for themselves and then for the students.

## THE WRITING TEXTBOOK ISSUE

Almost all writing textbooks at every level rely on skill-bound activities that refrain from integrating the isolated parts into the whole of a piece of written discourse and from explaining the theoretical basis of the skill. While I have treated this problem elsewhere, I point out in this context that the cries against terrible writing textbooks are ancient. Plato and Aristotle railed against them. Aristotle, in fact, in Book I of the *Rhetoric*, states that he intends to correct some of the problems with these books (usually translated into English as "handbooks"). The writing textbook market is a profitable source for the many conglomerate companies that now have them produced by professors, manufacture them, and then distribute them to teachers. The great majority of these books, particularly those that are in the current-traditional model and the romantic model, are boring. They are so because they rely, whether they admit it or submerge it, on skill-bound writing instruction. The activity of writing is divided up in various ways and the student is then tutored in these skills. The idea is that the student writer will integrate these skills into her or his writing. However, boredom usually reaches the student first. The third generation of writing textbooks, such as Rise B. Axelrod and Charles R. Cooper's *St. Martin's Guide to Writing*, depends on recursiveness that resists boredom. These heavily theoretical books disguise their theory. They are reputedly required by their market to disguise the theory. Since most of the buyers of writing textbooks are inhabiting the intellectual universe of skill-bound instruction, the mention of theory tends to put them off greatly. Axelrod and Cooper and some other textbook writers have subverted their own market by relying on current rhetoric and composition theory and then presenting it in a way that anti-theory writing instructors will believe. This step represents a breakthrough in contemporary rhetoric and composition studies. The problem that remains, of course, is that the skillbound writing instructors are still skillbound. They use better theories with the third generation of textbooks, but they remain unaware of the new theory, just as they were unaware of the current-traditional/objectivist theory that underlies the old-fashioned textbooks. So the third generation textbooks still have not found a way to train the writing instructor in the theory that always exists. With these books, the reciprocity of theory-unconscious textbooks and theory-unconscious writing instructors is broken. However, the theory-unconscious instructors still remain hostile to theory.

## RECOGNIZING THE EPISTEMOLOGICAL SIMILARITIES OF SPEECH COMMUNICATION AND ENGLISH

Because we have been in secondary orality for about 150 years (if one designates the beginning of secondary orality with the invention of the telegraph in the 1840s, when disembodied, electrical communication began), the combining of instruction in written discourse and spoken discourse has become more important than ever. The familiar pedagogical divorces between writing and speaking pedagogy cause many instructional problems for those who work in language training. The most prominent feature of the split is in the institutional reality that departments of English and departments of Speech Communication are separated, even though much of how and what they teach overlaps because it has the same theoretical grounding. The problem is not just a territorial issue, with one department seeking more power than another department. There are enough students to go around. The problem is dialogue/dialectic. These two very similar disciplines need to continue intellectual stimulation. The current vogue in administrations and funding agencies for interdisciplinary studies may help the split that began officially with the 1914 walkout by speech people in Chicago. Writing textbooks need to connect to the power of secondary orality by studying issues already well developed in the discipline of Speech Communication, for example, argument theory, interpersonal communication theory, and mass communication theory. Since orality has been rejuvenated by the secondary orality of electronic discourse, the disciplines of English and Speech Communication have more in common than is usually recognized. The spoken word is now electronic much of the time. Its relationship to the nonelectronic spoken word remains very great.

Writing textbook problems continue to dominate the potentially large market for advanced writing textbooks. These books have simply replicated the problems of the freshman writing books and will more frequently reside in the advanced writing classroom where positivist writing theory will continue and boredom advance.

Rhetorical and historical consciousness takes many forms. I have discussed some of them and realize that many others exist. Rhetoric and composition studies have always been partially constituted by pedagogy, from the time of Corax to the late twentieth century. Although some, as discussed, regard the pedagogical function as déclassé, nongenteel, and grubby in the general sense, rhetoric and composition studies have always, no matter what disguise they have taken historically, recognized teaching and its centrality to culture. In addition, rhetoric and composition studies have consistently, from Corax's time to our own, recognized production as much as reception. Encoding, whether in writing or in speaking, has been privileged over reception for 2500 years. Encoding is anti-passive.

## RECOGNIZING THE POWER IN THE ORDINARINESS
## OF LANGUAGE

When people recognize the power in the ordinariness, the dailiness, the internality, of language, they are able to help empower themselves and to participate in public life in a variety of ways. Ordinary language tends to be discounted by many people as "merely" utilitarian, as something that everyone has and that therefore is not valuable. In spite of this common attitude, which derives from positivist objectifying of language as a thing, an addition, or a useful decoration, the ordinariness of language in fact accounts for much of the power of written and spoken discourse.

One of the most ordinary uses of language occurs in interior discourse. Vygotsky's discussion of language and thinking in *Thought and Language* helps to highlight the issue of how we all talk to ourselves. Interior discourse—talking to ourselves—is one of the most important locations for language use. Cognitive psychologists tell us that we talk to ourselves most frequently about ourselves. What could each of us find more interesting and, of course, troublesome? Dysfunctional thoughts (the replacement term for the misappropriated word "neurotic") bother many language users. In other words, ineffective or even damaging language training in educational systems helps to create or promote dysfunctional thinking. If the ways that many people talk to themselves are dysfunctional (talking to themselves as victims or as persecutors, for instance, and not realizing that rhetorical stance), then the people will be unhappier than they might ordinarily be. Language accounts for interior communication as much as it does for exterior communication. They mutually affect each other as well. A person's internal discourse leaks out into exterior discourse. Habits of dysfunctional thoughts are able to be changed by changing the ways one talks to oneself. The relationship between exterior and interior discourse has not been widely explored in rhetoric and composition, although romantic composition-ists have done impressive work with the relationship between the two with free writing, journal keeping, personal writing, and other strate-gies.

No easy distinction exists between social language and private lan-guage. The two help to create each other. Bifurcating the two realms, as has conventionally been done through assumptions and objectivist language training, leads to painful conclusions. It leads to a diminishing of the power of interior discourse and exterior discourse, of communi-cation with oneself and communication with other people.

If classical rhetoric continues to be appropriated for Heritage School uses and, in turn, denounced by positivists of other schools, then it does not have any usefulness. The residue of elitism that clings to classical rhetoric continues to be malignant. The presumed authority of classical Greek and Latin studies and the presumed superiority of their essential natures are dangerous in a culture such as ours. It is imperative to recognize that slavery, rape, imperialism, and other forms of subjuga-tion were rules of classical Greek and Roman culture, not the excep-tions. As we appropriate classical rhetoric as a system of theories, practices, and analytical methods that interact with one another, we must keep in mind that the forces of subjugation defined the cultures that also produced these theories. Even if classical rhetoric could be isolated as a discrete entity removed from the cultures that produced it and received it—and it cannot be—it would have to be appropriated by late twentieth-century decoders. We do not have any other glasses to view the Sophists, Plato, Aristotle, Cicero, Quintilian, and the others through. Classical Greek and Roman cultures were dangerously and self-annihilatingly imperialist. They colonized other peoples (a barbar was a non-Greek), and they colonized women and slaves. Socioeco-nomic categories rigidly excluded people from traversing the social spectrum. In many respects, these cultures were backward, benighted, and not worthy of emulation. Sarah B. Pomeroy's *Goddesses, Whores, Wives, and Slaves: Women in Classical Antiquity* describes in its title and provides in its text one version of the condition of women in ancient Greece and Rome. It is not a pretty picture and it needs to be recalled and integrated into any study of classical rhetoric. The jingoism of classical superiority is quickly squelched when one reviews the catalogs of oppression, rape, and slavery that characterize so much ancient literary, rhetorical, mythological, and philosophical discourse. Centu-ries of genteel reception of classical rhetoric, literature, and culture have rigorously excluded the ancient everydayness of slavery, rape, and imperialism and so have tacitly asserted that they were not significant. Eva C. Keuls' *The Reign of the Phallus: Sexual Politics in Ancient Athens* presents a version of masculinity that reformulates thinking about classical Greek culture and gender issues that have been traditionally suppressed.

## ACKNOWLEDGING INTERPRETIVE OPTIONS
## AS CONNECTED TO VALUE SYSTEMS

No interpretive school is value free or theory free. The dominant ways of teaching English have implicitly asserted that one dialect of English is inherently, by its very nature, superior to other dialects of English, particularly Black English. The hegemony of "standard English" has created one of the most serious obstacles to the acquisition of student power in language. Standard English, or dominant culture English, needs to be taught as a dialect, as one kind of verbal form available to all writers and speakers. Students could then decide to acquire the dominant dialect or not. If the rewards of acquiring this dialect are shown to students—possible upward social mobility, better job opportunities, and other cultural rewards—then students will be eager to get a handbook of rules and learn the dialect. If dominant culture English is presented as inherently superior, as an innately better way of speaking English (a matter of *physis* and not of *nomos*), then they might feel that they are not acquiring just another dialect but are diminishing the dialect that they grew up with and that consequently constitutes much of their interior discourse. Dominant culture English would, then, become a choice for a student who wishes to empower herself or himself in various economic and social ways. It would not have to replace the student's own dialect. It would supplement it.

Dominant culture English is one of the most explosive theoretical issues facing all teachers of English. The continuing drilling through skill-based, theory-unconscious instruction that quietly asserts that dominant culture English is the most important, the most beautiful, and certainly the most wholesome way to write or speak English presents an unacknowledged value system. When instructors face the value system of dominant culture English and then confront their students with it, they are more likely to succeed in getting students to join the discourse community of dominant culture English. *Students' Right to Their Own Language* continues to teach us much.

One way to teach dominant culture English is to give up obsessive error correction in essay writing and to talk to students about the realities of socioeconomic status in the United States. The possibility of movement up and down on the social scale is a powerful attention-getter in the classroom. The fluidity of socioeconomic status in the United States needs to be exploited by instructors of the native tongue because it teaches students an awareness of class issues. Writing and speaking dominant culture English provide the fastest route to the huge middle class in the United States and all its various substrata. One might hope that, after excluded groups have been assimilated into the middle class, they can go on to subvert its many malignant aspects.

Even if we were successful in persuading writing and speech communication teachers that dominant culture English should be treated as just another dialect, the one that will bring more of the rewards the culture has to offer, we would not have achieved full access to one's value system. We can never have full access to our own value systems. Large areas of our behavior and our beliefs have to remain unknown to us.

The rhetorical stance that severs thought and language, such as that of the Heritage School and many other positivists, needs to be viewed as an issue of values. Assuming the positivist stance toward language as an entity separable from other issues such as beliefs, thinking, and ideology means giving up the real connections between language study and value systems. While many humanities scholars and instructors espouse the importance of values, few make the hard connections between humanities studies and value systems that inhere in class structure, class privilege, and the value-laden activities of supposedly neutral institutions such as the university and the academic department.

Recognizing the value systems implicit both in familiar logic and traditional logic also requires further work. The acknowledgment of the value systems in the "objective" sciences has to take place. Bleich has discussed the subjective stances of many important scientists. This message needs to be more widely disseminated before any real discussion of values can take place.

I have purposely refrained from using the words "ethical" and "moral" in the discussion of language and values. I find the two words to be, simply, old-fashioned for many readers, although certainly not for all. The connotations of "ethical" and "moral" have lost power since the revolutionary 1960s (a period of cultural/linguistic reform that I designate as taking hold in 1968 with the national broadcast of large-scale, nationwide student protests). For many readers now, the words connote boredom and issues that are detached from day-to-day living and interior discourse. Since I do not want to evoke those associations, I have chosen the words "values" and "value system."

## CLASSICAL RHETORIC AS ONE MEANS OF ACHIEVING RHETORICAL AND HISTORICAL CONSCIOUSNESS

Classical rhetoric provides for the moment the most complete system we have for producing, analyzing, and theorizing about any kind of text—

written, spoken, electronic, cultural, and other texts. Its completeness does not deny the power of other kinds of theories. Rather, the adaptability of classical rhetoric makes other theories—semiotics, Russian formalism, New Criticism, deconstruction, etc.—a part of the cultural conversation. In this book, although I privilege and foreground classical rhetoric, I do not intend to exclude the importance of other critical systems. Knowledge and application of many kinds of critical systems reinforce one another and are central to cultural and theoretical dialogues. Nevertheless, of all the various theories available to us now, classical rhetoric remains the system that emphasizes production of discourse as much as and sometimes more than reception of discourse. The critical systems just mentioned offer endless possibilities for the analysis of completed texts, and they tend to place encoding in the background. In contrast, the concern for production in all phases of classical rhetoric connects to the importance placed on dealing with whole people. A whole person has what we now call a psychology. Rhetoric is based on influencing the whole person, a hallmark of classical rhetoric. Plato's version of dialectic demands treating the whole person, as *Phaedrus* makes clear. Dialectic demands mutual encoding and works well in Bleich's conception of subjective criticism. Dialogue/dialectic presents a path away from acquiring knowledge as information (an objectivist stance) and instead acquiring knowledge as a dialectic of interior discourse. Knowledge then moves away from being a commodity to being a way of thinking and acting.

The subjectivity of interior dialectic constitutes the basis of culture. Recognizing the subjective while giving up nostalgia and elitism in the study of classical rhetoric as well as of traditional literary studies offers many intellectual/pedagogical possibilities. Acknowledging everyone's existence in a noetic field, as Berlin discusses in *Writing Instruction in Nineteenth-Century American Colleges*, can help promote this rhetorical stance. The range and adaptability of classical rhetoric offer us many strategies for action.

These strategies lie waiting for us in promoting rhetorical and historical consciousness. The ones that I have discussed here provide some options for working our way beyond the positivistic gridlock that controls so much intellectual action.

# 4

Appropriating Plato's
Rhetoric and Writing into
Contemporary Rhetoric and
Composition Studies

An interpretive option for historicists of classical rhetoric and composition lies waiting: Platonic rhetoric. Two primary issues need to be
reconceptualized and integrated into contemporary rhetoric and composition studies in order for this option to work: (1) what Plato says
about rhetoric and writing in dialogues such as *Phaedrus, Gorgias*, and
*Protagoras* and in Letter VII and (2) as significantly, the nature of Plato's
writing as writing. In other words, historicists are faced not only with
the familiar "what" issue (familiar because of our comfortableness with
the positivism discussed in Chapters One and Two) but with the rather
unfamiliar "how" issue. The latter problem of how Plato writes, including how he writes when he denounces writing itself, forms one
definitive aspect of his rhetoric. Classical rhetoric, from Corax to the
Sophists, to Plato and Aristotle, and on into the Romans, is consistently
regarded as a faculty, an ability, as much as it is conceived of as a subject
for study. Plato is not exempt from this stance toward rhetoric; he is a
part of this stance.

During all the seven hundred years of the emergence of rhetoric in the
classical period, rhetoric as a faculty, or an ability, formed one of its
centers. Disregarding rhetoric as a faculty leads to some large interpretation problems. Rhetoric as a faculty has been diminished since the

Middle Ages but found its most serious diminishment with the rise of scientism and Cartesian rationalism. The ability to do something became radically subordinated to whatness, or "content." This situation persists into the late twentieth century and accounts for many of the peculiar appropriations of classical rhetoric that we see and read all around us. Many aspects of rhetoric and composition have sunk into a swamp of content devoid of their functions as faculties or abilities. Rhetoric and composition without their vital functions as faculties ultimately become trivial and boring.

Because rhetoric is a faculty, it can be made to adapt to anything. Its life as a faculty provides its range and its adaptability. These two primary characteristics not only provide rhetoric with much of its power historically and currently, but they provide rhetoric with much of its controversy and even animosity both historically and currently. Plato and Isocrates were two of the first writers to explore the negative implications of rhetoric's adaptability and range, its chameleonlike ability to promote anything at all. Isocrates nonetheless praised rhetoric's adaptability; Plato exploited it and worried about it.

Plato realized that rhetoric could be used positively, negatively, or any way at all. In *Phaedrus* he is forthright in his interpretation of rhetoric's positive force. At the same time, Plato in *Phaedrus* acknowledges and denounces the capacity of rhetoric to be used negatively. Much of the subsequent historical commentary of Plato's appropriation of rhetoric has centered on these content issues of his negative and/or positive response. The act of his writing—his own stance as a rhetorician—has received less attention, particularly in the historicizing of rhetoric and composition studies. How Plato writes as a rhetorician and how contemporary appropriators of his theories write as rhetoricians are discourse issues that loom before us.

The reception of Plato's rhetoric in the rhetoric and composition focus since 1965 offers us an essential classical location for insight into our own stances toward language as we struggle with new theories of rhetoric and composition. In Heritage School presentations of Plato on rhetoric—especially in the tacit historicizing of rhetoric and composition that characterizes that theory—Plato has been made to disappear or has been made to stand against rhetoric. Both interpretive options have serious consequences for the theoretical bases of current work in rhetoric and composition studies; they determine to a large extent how rhetoric and composition exist for us. Such receptions show us the results of the rhetorical unconscious or the denial that all language study depends on theory and necessarily includes value systems. Partly because Plato's rhetoric is so often theoretical, that is, so concerned with systems of underlying relationships and principles that inform surface language issues, many contemporary scholars in rhetoric and composition have ignored Plato. Doing so has been made easier because tacit permission has been granted by the writers who dispense with Plato's rhetoric by writing as if it did not exist or as if he disowned all of rhetoric. Further tacit permission has been granted by those who treat theory and practice as completely separate activities rather than as interrelated areas of inquiry. This chapter focuses on three prominent versions of the contemporary reception of Platonic rhetoric: (1) the position that Plato is antirhetoric; (2) the position that Plato has nothing to do with rhetoric; and (3) the position that dialectically engages Plato's rhetoric. These different receptions allow us to construct historical rhetoric in different ways, and to consider how contemporary composition and rhetoric is in large part created by them.

## PLATO'S REMOVAL FROM RHETORIC AND HIS RELATIONSHIP TO THE FIVE CANONS

The first kind of reception, the removal of Plato from historical rhetoric, focuses on the form that many contemporary discussions of classical rhetoric assume. One representative example is John H. Mackin's *Classical Rhetoric for Modern Discourse*. The subtitle of this 1969 book, *An Art of Invention, Arrangement and Style for Readers, Speakers and Writers*, indicates its deletion of two of the five canons. The structure consists of ordering the material of discourse into the categories of the first three of the five canons of rhetoric: invention, arrangement, and style.

While the five departments of rhetoric were not canonized until Roman rhetoric, they are in fact apparent in Greek rhetoric. Aldo Scaglione writes in *The Classical Theory of Composition* that the five canons (which he calls functions) can be found in Aristotle (p. 14). Ray Nadeau, in "Delivery in Ancient Times: Homer to Quintilian," demonstrates that the fourth canon held great importance for Isocrates, Aristotle, and other Greek rhetoricians (pp. 53–54). He cites the many quotations of Demosthenes claiming "rhetoric is delivery" (p. 54). The centrality of the fifth canon, memory, in Greek rhetoric is argued by Frances A. Yates in *The Art of Memory*, where she connects the Roman treatise *Rhetorica Ad Herennium* to earlier Greek work:

> An immense weight of history presses on the memory section of *Ad Herennium*. It is drawing on Greek sources of memory teaching, probably in Greek treatises on rhetoric all of which are lost. It is the only Latin treatise on the subject to be preserved, for Cicero's and Quintilian's remarks are not full treatises and assume that the reader is already familiar

with the artificial memory and its terminology. It is thus really the main source, and indeed the only complete source, for the classical art of memory both in the Greek and in the Latin world. (p. 5)

Scaglione, Nadeau, and Yates show the existence and the importance of the five canons during Plato's time. The Greek names of the five canons (*erga*) were available, as Scaglione mentions (p. 14): *heuresis, taxis, lexis, mneme,* and *hypocrisis.*

Constructions such as Mackin's three-part canons could not exist if Plato's rhetoric were included. In fact, Mackin's construction does not appear to be radical because we are all so familiar with it; the deletion has become a commonplace in rhetoric and composition studies. Familiarity disguises its revolutionary consequences and conditions us to experience the removal as "normal." For example, the first three canons organize the vast majority of contemporary writing textbooks. An analysis of the results of eliminating two of the classical canons can reveal some of the unconscious uses of language theory. Looking at the deletion of two-fifths of the canons can show us something about Plato's conceptualization of rhetoric. If memory and delivery are ignored, we have effectively ignored much of the contribution Plato made to rhetoric.

All composing is recursive and dependent on the organic interrelationships of the recursive movements. In other words, composing is not linear and divisible into discrete parts. It is noteworthy that the Greek word for composition is "synthesis." All aspects of composing merge in various ways with one another. Invention, for example, is a primary generating issue in all five canons. While we can isolate it—as much excellent research in invention in the last fifteen years amply shows us—we need to maintain its sense of recursiveness and recognize its presence in every aspect of composing, regardless of whether we order it according to the classical canons or according to some other structure. Form partakes of the same recursiveness, as do style, memory, and delivery. The five canons work together to maintain this synergistic, mutually dependent relationship. Part of this inclusiveness derives from the contact with culture and public life that characterizes all seven hundred years of classical rhetoric in Greece and Rome. The power of classical rhetoric always resided in its symbiotic relationship with Greek and Roman culture and politics. When the canons are reduced to three composing issues—invention, arrangement, and style—not only is the definitive energy of the fluctuation among them deeply affected, but the relationship to culture assured by delivery disappears and the idea of category-for-category's sake is able to acquire more importance. The deletion of memory and delivery from any canonical system undercuts the intentions and rhetorical fullness of the five-part structure. In addition, their deletion by us ignores the orally based rhetoric that was the foundation for writing.

The motives for memory and delivery's consistent removal usually center on the association of memory and delivery with the dominance of oral discourse. However, the widespread assumption that oral dominance and writing dominance are easily separable and that writing dominance did not occur until after the height of classical rhetoric is refuted by the research of Eric A. Havelock, Walter J. Ong, and Tony M. Lentz, among others. Their work shows that written discourse began assuming major rhetorical importance by the fourth century B.C. when Plato was writing his dialogues (Havelock, "Alphabetization of Homer" p. 4). Certainly by the time of the writing of the *Rhetorica Ad Herennium*, where the canons were first codified explicitly in a document, writing had been thoroughly interiorized and was regarded as crucial to thinking. While orality was more important to the formation of consciousness (and, we might say, unconsciousness) in the classical period than it is in our own, writing was fully interiorized by the fourth century B.C. We cannot ignore this phenomenon in our conceptualization of classical rhetoric, nor can we neatly divide oral dominance and writing dominance in ancient Greece. Orality and literacy need to be considered together, because they worked together.

Tony M. Lentz demonstrates this point in *Orality and Literacy in Hellenic Greece:*

> The most significant conclusion I draw is that the symbiosis of writing and oral culture may have been a vital part of the origins of Western culture itself. That is, the vital element for the creation of philosophy and science was not the dominance of written abstraction or oral culture but the relationship between the two. First, the "tense" relationship between the two continues unabated throughout the period. The evidence does not support a conception of "victory" by one medium over the other. Second, the tension between the two modes of thought and communication is beneficial to the culture. (pp. 175–176)

Lentz's analysis shows the way for subsequent recognition of the interaction of orality and literacy. Nevertheless, Heritage School inertia will be difficult to overcome: the dichotomizing of orality and literacy has acted as a powerful binary opposition.

Plato's work developed significantly because of the interaction of orality and literacy. The common division of these two forms of discourse, referred to in many asides on rhetoric, constitutes a factual error. In fact, the mutuality in their coexistence exerted powerful language and consciousness changes, as Ong shows. Many of the critics who remove memory and delivery from the canons regard them as mere rote memorization and as simple gesture. Yet a more careful review of these assumptions informs both our rehistoricizing of classical rhetoric and Plato's relationship to it.

The depth and complexity of memory in all stages of classical rhetoric, from Corax to Plato to Quintilian, are called to mind by George Steiner's striking explication of the commonplace phrase "by heart" as a way of indicating memorization. Remembering something, carrying something around with oneself, takes place at the center of one's being. Eugenio Montale makes the same point in his essay "The Second Life of Art." The experience that the decoder takes away from the experience of art — the reflecting and mulling that accompany the activity of experiencing effective art — is the real source of art's power. If one's *memoria* is not changed by the experience of art, if the experience is not taken away, then it has not been deeply felt. Both Steiner, in *After Babel*, and Montale, in "The Second Life of Art," evoke the centrality of memory to all discourse and point to the phenomenon that memory is power.

Perhaps the most important connection that memory as a canon of rhetoric gives us is its explicit pointing to psychology. Research in cognitive psychology reveals the relationship between memory and creativity, as the work of John R. Anderson and John R. Hayes, among others, has shown. While the canon of memory is certainly not the only approach to psychology and discourse, it remains an important one. Moreover, memory does not decrease in importance with the rise of writing dominance, but it changes emphasis, particularly in the formation of consciousness as it relates to technology (Ong, *Orality*, pp. 78–116). David S. Kaufer demonstrates Plato's connection of rhetoric and psychology. Kaufer states that "there is a systematic connection between rhetoric and psychology in the *Dialogues*, and it comes to this: Plato knew there was a way of using words to affect the soul for good or evil and, as he saw it, one of the tasks of psychology was to explain the moral difference between the two" (p. 64).

When we reconstitute memory as a crucial aspect of Greek systems of rhetoric, one of the first things we discover is that memory is not merely a component of Plato's rhetoric. Memory is, as Yates claims in *The Art of Memory*, inherent in his rhetoric because rhetoric partakes of the Forms, and the soul's attempt through language to have access to them. Yates writes, "Memory is not a 'section' of this treatise, as one part of the art of rhetoric; memory in the Platonic sense is the groundwork of the whole" (p. 37). Memory is also the existence of the past within the present. It is there that culture and rhetoric largely exist, for Plato and for us.

Similarly, the canon of delivery has important implications for rhetoric and composition. Rather than limiting delivery to the physical gesture and expression that take place during speaking, we can relate it to the idea of medium. This point is made in Patrick Mahony's article "Marshall McLuhan in the Light of Classical Rhetoric" when he reveals that the fifth canon ultimately signifies medium. Mahony states, "As a theoretician of rhetoric, McLuhan's main contribution lies in the fact that he has developed and broadened the fifth category of traditional rhetoric" (p. 12). If delivery is regarded as medium, then the dynamics of the canon are reinvested with their original power. Medium in classical and contemporary rhetorical theory, as Ong, McLuhan, and Lucien Febvre demonstrate, determines the power of rhetoric. A major reason for the similarly intense study of rhetorical theory in ancient Greece and in contemporary America derives from shifts in consciousness—the movement from orality to literacy—set in motion by radical change in the fifth canon. In classical Greece, the gradual interiorization of the phonetic alphabet from the eighth to the fourth centuries B.C. led to these changes in discourse, and in the contemporary period, the interiorization of electronic media in the last one hundred years has been changing gradually our relationship with all kinds of discourse (Ong, *Orality*, p. 79). These changes are major factors in the enormous interest in rhetoric in the classical and contemporary periods and help to tie the two periods together. In *The Presence of the Word*, Ong states, "Our entire understanding of classical culture now has to be revised—and with it our understanding of later cultures up to our own time—in terms of our new awareness of the role of the media in structuring the human psyche and civilization itself" (p. 18). So the fifth canon, particularly in its interaction with the four other canons and with a recognition of its recursiveness, offers us important and largely unexplored interpretive options in contemporary rhetoric.

Removing memory and delivery from the canons can undermine contemporary work in rhetoric by diminishing its range. If we are going to rely on the structure of the five canons of classical rhetoric, we need either to use that structure or to explain its adaptation with great care, for the removal of two-fifths of the canons is not an adaptation but a wholly new structure that denies the central language issues of culture and power. Classical rhetoric as a [word] system of discourse theory remains unique among the various critical theories available to us because it connects to history, politics, and the everyday uses of language. In addition, it takes full account of the production of discourse. The central language issues of memory and delivery, which assumed importance in Greek rhetoric and were canonized in Roman rhetoric, are connectors to history, culture, and the life of the polis. If Plato's views were allowed to exist in interpretations of classical rhetoric, then a structure like the truncated canons could not function. To reduce the classical canons from five to three has the same consequences as saying that Plato opposes all of rhetoric. Both these interpretations of classical rhetoric diminish its effectiveness, its range, and its usefulness as anything more than an attractive antique.

## THE INTERPRETIVE OPTION THAT PLATO OPPOSES RHETORIC

Plato's rhetoric bypasses helpful categorization (of the kind that Aristotle has made us so comfortable with) and relies instead on the active interchange of rhetoric and dialectic between two sides actively engaged in a search. Plato attacked his version of sophistic rhetoric. He embraced dialectical rhetoric. This oppositional view accounts for one source of confusion in the reception of Plato's rhetoric. Plato does not so much contradict himself as he distinguishes between his version of sophistic rhetoric and his version of dialectical rhetoric. He denounces the former and praises the latter kind. Plato's defense of dialectical rhetoric appears in *Phaedrus* explicitly and in *Gorgias* implicitly. In Plato's heated attack against sophistic rhetoric in *Gorgias*, he complained about the prescriptions that the sophistic handbooks relied on. He railed against the illusory power of discourse that lacked vital connections to human thought and essential principles. He worked against the absence of intellectual inquiry in some of these handbooks and the teachers who used them. He opposed their relativistic bias because it denied his ontology of the Forms and the soul's relationship to them. Even more importantly, Plato could not envision a genuine rhetoric that does not deal with activity between the encoder and the decoder. Plato attacked his version of sophistic rhetoric not only because it denied his conception of reality but, crucially, because much sophistic rhetoric seemed to him to deny activity between the message sender and receiver, and therefore allowed the soul to atrophy, or to use the imagery from *Phaedrus*, his version of sophistic rhetoric pulled the soul back to the earth rather than allowing the soul to soar. Plato believed that the Sophists' rhetoric ignored the nature of dialectical inquiry.[1]

Plato praised dialectical rhetoric because it depends on the active use

---

[1]Edwin Black, in "Plato's View of Rhetoric," argues that more than one kind of rhetoric is treated in *Gorgias*. Black states, "It is impossible to maintain that Plato intended the *Gorgias* to be a total condemnation of all rhetoric as a 'knack' and a 'counterfeit of politics' when, in that very dialogue, he already sketches out some of the conditions of a rhetoric which would deserve the name of art" (p. 179).

of dialectic. Passivity precludes dialectic. The activity, the interdependent exchange of ideas and emotions, the push and pull of spiralling intellectual and psychological inquiry, constitute Plato's conception of philosophical rhetoric in *Phaedrus*. Without dialectic, there is no real rhetoric for Plato. In the presentation of all his writing—the letters as well as the dialogues—he indicates that rhetoric is crucial to his effective working out of dialectic. They are intertwined for him. Consequently, the categories that deny connection and therefore activity cannot be a part of his rhetoric.

Because of Plato's unwillingness to categorize his rhetoric, it is more difficult to describe his dialectical rhetoric than Aristotle's, whose extant lecture notes invite others to formulize his rhetoric. We cannot simply excerpt a few lines—as we do so nicely with Aristotle—and provide a definition of Platonic rhetoric. We have to consult the rhetorical form of Plato's work, the interaction of rhetoric and dialectic, and the psychological activity of the speaker or writer with the listener or reader. The medium of writing (that is, Plato's use of the canon of delivery) and the psychology of discourse (Plato's use of the canon of memory) combine with the canons of invention, arrangement, and style to provide a Platonic definition of rhetoric.

Plato's rhetoric is much less concerned with a large assembly of hearers or readers than with a series of one-to-one dialectics formed by rhetoric. Consider, for example, three of his middle group of dialogues—*Phaedrus*, *Symposium*, and *Republic*. In these pieces the literary characters of Phaedrus, Alcibiades, and Thrasymachus are presented as memorable individuals who interact not only with the dialogue character of Socrates but with the environments they populate. The individuals, set in the scene of a particular Athens, are active interlocutors who challenge and are challenged by Socrates. There is no Platonic dialogue without this verbal interchange of persuasion and belief. They are so carefully wrought that, as Walter Pater has discussed in *Plato and Platonism*, the dialogues themselves become individuals with whom we interact.

The tendency to consider classical rhetoric exclusively as a public art—to envision a formal speech delivered to an assembly—has dominated contemporary studies of rhetoric. Just as important as public discourse was the individual correspondence, clash, and movement of the Platonic, "personal" rhetoric. This conceptualization of rhetoric does not depend as thoroughly on the construction of political interactions as public rhetoric does. It changes as the state changes, but it does not disappear, as legislative rhetoric does with the disappearance of democracy. In the last section of *Phaedrus*, Socrates makes the following extension of rhetoric:

> Is not rhetoric, taken generally, a universal art of enchanting the mind by arguments; which is practiced not only in courts and public assemblies, but in private houses also, having to do with all matters, great as well as small, good and bad alike, and is in all equally right, and equally to be esteemed—that is what you have heard? (Jowett, p. 305)

After an illustration of the personal kind of rhetoric that exists alongside public rhetoric, Socrates goes on to instruct young Phaedrus: "The art of disputation, then, is not confined to the courts and the assembly, but is one and the same in *every use of language*" (Jowett, p. 306, my emphasis).

Plato's rhetoric is more difficult than virtually any other rhetoricians' because it derives from the mutuality of dialectic and its connection to Plato's construction of basic realities. Two people interact only because each rhetorical partner actively exists. The emphasis on individual responsibility in the rhetorical, dialectical act is not as easy to capture, to codify, even to prescribe, as rhetoric before a large audience whose interaction must by its very nature be difficult to assess. In a public forum, the audience works as a group and in many ways is externally passive, or can choose to be utterly passive. The rhetoric of the public speaker does not depend as thoroughly on the audience as the individual, dialectical version of rhetoric does. Plato makes the reader of the dialogue join Socrates and his companions in the art of private rhetoric and dialectic.

Those critics who interpret Plato as completely opposed to rhetoric tend not to consider the existence of the dialogue form in Plato and the fact that it requires active reading. They disregard the readerly resistance that Plato demands in the form of the dialogue, a resistance that assures participation by the reader. The negative critics emphasize a limited aspect of Plato's conceptualization of rhetoric: they turn exclusively to his attack on the sophistic rhetoric he sets up in the early *Gorgias*. Plato sets up his often-quoted, graphic, analogical series of dangers in presenting Gorgias's kind of rhetoric as a trivialization of something important. Just as gymnastics and medicine can be reduced from arts to knacks by reducing them to cosmetics and cookery, so rhetoric can be reduced (*Gorgias*, p. 465).[2] The crucial interpretive question in Plato's analogical reasoning consists of two parts. Those critics who interpret Plato as thoroughly attacking rhetoric in this frequently cited passage are attending to only one half of each analogy, namely, cosmetics and cookery. Their worthy counterparts, gymnastics and medicine, are ignored in this interpretation. In his extensive use of

---

[2]See Dodds, pp. 229–230, and Kennedy, *Classical Rhetoric and Its Christian and Secular Tradition from Ancient to Modern Times*, p. 49.

these ratios, Plato's Socrates points to an alternative rhetoric, one based on the pursuit of justice (*dike,* or balance) and the good rather than on pleasure. So even in *Gorgias,* a dialogue often dismissed as thoroughly against all rhetoric, Plato treats and enacts dialectical rhetoric. The form of the dialogue itself remains a primary enactment of Plato's rhetoric. Cicero, in *On the Character of the Orator,* states that Plato is a very effective rhetorician in arguing against sophistic rhetoric (p. 18). Critics who attend only to Plato's condemnation of his version of sophistic rhetoric go beyond the interpretation problem of ignoring half of Plato's analogies to rhetoric. They inaccurately make a synecdoche out of the part of the analogy they do respond to; they claim, in effect, that half the analogy stands for all of Plato's conception of rhetoric and they ignore the fact that only a rhetorician passionately committed to the possibilities of dialectical rhetoric could damn its misuse so thoroughly.

The extension of Plato's attack against his version of sophistic rhetoric to include theoretical rhetoric is a primary characteristic of the contemporary reception of classical rhetoric. As we saw with Knoblauch and Brannon's *Rhetorical Traditions and the Teaching of Writing,* Plato's attack on his version of sophistic rhetoric moves forward their argument that classical rhetoric largely created such modern problems in the teaching of writing as the current-traditional paradigm. Theoretical rhetoric in Plato does not exist for them. The mere repetition of the concept that Plato does not exist for rhetoric has provided this interpretation with much of its power.

From the anti-rhetoric interpretation of Plato, it is a logical step to a different but related incarnation of the contemporary reception of Plato's rhetoric. This reception excludes Plato altogether in the contemporary historicizing of rhetoric. All of rhetoric is made to begin with Aristotle. The editors of *Reinventing the Rhetorical Tradition,* Aviva Freedman and Ian Pringle, for example, follow this path, as does Douglas Ehninger in "On Systems of Rhetoric." Critics who exclude Plato tend to depart from the questions of theoretical rhetoric because they do not engage dialectic, its attendant psychological interactions (that is, the advancement that the canon of memory provides), and the activity found in whole discourses. It is a small step from the exclusion of dialectical rhetoric to the reduction of interactive whole discourse, to fragments of discourse and the reduction of a whole, psychological being whose essential formation, whose realization of a best self, occurs with discourse. The avenue toward the formulizing of rhetoric therefore lies open. Rhetoric is well on its way to becoming trivial, if such a view is adopted.

The denial of dialectical rhetoric leads the way to a third kind of classical rhetoric: technical rhetoric, a dry, prescriptive, microscopic form of language use that holds the power today that some versions of sophistic rhetoric held in Plato's time.[3] Almost all freshman writing books, as Mike Rose, Richard Ohmann, and others have demonstrated, emphasize this kind of static, rule-centered rhetoric. Plato's version of sophistic rhetoric and technical rhetoric share in their denial of the essential power of dialectical rhetoric, what some critics call "true rhetoric" (for example, Erickson in *Plato: True and Sophistic Rhetoric*). The assorted versions of sophistic rhetoric enjoy the advantage over technical rhetoric of at least treating psychology (forms of memory) and whole people. Technical rhetoric characterizes itself by a focus on fragmentary, prescribed discourse.

Leaving Plato out of our construction of rhetoric virtually assures a lapse into the prescriptions of technical rhetoric. This absence promotes the nontheoretical thinker whom Terry Eagleton, William M. A. Grimaldi, and others have complained of, and so sets the stage for a static, rule-bound rhetoric that evades the issues of thinking, performance, and discourse.

## THE INTERPRETIVE OPTION THAT DIALECTICALLY ENGAGES PLATO'S RHETORIC AS A FACULTY AND AS A SUBJECT

Fortunately, a third kind of reception of classical rhetoric exists. Some writers in contemporary rhetoric and composition have understood the consequences of making Plato anti-rhetoric or of deleting him from rhetoric altogether. Such rhetoric critics as George Kennedy, especially in *Classical Rhetoric and Its Christian and Secular Tradition from Ancient to Modern Times*, Ong in *Orality and Literacy* and other places, Lunsford and Ede in "On Distinctions between Classical and Modern Rhetoric," and Jasper Neel in *Plato, Derrida, and Writing* represent an alternative contemporary reception of classical rhetoric by beginning with careful readings of Plato's dialogues, making connections among them, and understanding Plato's rhetoric as part of his dialectical system. These writers address Plato's rhetoric and dialectic by participating in it; Kennedy, Ong, Lunsford and Ede, and Neel are active dialecticians themselves in their studies of Plato's rhetoric.

In *Classical Rhetoric in Its Christian and Secular Tradition from Ancient to Modern Times*, Kennedy reads *Phaedrus* for us in a way that not only

---

[3]Classical technical rhetoric, as George Kennedy and others define it, differs from the contemporary field of technical writing. Contemporary technical writing is a form of reference discourse and deals with strategies for conveying specialized information.

synthesizes but rehistoricizes subsequent views of classical rhetoric.[4] Plato "lays the foundation for basic features of Aristotle's *Rhetoric* and he integrates rhetoric into his other philosophical ideas in a way not attempted elsewhere" (pp. 52–53). Kennedy rereads himself (in *The Art of Persuasion in Greece*) and shows us the psychological, erotic, and even divine attributes of Plato's rhetoric. Kennedy removes us from hyperlogical classical rhetoric as Plato himself did. Kennedy shows us how to recognize the enormous power of rhetoric and to see that it cannot be explained by cordoning off the logical aspect of the mind and separating it from the whole person. While his stance is objectivist/positivist, Kennedy nonetheless offers alternative interpretive options.

Like Kennedy, Ong provides a different kind of Platonic interpretation that also depends on explication of Plato's dialogues and a careful setting up of his language, context, and culture. Ong also rehistoricizes classical rhetoric by showing us that oral dominance and writing dominance are not separate spheres and that the technology of language shapes the unconscious and the conscious mind (*Orality*, pp. 78–79). Most importantly for contemporary rhetoric and composition studies, Ong connects the technology struggle of Plato's time with the technology struggle we experience now with electronic media. At issue is the shaping of consciousness from which all encoding derives. In other words, Ong explains the psychology of rhetoric in Plato's context and in our own. Plato realized that writing his ideas enabled him to preserve them, in spite of his complaints against writing. With the form of the dialogue, he chose a kind of writing that resembles speaking. Psychology, particularly in its relationship to consciousness and language, is an area that most contemporary studies of classical rhetoric have ignored. This inattention has led to the removal of Plato in the historicizing of rhetoric, to a hyperlogical reduction of Aristotle's rhetoric, and to a denial of the power we derive from technology-induced shifts in consciousness. Ong states: "Technologies are artificial, but—paradox again—artificiality is natural to human beings. Technology, properly interiorized, does not degrade human life but on the contrary enhances it" (pp. 82–83). We must face the interiorization of electronic media as Plato in his rhetoric faced the interiorization of the phonetic alphabet. This treatment requires treating whole people. Plato resisted the new technology of writing even as he artistically manipulated it.

Plato's rhetoric is very much like our own rhetoric as it is treated in Lunsford and Ede's essay "On Distinctions between Classical and

---

[4]See Keith V. Erickson's "The Lost Rhetorics of Aristotle" for an analysis of Aristotle's development as a rhetorical theorist. Erickson shows how Aristotle also modified his attitudes toward rhetoric.

Modern Rhetoric." They rehistoricize rhetoric for us by analyzing an influential segment of the reception of rhetorical thought into a false dichotomy. By revealing the reductionism that has turned Aristotle, for instance, into a hyperlogical language theorist—and, by implication, Plato—they reread Aristotle by placing him within his own philosophical system. Lunsford and Ede reintegrate common reductions of classical rhetoric—such as interpreting classical rhetoric as logic dominant—into a wide-ranging theory of discourse. Their analysis of the contemporary reception of classical rhetoric depends on the recognition of Plato as a primary classical rhetorician.

## REDIRECTING THE CRITICAL CONVERSATION: NEEL ON PLATO'S WRITING

Plato's position in contemporary rhetoric and composition studies has been reappropriated by Jasper Neel's 1988 *Plato, Derrida, and Writing*. Neel's rhetorical stance in the book perhaps most significantly relies on including Plato's work on rhetoric and writing in the context of composition studies. He makes Plato a part of the current critical conversation. By appropriating Platonic rhetoric and writing in this radical way, Neel brings new kinds of discourse into the conversation. Boldly setting aside various historical claims about the dominance of philosophy over rhetoric, Neel brings to light many assumptions about the historicizing of rhetoric that had not previously been available. Neel writes: "My purpose in working through the long struggle that precedes this chapter has been to clear a space in which composition studies finally can be liberated from philosophy" (p. 202). By reappropriating the traditional power of the discipline of philosophy, Neel has repositioned not only rhetoric but writing as well. This strategic move enables writing to exist as a faculty (as a process) more fully than other constructions have allowed.

Neel, through the course of his book, engages readers in his own dialectical struggle. He announces in his preface ("Renvoi") that Plato, "the most powerful voice of the West," . . . "must be silenced" (p. xi). Nevertheless, Neel gives eloquence to Plato. Just as Plato, on writing, says one thing and enacts another (explaining in a letter or a dialogue the dangers of writing but doing so in carefully crafted prose), so Neel announces the importance of silencing Plato while he enlivens all of Plato's work. We are taken through a careful explanation of *Phaedrus* and, more importantly, we are placed in Neel's dialectic with himself on Plato's relationship to writing and his unhappy relationship to philosophy. By recognizing the impossibility of the task he has set himself, Neel empowers himself as a writer and represents Plato's rhetoric in a way that makes us more aware of Plato's own dialectic. The texts on writing by Plato and Neel dialectically engage the reader by providing resistance and compelling questioning.

Neel's statements about Plato as the most powerful *voice* of the West will surprise many writers in rhetoric and composition studies who see Aristotle as the genuine source of power traditionally. Aristotle's scientism especially enabled his writing (or lecture notes) to define many disciplines. His categories remain very adaptable. Neel writes that he needs "to admit from the beginning that the success of my text depends on my ability to discover and to use the available means of persuasion," an acknowledgment of Aristotle's definition of rhetoric.

The brief explicit appearances of Aristotle in this book speak eloquently. The three direct comments on Aristotle (pp. 5, 12, 47) historicize rhetoric and writing in important ways. By expropriating Aristotle from Neel's dialectic, Neel has reorganized the critical conversation to begin the history of rhetoric and writing where the documents (the writings) appear to begin, with the Sophists and with Plato. This tonic to the hyper-Aristotelian stance that has dominated much rhetorical and literary discussion of the twentieth century enables Neel and his readers to rehistoricize rhetoric and composition studies with different insights and goals.

Neel probes keywords such as *pharmakon*, he exploits the power available in translation, and he understands that classical rhetoric cannot usefully exist as a seven-hundred-year monolith. In addition, Neel as a writer does not merely feed his readers. He requires that we join him in his own dialectic as a writer writing first to himself. Consequently, the form of Neel's book resembles the form of Plato's own writing more than many previous commentaries have done. He deconstructs *Phaedrus* according to Derrida's procedure, he rehabilitates Plato, and he then calls for an emphasis on sophistic rhetoric.

Neel, then, writes as a Dialectical Critic. Like Ong, in the third category of Platonic/rhetorical reception that I have set up in this chapter, Neel understands the psychological issues involved in Plato's relationship to writing. But unlike Ong, Neel displaces the orality-literacy hypothesis and Plato's own emergence in a culture that was rapidly interiorizing writing. Throughout Neel's book, he responds negatively to the disjunction between what Plato says about writing and how he appropriates writing. Neel is careful throughout the book to present explicitly his bias against Plato; this presentation is provocative and heightens reader interest. He believes that Plato has tried to usurp writing, to put one over on us. Neel's project is partly to overturn this agenda. Most of Neel's complaints about Plato's usurping of writing can be accounted for by Plato's position in the crucial early history of writing as a technology. The motives imputed to Plato could not have been available to any writer of the fourth century B.C. What appears to a late twentieth-century reader like Neel actually resulted from the struggle of writing to exist as more than a recorder of information. Plato's motives as a writer and our motives as readers are more carefully understood by the orality-literacy hypothesis.

The work of Kennedy, Ong, Lunsford and Ede, and Neel—exemplifying the third reception of classical rhetoric that I have set up in this chapter—represent successful attempts to reconnect rhetoric with thinking and performance, rather than with mere formulizing. These writers do not trade on Plato's image and Aristotle's authority but engage in the active search that informed all of their writing. By showing us this kind of textual interaction, Kennedy, Ong, Lunsford and Ede, and Neel remove classical rhetoric from its skill-bound appropriators and help us restore discourse and thought to the center of the rhetoric and composition curriculum, usurping the static formulas and exhortations that persuade many people that it is better to dispense with classical rhetoric.

This chapter presents one symptomatic reading of contemporary rhetoric and composition studies: that the kind of reception we give classical rhetoric—and by extension the rest of historical rhetoric and composition—informs how we study the discipline today. We can turn now to the issue of how we can change the condition of language study so that dialectical rhetoric, language and thinking interdependent in Vygotsky's sense, gains dominance over the necessarily fragmentary, skill-bound rhetoric. One strategy is to consult the struggle between skill-bound rhetoric and dialectical rhetoric that has been going on since the fourth century B.C. We need an awareness of how the twentieth-century rhetoric and composition resurgence fits into historicizing. When we better understand the reasons why rhetoric and composition have assumed great importance again, we may be able to exploit better what Terry Eagleton calls the "forms of power and performance" that rhetoric gives us (*Literary Theory*, p. 205). In other words, we need to remember that we historicize ourselves as we rehistoricize Plato's work on rhetoric.

Contemporary rhetoric cannot consult the "forms of power and performance" without recognizing the struggle Plato went through with the new technology of writing. By the time Plato complains (ironically, in literary texts) that writing threatens intelligence, or the discourse status quo, there was no turning back to primary orality, a point that both Ong and Havelock have made repeatedly. Writing had pervaded the general consciousness; it had changed not merely what people thought about but *how* they thought about it. In a similar way, we can see that the electronic media have already changed the way consciousness is formed. We cannot choose to avoid this change. In spite of this phenomenon, reaction to change is all around us in blanket denunciations of video, especially in the form of television and the attendant proclamations of impending universal illiteracy. Such a struggle is a struggle over rhetoric; it is analogous to the struggle between writing and speaking dominance that preoccupied Plato so acutely in *Phaedrus* and the Seventh Letter. As teachers and writers of rhetoric and composition, we witness a striking example of the conflict between writing and electronic media. It comes to us in the form of a schism between traditional literary studies, which tends to emphasize history, theme, and artistic expression (field coverage with some aesthetics), and rhetoric and composition studies, which examine any kind of writing occurring anywhere as well as the production of all kinds of discourse. In this schism, critical theory is on the same side as rhetoric and composition studies. Many aspects of rhetoric and composition studies and critical theory examine the assumptions of language study and radically extend the kinds of discourse to be studied. This extension of discourse study and, more importantly, the reorganization of assumptions of language study, is frequently regarded negatively by some traditionalists. The struggle of rhetoric and composition studies and critical theory to assert themselves institutionally in departments is analogous to the struggle that written discourse underwent in Plato's Athens. Shifts in consciousness do not occur easily and without rancor.

When Plato appears to be ambivalent about writing and rhetoric, he was responding to his version of sophistic rhetoric, to skill-bound rhetoric, and to his sense of how these two versions of rhetoric were exploiting very effectively the burgeoning power of the written word. He chose to respond with his own elaborate writing, his own conception of philosophical rhetoric, and his own *paideia.* In other words, he reinscribed what he regarded as harmful material. So Plato was concerned not with obliterating rhetoric and its increasingly familiar discourse partner writing, but with appropriating them to his own beliefs and directing that meaning of rhetoric to others.

Just as Plato's intense understanding of the physical world has frequently been denied in favor of a blatant, dualistic interpretation that places Plato in an ethereal world of invisible Forms, so Plato's equally intense understanding of the centrality of rhetoric to dialectic and philosophy has been denied. Both denials deprive us of Plato's power and insight. In addition, similar denials deprive current rhetoric and composition studies of power. The revolutionary aspect of Plato's writing resides in his use of dialectic *and* rhetoric, his connection of form to human activity. Dialectic in Plato's sense has particular importance for current rhetoric and composition pedagogy. At the center of dialectic lies activity between two (or more) fully participating sides. Platonic dialectic denies passivity, the attribute that most characterizes contemporary education and that depends completely on a denial of individual power. In other words, passivity denies the dynamic capacity of student *ethos*, traps them in triviality, and therefore stifles their power. From this point of view, from Plato's point of view in *Phaedrus,* and from Neel's point of view in *Plato, Derrida, and Writing,* the teaching of rhetoric and dialectic is a subversive act, a call to mutual activity that obliterates the familiar passiveness of the classroom.

Plato cannot divide the activity of dialectic from rhetoric, as Aristotle does in his simultaneous elevation and cordoning off of rhetoric in Book I. When Aristotle states that rhetoric is the counterpart (the *antistrophe*) of dialectic in the first sentence of the *Rhetoric,* he has separated the two activities. For Plato, rhetoric without dialectic diminishes it to the status of cookery and cosmetics. Dialectical rhetoric must partake of the mutuality that speakers and writers necessarily have with their audiences. The mutuality requires that the audience become an encoder as well. Rhetoric can be profoundly good or profoundly bad for Plato, depending on its relationship to dialectic, its relationship to ultimate reality, and the striving for contact with it. Again, the adaptability of classical rhetoric reveals itself. There can be no dialectical rhetoric if whole pieces of discourse are not used. Nor can there be dialectical rhetoric if all five canons are not included. The famous passage in *Phaedrus* discussing discourse as an organic body provides one of Plato's strikingly graphic explanations for this attitude toward the potential power of language (Jowett translation, p. 309). If understanding is to emerge from the discourse, if language is given the opportunity to achieve its power, language must be performed interactively and must aspire to contact beyond the apparent world.

Given the kind of connection and dialectical interaction Plato requires, the reader can see why skill-bound rhetoric—the kind represented in different ways by Polus, Callicles, and Gorgias in *Gorgias*—would not work for Plato. This version of rhetoric did not engage whole human beings. Skill-bound rhetoric, the kind propounded in the many handbooks then in circulation promising quick language fixes of power, engaged even less of the essential person than Plato's version of sophistic rhetoric. Plato overcomes these two kinds of rhetoric by repeatedly showing us his conception of dialectical rhetoric, the interaction of dialectic and rhetoric. In other words, the form of each dialogue acts as another utterance of this primary fact.

Two of the familiar forms of the contemporary use and reception of classical rhetoric rely on leaving Plato out of classical rhetoric or, worse, claiming he rejected rhetoric. This historicizing leads to formulizing of the kind we see in the truncated canons of contemporary presentations of classical rhetoric: a categorical structure that contains only remnants of an entire theory. If contemporary movements in rhetoric and composition studies are going to work, they are going to have to follow such writers as Kennedy, Ong, Lunsford and Ede, and Neel in more elaborately reinscribing Plato's rhetoric.

# 5

Appropriating Competing
Systems of Classical Greek
Rhetoric: Considering
Isocrates and Gorgias with
Plato in the New Rhetoric
of the Fourth Century B.C.

> The most widespread early criticism on historical record was not, in
> our sense, 'aesthetic'; it was a mode of what we would now call
> 'discourse theory,' devoted to analyzing the material effects of
> particular uses of language in particular social conjunctures. . . . Its
> intention, quite consciously, was systematically to theorize the
> articulations of discourse and power. . . . The name of this form of
> criticism was rhetoric. From its earliest formulations by Corax of
> Syracuse in fifth-century Greece, rhetoric came in Roman schools to
> be practically equivalent to higher education as such.
> —Terry Eagleton, *Walter Benjamin*

"Classical rhetoric" is very susceptible to interpretations other than the
ones offered by the Heritage School, in which once-useful formulas
impose a benign means of organizing the written and spoken language
of the seven hundred years of this era. Alternative appropriations of

classical rhetoric locate its systematic beginning in the fifth century with Corax's manipulation of power in public speaking and in teaching.[1] Systematic rhetoric acquired increasing importance in the fifth century B.C. as spoken and written presentations for law courts increased and as the writing of dramatic literature—notably by Aeschylus, Euripides, Sophocles, and Aristophanes—achieved new levels of complexity and artistic achievement. Rhetoric gathered momentum in the fourth century B.C. as astonishingly successful schools of rhetoric emerged from the enthusiastic desire of large segments of the population to train with rhetors. The changing political systems contributed to the new pedagogical awareness. With this intense interest in language training, schools of rhetoric began to compete with one another. Historicizing rhetoric by beginning with Corax accounts for the fifth and fourth century B.C. contexts of rhetoric and provides a version of rhetoric and composition that constitutes a radical and complete system for the production of written discourse and spoken discourse, for the practice of them, and for the theorizing of them. To begin the history of rhetoric and composition with Aristotle, whose work appeared generations after that of Corax, is to remove a crucial segment of early rhetorical history. This familiar kind of historicizing, investigated in Chapter One, necessarily removes Aristotle from the intellectual context that enabled him to produce his writing and speaking. In this familiar construction, Aristotle's part in the critical conversation is converted into a monologue.

The unique completeness of classical rhetoric recognized by Eagleton and others relies partly on beginning this part of discourse history with Corax in Syracuse in the fifth century B.C. rather than with Aristotle in Athens in the fourth century B.C.

In addition to a historical change in the locatable beginnings of classical rhetoric, the unique completeness of classical rhetoric that Eagleton and other critics have written about (see, for example, Corbett, *Classical*, pp. 594–630; Mackin, pp. 1–48; and Kennedy, *Art*, pp. 3–25) lies in its ability to account for all aspects of written and spoken discourse: producing both kinds of discourse, analyzing them, and manipulating and responding to the cultural and political contexts from which discourse must emerge. In each of these interrelated capacities, an emphasis on function is always present. The functionalism of

---

[1] I use the term "systematic" here to take account of Homeric rhetoric. The many speeches in the written-down versions of the *Iliad* and the *Odyssey* (as opposed to their earlier spoken manifestations) constitute one part of Homeric rhetoric. A traditional consensus places the beginning of Greek rhetoric as a self-conscious system with Corax and Tisias (see, for example, Murphy, *Synoptic*, pp. 3–18).

language, a new awareness of its capacities, appears with the many teachers and schools of rhetoric. In Corax's case, the use of probability to sway opinion occupied a central place.[2] The Sophists, from Gorgias to Isocrates, to many whose work is obscured for us because their material was either not written down or was lost, promised and often delivered very practical instruction in how to get what one wants.[3] The teacher-student relationship provided an opportunity for the dissemination of knowledge of rhetoric as well as its practice. The teachers' emphasis on success in private and in public life consistently concerned itself with functionalism. How to succeed in the law courts in an increasingly litigious society formed one important aim in rhetorical training and was oral-dominant in the earlier stages. One of many important voices in this progression of Greek rhetoric is Plato, whose aggressively complex and irreducible rhetoric (as we saw in the last chapter) depended for its existence on dialectic as well as other parts of his interactive, dualistic epistemology. Later, in a way that differed from Corax and from the Sophists, and less radically from his teacher Plato, Aristotle emphasized practicality in his development of rhetorical theory. He provided a systematic rendering of discourse theory, breaking it down into sets and subsets not unlike his studies of animals or of astronomy. Corax, the various Sophists, Plato, and Aristotle were all preoccupied with useful ness in various ways. Traditionally, many readers have interpreted Corax, the Sophists, and Aristotle as very practical people. Plato, too, as we saw in Chapter Four, was practical in that his system accounted for the totality of life (taking account of the soul even before and after birth), ultimate reality, and therefore to some extent, meaning. In addition, Plato emphasized—through dialogue—that private rhetoric was as important as public rhetoric.

The radical nature of classical rhetoric cannot exist for us now if the crucial first two hundred years of its emergence and development are ignored or suppressed. The familiar constructions of classical rhetoric that begin with Aristotle rather than with Corax, the Sophists, and others bypass the undulations of change and thought that enable Aristotle's language theory to exist in the first place. Aristotle's work emerged from the context of Plato's school, the Sophists' work, and the investigations of the cosmologists as well as the post-Peloponnesian political situation of the early third century B.C.

---

[2]For an analysis of what is known about the work of the earliest known rhetoricians, see D.A.G. Hinks, "Tisias and Corax and the Invention of Rhetoric."

[3]See Guthrie, *The Sophists*; Mario Untersteiner, *The Sophists*; G. B. Kerford, *The Sophistic Movement*; and Susan C. Jarratt, "The First Sophists and the Uses of History" and "Toward a Sophistic Historiography" for five important presentations of the Sophists.

The emphasis on completeness and usefulness in the first systematic rhetorics tapped into growing language power in a unique way. All these versions of Greek rhetoric depended on the utilitarianism of language as well as on its aesthetic and theoretical properties. From another point of view, one could say that aestheticism and theory were functional for these thinkers in rhetoric. An illuminating example of functionalism coexisting with theory and aesthetics in rhetoric is Isocrates' *Antidosis* (354 B.C.–353 B.C.), a written text that maintains the fiction that it is meant to be spoken. Isocrates discusses taxation (an enlightened form of taxation in which rich people are compelled to pay for, say, a military weapon). His elaborate discussion assumes aesthetically pleasing proportions that work to persuade readers of his point about the taxation of the reputedly wealthy. The everyday issues of supporting a government in its military activity through selective taxation takes on layers of meaning that impinge on public perception of rich citizens like Isocrates, the daily tasks of government, and the ability of language to create change. *Antidosis* acts as a public policy statement, an autobiography, an investigation of the ways that public attitudes are formed, and as literary discourse whose language transcends the quotidian ordinariness of complaining about taxes or of defending the way that one has led one's life.

By treating issues that affected ordinary living, Isocrates, in *Antidosis* and elsewhere, was able to exploit the power inherent in discourse that is used every day. A recognition of this power of the everyday use of language runs from Corax through Aristotle in Greek rhetoric. An understanding of the nature of language as it is used in ordinary circumstances occurs in all the theories of classical rhetoric. The daily uses of language were not looked down on and were not ignored as trivial; rather, they were recognized as holding important keys to thinking. The daily repetition of language and the dependence that people inherently have on it were recognized and exploited by these rhetoricians. This connection to the ordinary did not always enjoy the same degree of completeness in post-classical systems of rhetoric.[4]

Rhetoric accounted for and helped to develop the everyday uses of language, in which repetition of words and syntactic structures (including many recently developed ones) constantly reinforced the power of discourse. It consequently treated social, political, and psychological issues. There was everywhere apparent in the fullness of rhetoric a

---

[4]For comparisons of classical rhetoric to later systems, see, for example, Kennedy, *Classical Rhetoric and Its Christian and Secular Tradition from Ancient to Modern Times*; Richard M. Weaver, *The Ethics of Rhetoric*; James J. Murphy (Ed.), *The Rhetorical Tradition and Modern Writing*; and Winifred Bryan Horner (Ed.), *The Present State of Scholarship in Historical and Contemporary Rhetoric*.

sense of bringing about change. Rhetoric's wide-ranging capacity depends partly on its not being confined to a specific subject matter. But as Richard McKeon has pointed out, although rhetoric does not have a specific subject matter, it does in fact treat subjects.[5] In his perplexing *Speculum* article on patterns in the rehistoricizing of rhetoric, McKeon writes: "The history of rhetoric should have as subject an art which, although it has no special subject matter according to most rhetoricians, nonetheless must be discussed in appreciation to some subject matter: rhetoric is applied to many incommensurate subject matters" (p. 3). The faculty of rhetoric is able and in fact needs to attach itself to virtually any subject matter (making McKeon's "incommensurate subject matters" irrelevant), including the daily matters of living, aesthetic discourse, and everything in between. Unlike, for instance, much of New Criticism, with its emphasis on the textual object,[6] and the aesthetic implications that revolve around that object,[7] classical rhetoric formed an inclusive system that accounted not only for the aesthetic but for the utilitarian aspects of discourse. One might say that classical rhetoric makes the aesthetic utilitarian. When a system of language criticism exploits the ubiquitous power of discourse that derives from its use every day, then it enables people to analyze and to produce both written and spoken discourse more effectively. Ordinary language and extraordinary language (or everyday discourse and artistic discourse) can benefit from each other. When these two kinds of languages are recognized as not merely informing each other but helping to create each other, then discourse in general is empowered. The systems of classical rhetoric as they developed in the fifth and the fourth centuries B.C., most tellingly with Gorgias, Isocrates, Plato, and Aristotle fully exploited the central relationship that exists between everyday language and artistic language. Far from regarding everyday language as in some way inferior to what we now call literary language, Gorgias, Isocrates, and Plato regarded it, in these vivid years of language development in general and rhetorical theory in particular, as a center of thought, performance, and education. Gorgias did so with his emphasis on the power of *logos* (a concept that meant for him, among other things, reason and language) that he found to be everywhere present. In addition to his interest in *logos* as a central aspect of human thought and action, Gorgias promoted the use of poetic devices (of the kind, for example, found in the written-down Homeric poems) in the rapidly developing genre of prose. Many presentations of Gorgias's thought suggest that his concern with

---

[5]"Rhetoric in the Middle Ages." *Speculum*, 17 (January, 1942), (p. 3).

[6]For a conventional examination of textual preoccupation since Romanticism, see M. H. Abrams' *The Mirror and the Lamp: Romantic Theory and the Critical Tradition* (especially pp. 3–29).

[7]See, for example, John Crowe Ransom and Allen Tate, discussed in Chapter One.

*logos* and his concern with "style" are separate. They are actually interdependent concepts, as Jacqueline de Romilly and John Poulakos, among others, have demonstrated.[8]

Gorgias's pupil Isocrates goes even farther than Gorgias in promoting the intertwining nature of utilitarian and literary language. Isocrates, like Gorgias, was prominent in the radical language and the cultural changes of the fourth-century B.C. He experimented in the post-war era with the growing possibilities of prose and put his discoveries to work in his school of rhetoric. Isocrates first established his school, in 393 B.C., in Chios. He later opened a school in Athens, where thinkers of various kinds were drawn because of its intellectual and cultural freedom and dynamism. His extensive course of study was so complete that it provided a model of education for at least 2200 years and led to Isocrates' commonplace designation as one of the founders of the liberal arts. Isocrates approached written and spoken language as mutually reinforcing.

As one of the ten Attic orators, a rather arbitrarily devised group, Isocrates, as well as Antiphon, Lysias, Andocides, Isaeus, Demosthenes, Aeschines, Lycurgus, Hyperides, and Dinarchus, composed what George Kennedy has called a literary genre.[9] Part of their writing came about in their roles as logographers, or writers paid to compose court speeches, a growing utilitarian function. They flourished in the context of rising judicial importance, the consequent empowerment of many individuals, and the remarkable desire to litigate that partly characterized the culture. In fact, Greek oratory, including Isocrates' work, consisted partly of court speeches written by the sometimes invisible logographers. In other words, even "oral" discourse was largely written discourse during the fourth century B.C. Isocrates, who worked as a logographer for ten years until 403 B.C., wrote discourse that was to be read as well as spoken, such as the court speeches. His career illustrates the unique relationship of writing and speaking in the fourth-century B.C.[10]

One of the reasons that Isocrates was able to avoid absorption into the increasingly negative *ethos* of Sophism in the fourth century B.C. was

---

[8]*Magic and Rhetoric in Ancient Greece* (pp. 1–22). The modern preoccupation with "style" as a discrete part of discourse lies, of course, partly in the Ramistic cordoning off of the functions of rhetoric. See Walter J. Ong, *Ramus, Method and the Decay of Dialogue: From the Art of Discourse to the Art of Reason* (especially pp. 1–16 and pp. 270–292). Post-Ramistic connotations of "style" create interpretive dislocations in the reading of Gorgias's theory. For Poulakos's rehistoricizing of Gorgias's rhetoric, see "Gorgias' *Encomium to Helen* and the Defense of Rhetoric."

[9]The canon of the ten Attic orators comes to us in the form of writing and is either Alexandrian or from the Roman Caecilius of Calacte. The list is probably an arbitrary one. See Kennedy's *The Art of Persuasion in Greece* (pp. 125–263).

[10]I. J. Gelb, in *A Study of Writing,* provides a detailed analysis of alphabets that failed and the characteristics that helped the Greek alphabet to operate with great efficiency.

his sustained commitment to educational theory. In this theory, he continually recognized and promoted the intertwining concern of the utilitarianism of language and the literary power of language. While many Sophists focused on microscopic methods of language manipulation, Isocrates stressed rhetoric as an extensive system incorporating everyday usefulness as well as artistic uses. His work, therefore, was based on language theory and so transcended the familiar Sophistic goal of learning how to get what one wants. In contrast, his system of education depended on approaching the whole person and on the importance of a wide-ranging educational curriculum. The intellectual and value-laden development of whole people with wide-ranging capacities defined Isocrates' chief pedagogical aim, his theoretical bases, and consequently the course of study at his school. This system relied on rhetoric and included work that we would now call literary studies. Isocrates' definition of his pedagogical theories in opposition to Sophism in general appears in the fragmentary *Against the Sophists* (written about 390 B.C.) Here he distances his school from other schools, asserting that his emphasis on value systems and their relationship to rhetoric makes his school superior to the others. Like Plato, he consistently connected individual education to the health of Greek culture. Deemphasizing the merely factual in education, he maintained that knowledge, understanding, and values should form the center of education. He believed that this emphasis would then lead to a healthy culture.

Both Isocrates and Plato emphasized the educational development of whole human beings and the importance of ethics. Both thinkers also based their educational theories on what each called "philosophy," although they differed substantially on the definition of that concept. While Plato promoted the idea of the immutable and transcendental Forms, and the relationship of those Forms to the soul and to knowledge, Isocrates did not claim to understand ultimate reality. He was more concerned with the palpable issues of practical education, the establishment of a unified Greek culture, and the inculcation of values. Isocrates was closer to the relativism of Protagoras than to the idealism of Plato, according to W.K.C. Guthrie. Isocrates and Plato were especially close in their use of the new technology of writing and both thinkers developed educational theories that reflected their concern with the new technology. Isocrates chose to work in written discourse, revealing some awareness of the burgeoning power of the new technology of writing. He makes claims about the centrality of speaking, but he reveals a commitment to writing in his choice of the language medium of writing. Isocrates and Plato, two striking figures in the emergence of ancient rhetorical theory, resembled each other on many pedagogical issues and on value systems, even though their theories diverge in various ways.

## GORGIAS'S RHETORIC AS PERFORMANCE

Isocrates was only nine years old when Gorgias arrived in Athens from Leontini. He appears to have had a substantial influence on the younger Isocrates. From Isocrates' extant writing, especially the *Antidosis* (*Isocrates*, Vol. II), we can see that Gorgias' emphasis on *logos*, on Greek unity, and on the power of written language affected Isocrates significantly. Gorgias, as we saw earlier, enjoyed energetic popularity in Athens and was contributing to the development of a new genre of discourse. Gorgias's dynamic, innovative, and provocative uses of written and spoken language delighted Isocrates as it did many Athenians. As is frequently the historical case in language innovation, Gorgias's uniqueness and iconoclasm angered many other people. Partly because of his energized and energizing language use, he provoked high praise and high blame. The traditional critical tradition, from Isocrates' time through the present, tends to reflect these diverse reactions by portraying the Gorgianic influence on Isocrates as an aspect to be admired or tolerated. The influence is difficult to interpret now because not many of Gorgias's speeches have survived (see Freeman, pp. 127–139). From the writing of Gorgias that does survive, the connection between the utilitarian in language and its poetic force is clear, especially in the *Encomium on Helen*. The writing of Isocrates and Gorgias can be characterized as centering on what has come to be called "critical thinking." This kind of intellectual action embraces not only the important issues of decoding artistic expression, but includes definitively the application of sophisticated judgment of issues that occur in everyday living; it signifies an ability to apply judgment well in specifically unpredictable situations.[11]

Isocrates' school opened partly in response to the political and economic realities brought about by the effects of the Peloponnesian War, which ended in 404 B.C. Having lost his substantial inheritance as

---

[11]Isocrates' school enabled him to recover the wealth he had lost during the war. But that wealth, interestingly, did not damage his reputation. He succeeded at a unique balancing act: he collected large fees at his school but distanced himself from other Sophists whose equally large fees contributed to their bad reputations. Plato and the Platonic Socrates represent a prevalent opinion in their attacks and sarcastic asides against the fees charged by many Sophists. In spite of this condemnation of many of his peers, Isocrates is praised at the end of Plato's *Phaedrus*. This significant allusion to Isocrates shows the importance his ideas held even among those who disagreed with much of his writing and action. For a careful and recent analysis of Isocrates' *Helen*, see John Poulakos, "Argument, Practicality, and Eloquence in Isocrates' *Helen*." In his rehistoricizing of this primary text, Poulakos states: "Grounded historically and textually, this [Poulakos's] interpretation will posit that the *Helen* argues that rhetoric, as Isocrates understands it, is the best kind of education in Athens" (p. 5).

a result of the war, Isocrates opened his Chios school where students were taught to develop judgment that could be applied to any situation. In his general curriculum, Isocrates relied on challenging students with difficult material and requiring them to work at a variety of intellectual tasks. Isocrates' school differs from those of most of the Sophists because he did not, as was typical of the Sophists, travel around to teach and to present public speeches. Like Plato, and unlike Gorgias, he created a permanent school, requiring students to come to him. Given the serious physical requirements of travel in ancient Greece, a point that Richard Leo Enos has explored,[12] the establishing of one location for his pedagogical experiment enabled Isocrates to devote more time to writing and to teaching, two activities that he found to be mutually reinforcing. Having chosen not to undergo the rigors of travel over difficult land and water, Isocrates focused his energy on his writing and on his school. One wonders if Gorgias might not have written more if he had stayed longer in one place.

The technology of writing, as Ong and Havelock have pointed out, leads to a way of living that is more solitary than orally based living is. The requirements of abstraction, among other issues, and the psychological changes in memory brought on by thinking in writing lead to behavior different from that brought about by speaking. One change derives from the fact that the writer requires more time alone. By replacing the work of travelling from place to place with writing in one location, Isocrates was able to produce more prose than many other Sophists and to devote time to the development of pedagogical theory. The permanence of this prose, as opposed to the ephemeral nature of spoken discourse, led also to Isocrates' prose exerting extraordinary power for many centuries. While his reputed shyness in public speaking may have caused Isocrates some difficulties, his retreat from the public and from travel to the more confining circumstances of writing ultimately contributed to his success. Gorgias did not share the problem of shyness. He apparently responded very well to the participation of audiences in his speaking. His performance-centered rhetoric required the give-and-take that a live audience can provide a dynamic speaker.

## ANCIENT GREEK RHETORIC, DRAMA, AND EDUCATIONAL SYSTEMS

The writing down of speeches and dialogues by Plato, Isocrates, and Gorgias resembles generically the fifth- and fourth-century B.C. writing

---

[12]See "The Composing Process of the Sophist." See also his "The Hellenic Rhapsode."

down of dramatic pieces by Aeschylus, Aristophanes, Sophocles, and others. The spoken word and the written word find a unique merger in both oratorical literature and dramatic literature produced in abundance in this period. Again, the utilitarian and the artistic exist together in these two kinds of writing/speaking to create extraordinary effects. It is not a coincidence that these two genres achieved dominance at the same time.[13] The burgeoning power of writing was challenging but not overcoming the hegemony of recitation as Gorgias's career partly illustrates. Oratorical literature, dramatic literature, and philosophical literature (in the sense that Plato, rather than Isocrates, was able to appropriate it) depended equally on ways of thinking that derive from both speaking and writing. In other words, a new epistemology was forming. Oratorical literature, dramatic literature, and philosophical literature arose in and helped to perpetuate a social context that was undergoing radical change because of changes in communication technology, in political structures, and ultimately in thinking. The psychological realities created by the new contexts of writing and reading gradually empowered what came to be three "genres." Oratorical, dramatic, and philosophical literature accommodated the demands of traditional oral-based discourse while partaking of the power of the relatively new (about 300 years old[14]) written discourse.

The merging of the utilitarianism of everyday language and poetic language and their transformations deriving from literacy led necessarily to competing theories of education. The centrality of functionalism and education to Greek culture is revealed in every branch of classical rhetoric, from Corax, to the Sophists, to Plato, to Aristotle, and eventually to Roman rhetorics. The organization of language theory that appears in classical rhetorics always included educational theory. In fact, part of the lasting power of classical rhetoric has been the persistent inclusion of education as a central social, political, ideological, and language issue. This pedagogical focus, which continued with force

---

[13]The division of the study of fifth-century B.C. drama in literary disciplines and the study of written and spoken speeches in the disciplines of English and Speech Communication has led, during at least the years from 1945 to the present, to a fundamentally curious split between the very similar writings of rhetoricians and dramatists. A second division occurs because the study of "philosophical" texts has been assigned almost exclusively to the discipline of philosophy. While Plato's *Ion* might appear in an anthology of texts intended for the discipline of English (see Hazard Adams' *Critical Theory Since Plato*), *Phaedrus* and *Gorgias*, until about 1965, had been assigned to Speech Communication. The fifth-century B.C. plays have resided in classics departments and in "World Literature" courses in the discipline of English. It is not difficult to see the problems that arise for students who are shown (even if they are not told) that all these texts from the same historical era are unrelated and belong to apparently unrelated disciplines.

[14]See I. J. Gelb, *A Study of Writing* (especially pp. 183–189, "Alphabet's Conquest of the World").

until the Ramistic cordoning off of the parts of rhetoric in the sixteenth century, accounts for much of Isocrates' influence and for his appeal to a broadly based audience through many eras and cultures. Isocratean rhetoric, like Gorgianic rhetoric, Platonic rhetoric, and Aristotelian rhetoric, always spoke to a wide audience rather than to a limited audience of specialists. Far from suffering the silence that pedagogy has frequently experienced in the modern period, educational theory was regarded as a matter central to all intellectual concern and to the well-being of the culture. Various forms of language training constituted an essential aspect of fourth-century B.C. systems of education.

## ISOCRATES' AGENDA FOR RHETORIC

Rhetoric and its utilitarian as well as its poetic nature formed the central part of education theories. Isocrates' *Art of Rhetoric* is lost, but his theory of rhetoric and its application to pedagogy can be determined from his other work. The cornerstones of Isocratean rhetoric are the utilitarian appeal to many aspects of the listener or reader and an emphasis on values, two ideas that diverged from the guiding principles of many Sophists, who sometimes confined themselves to exclusively utilitarian themes. To bring about multi-faceted persuasion, the speaker or writer needed to rely on both broad rhetorical training and a self-presentation in prose or in speaking that assured the ability to be believed. To persuade a whole person requires variation in training. The psychological issues attending the idea of the speaker's or writer's integrity led Isocrates to emphasize value-laden conduct. Isocrates' emphasis on this training became an important basis for Cicero's ideal orator (*vir bonus,* or the good person) and later Quintilian's ideal orator (*vir bonus dicendi peritus,* or the good person speaking well). The emphasis on maintaining high standards of conduct and, as importantly, the appearance of that good conduct, are two of the reasons that Isocrates' school had a better reputation than those of the Sophists who did not emphasize this aspect of rhetoric. Isocrates, then, enacted his own training: he presented his own high standards in a way that contributed significantly to his school's excellent reputation and to his own. In other words, he understood very well the concept of *ethos,* the general idea of the character presented by a writer or a speaker, and used it to his advantage in his writing and in his curriculum. His understanding of *ethos* set him apart from those Sophists who did not share his belief in its importance. With this attitude, Isocrates taught his students the first issue in persuasion, credibility. He educated his students in how to engender belief.

The connection of rhetoric, education, and value systems appears forcefully in *Antidosis*. Isocrates, like Plato, extends rhetoric beyond the argumentation of law courts. He privileges instead his idea of "philosophy." He in fact uses the fiction of a legal defense as a frame for this autobiographical writing. With this writing strategy, he provides an example of how to extend legal oratory. He writes, "while those who are thought to be adept at court procedure are tolerated only for the day when they are engaged in the trial, the devotees of philosophy are honored and held in high esteem in every society and at all times" (II, pp. 213–214). His philosophy consists of work in rhetoric that includes the upholding of values.

> It remains to tell you about "wisdom" and "philosophy." It is true that if one were pleading a case on any other issue it would be out of place to discuss these words (for they are foreign to all litigation), but it is appropriate for me, since I am being tried on such an issue, and since I hold that what some people call philosophy is not entitled to that name, to define and explain to you what philosophy, properly conceived, really is. . . . For since it is not in the nature of man to attain a science by the possession of which we can know positively what we should do or what we should say, in the next resort I hold that man to be wise who is able by his powers of conjecture to arrive generally at the best course, and I hold that man to be a philosopher who occupies himself with the studies from which he will most quickly gain that kind of insight. (II, p. 335)

This use of judgment is intended to go beyond speaking in law courts. In other words, legal oratory did not embrace enough utilitarian issues to define either rhetoric or philosophy, which in the Isocratean world view applied to every area of human activity.[15] Because responses to situations cannot usually be completely predicted, the development of a critical faculty through work on rhetoric, "philosophy," and values enables the individual to meet any circumstances well. Isocrates established his point about the interrelated issues of rhetoric, philosophy, and critical thinking by quoting extensively in *Antidosis* from some of his earlier works.[16]

---

[15]McKeon complains about the limiting of rhetorical history to judicial oratory and excluding rhetoric's many other uses, including its influence on philosophy ("Rhetoric in the Middle Ages," p. 1).

[16]To some extent, the work acts as an anthology of his writing annotated by himself at the age of eighty-two. The excerpts from his earlier work serve two functions: to explain his life work and to act as an autobiographical argument. Like many autobiographies, the *Antidosis* reads subtextually as a sustained justification of the writer's life and work. The complex connections between the exposition of ideas and the narration of selected life events lead to a prose form that eventually reads like a justification, even though that motive may not be stated. The submerged argument of self justification has for many

The utilitarian nature of rhetorical theory and education remains a focus in Isocrates' discussion of the relationship of education and language in *Antidosis:*

> We ought, therefore, to think of the art of discourse just as we think of the other arts, and not to form opposite judgments about similar things, nor show ourselves intolerant toward that power which, of all the faculties which belong to the nature of man, is the source of most of our blessings. For in the other powers which we possess, as I have already said on a former occasion, we are in no respect superior to other living creatures; . . . but, because there has been implanted in us the power to persuade each other and to make clear to each other whatever we desire, not only have we escaped the life of wild beasts, but we have come together and founded cities and made laws and invented arts; . . . for the power to speak well is taken as the surest index of a sound understanding. (II, p. 327)

Language for Isocrates permeates every aspect of human existence, and is utterly utilitarian; and so the development of this ability assumes central importance in the education of the individual.

Isocrates defines the differences between his educational theory and competing theories in the opening of the *Encomium on Helen,* an excellent early example of the genre of encomium. Isocrates asserts that the rival schools ought to "pursue the truth, to instruct their pupils in the practical affairs of our government and train to expertness therein, bearing in mind that likely conjecture about useful things is far preferable to exact knowledge of the useless" (III, p. 63). In this passage and throughout his long writing career, Isocrates, as we have seen, strived to connect education to the useful, including the political and economic usefulness of a unified Greek culture. He viewed Athens as the center of this culture. While this idea was held by Gorgias and other thinkers, Isocrates carried the concept farther than other writers did. He promoted a transfer of fighting among Greek groups to fighting against the Persian empire. In this light, he praises Helen, who had been a familiar target for abuse: "it is owing to Helen that we are not the slaves of the barbarians. For we shall find that it was because of her that the Greeks became united in harmonious accord and organized a common expedition against the barbarians, and that it was then for the first time that Europe set up a trophy of victory over Asia" (III, p. 97).[17] Isocrates promoted imperialism as much as he promoted rhetoric.

---

critics read like a treatise of self promotion and has contributed significantly to Isocrates' reputation as a person dominated by egocentrism.

[17]Isocrates helped to establish this topic as a typical exercise in rhetorical education. The encomium on Busiris, a mythical king of Egypt, functions in a similar way.

The health of the state and the health of language education recur as themes in the nine extant letters of Isocrates. All the letters are written to leaders and are characterized by Isocrates' desire for Greek unity through an invasion of Persia. In his letter to the young Alexander (who Van Hook in Volume III says had probably just begun his instruction with Aristotle), Isocrates reiterates the centrality of rhetoric: "By means of this study [rhetoric] you will come to know how at the present time to form reasonably sound opinions about the future, how not ineptly to instruct your subject peoples what each should do, how to form correct judgments about the right and the just and their opposites and, besides, to reward and chastise each class as it deserves" (III, p. 429). The other letters—to Philip, to Dionysius, to Antipater, among others in Volumes I and III—comprise a kind of personal history.

Isocrates' concept of Greek unity and his system of education based on the utilitarianism and aesthetics of rhetoric affected ancient Greek history and subsequently Roman culture. Werner Jaeger summarizes his contribution in the following way:

> From all his words we can feel the living breath of Hellenism. The new era actually did fall into the forms which Isocrates had thought out before its advent. Without the idea which he here expresses for the first time, the idea that Greek *paideia* was something universally valuable, there would have been no Macedonian Greek world-empire, and the universal culture which we call Hellenistic would never have existed. (pp. 80–81, Vol. III) (pp. 80–81, Vol. III)

Isocrates was read and quoted extensively partly because his ideas combined cultural, political, utilitarian, and aesthetic issues with an agenda for individual education. A major reason for this sustained influence was his readable and evocative prose style. In other words, he enacted rhetoric and taught it; that is, he regarded it both as a faculty and as a subject matter. These two uses of rhetoric contributed substantially to the remarkable success of Attic prose, helping to extend its limits and to create new structures of thought.[18]

As we have seen in the discussion of Isocrates' innovative school,

---

[18]His influence in post-classical cultures was strong as well. Partly through Cicero, Isocrates has had an effect on all western cultures. With the serious resurgence of classical rhetoric since 1965, interest in Isocrates and the other Sophists has grown considerably. The Sophists have been receiving significant scholarly attention, and much of the new research reformulates the negative stance toward the Sophists that occurs in the work of Plato and Aristotle. Instead of presenting Plato's and Aristotle's views of the Sophists, as has traditionally been done, new research examines the work of the Sophists according to other perspectives. See, for example, Poulakos, Jarratt, Lentz, Neel, and Enos.

rhetoric had come to be the center of education and both were acquiring more and more cultural power. Two basic kinds of schools existed in the fourth century B.C.: (1) schools located in one place; and (2) schools whose teachers travelled around from place to place. The first kind, the stationary school, was favored, as we have seen, by Isocrates, who opened his school in Chios in 393 B.C.; by Plato, who opened his Academy in Athens in about 385 B.C.; and by Aristotle, who founded his school outside Athens in 335 B.C. These schools enjoyed a stability that the second kind of school did not. The schools of the Sophists were not place-dominant but almost exclusively person-dominant. Gorgias, for example, travelled from place to place delivering apparently dazzling lectures. He, like many other Sophists, travelled to his students, rather than having students travel to him. The considerable expenditure of energy that this travelling demanded has been explored by Enos, who has investigated the sheer difficulty involved in travelling over rough land and water in ancient times. These journeys, although they proved profitable for many Sophists (as Plato and other critics were fond of pointing out) required an effort that may be impossible for modern people to understand. The interruptions of inclement weather, the hazards of nature and of hostile people, and the slowness of movement all contributed in varying degrees to a major drain of energy for any traveller. It is interesting to speculate that the work of the classical Greek rhetoricians who maintained schools in one place has exerted a historical influence that the travelling Sophists have not shared. The placement of resources in teaching and in writing, as we saw in the case of Isocrates, rather than in withstanding travel, may have accounted for part of this discrepancy.

Students for these schools and audiences for these speakers existed in great numbers largely because a palpable usefulness was perceived in rhetoric. Its functionalism was readily apparent. The training answered deeply felt needs and provided practical training. The enormous popularity of the schools did not derive from the manipulation of a group of clever rhetoricians, who somehow fooled the public into listening to them. Rather, the social and political changes created a climate of possibility in the population. A general realization that access to language ability led to access to power made the offerings of teachers of many kinds very attractive. In other words, the schools answered serious cultural needs. Rhetoric burst forth from the fifth to the third centuries B.C. because of need. It did not emerge because articulate teachers one-sidedly provoked the population, a presentation of classical rhetoric that the Heritage School has promoted.[19] Rhetoricians did not create the power

---

[19]See, for example, the classical rhetoric section of Ehninger's "On Systems of Rhetoric" (pp. 50–51). See also McKeon's comments—unusual for 1942—on the historicizing of

of rhetoric. Rather, a confluence of circumstances, including the phenomenon of literacy, created the power of rhetoric, and rhetoricians exploited that power and necessity. This acquisition of greater power by individuals led to a desire for using that power in the form of rhetoric. The utilitarianism of rhetoric provided much of its appeal. Training in rhetoric accounted for a multiplicity of language functions. Perhaps in no other era was language study as all-inclusive as it was from the fifth through the fourth centuries B.C. The work in rhetoric produced by the Sophists during this period provided much of the material that Plato used in the development of his own rhetoric. Plato carefully took advantage of the substantial material on rhetoric that surrounded him. Part of his response was negative. He, like his contemporary Isocrates, believed that rhetoric required a grounding in a value system. For him, this value-laden stance required moving away from the relativism of a Protagoras and the skepticism of a Gorgias over to a recognition of immutable reality expressed in his developing theory of Forms.[20]

## PLATO'S DEPARTURE FROM ISOCRATES

Plato's construction of rhetoric, which included the demolishing of his version of sophistic rhetoric, and his presentation of pedagogical theory, are essential for an understanding of classical rhetoric as a whole, as we saw in Chapter Four. In his setting up of rhetoric, primarily in *Protagoras, Gorgias,* and *Phaedrus,* Plato exploited rhetoric in written discourse to the fullest and, through elaborate writing devices, illustrated how good rhetoric operates.[21] From the *Gorgias,* written rather early in his career, to the late-middle *Phaedrus,* Plato revealed a persistent awareness of how much power rhetoric was exerting in his culture. He was appalled at what he saw as the anarchic use of rhetoric and at the fact that many rhetoricians did not take account of larger cultural

---

rhetoric: "The history of rhetoric as it has been written since the Renaissance is therefore in part the distressing record of the obtuseness of writers who failed to study the classics and to apply rhetoric to literature, and in part the monotonous enumeration of doctrines, or preferably sentences, repeated from Cicero or commentators on Cicero" ("Rhetoric in the Middle Ages," p. 1).

[20]See, for example, *Phaedo.*

[21]Swearingen, in "The Rhetor as Eiron: Plato's Defense of Dialogue," writes:

Because we live and interpret in contexts unknown by Plato, it is useful, I think, to observe what he warned against, and to test our assumptions against his provocative guesses about what would happen should rhetoric and textuality become pervasive discourse norms (p. 329).

issues. His indignant response to this situation was nearly extreme, as his presentation of sophistic rhetoric in *Gorgias* indicates.

A central characteristic of Plato's rhetoric and one connected to its utilitarianism is its malleability. Rhetoric, like love, two central and intertwining concerns of *Phaedrus*, can be misused, according to Plato's presentation in that dialogue. And rhetoric, like love, can inflict damage. Plato, more than other Greek rhetoricians, confronted the issue that rhetoric has the potential for inflicting damage and the potential for promoting social and individual health. Corax, many of the Sophists, and Aristotle chose to emphasize the practical benefits of rhetoric and its systemic features. A usually tacit assumption appears throughout the work of these writers that their audiences will apply their rhetorical theory positively. Plato finds this assumption about values to be naive, and ultimately dangerous. The assumption that rhetoric will be positively applied denies for Plato its inherent malleability, its chameleonlike essence. Even more seriously, the definition of "the ethical" and widespread, unconscious assumptions about the nature of reality worried Plato. For Plato, the malleability of rhetoric is part of its attractive power. But it is its danger as well. Only Isocrates and Socrates appear to have shared Plato's denial that rhetoric will be used according to a worthy set of values. To deal with the changeability of rhetoric, to see its potential for corruption, was crucial to Plato. The cultural flux that informed classical Greece increased rhetoric's power, and Plato was aware of this phenomenon. He was equally aware that without a value system, the power of rhetoric posed large dangers. Plato insisted on recognizing rhetoric's capacity for what he regarded as good or evil, or areas in between, and its capacity for inflicting great damage or great good. He was fond of illustrating the damage by pointing to much of the work of the Sophists, the excitable and nonthinking Polus presented in *Gorgias*, for example. The erratic nature of rhetoric needed to be controlled. Plato's imposition of control appeared in connecting rhetoric to his epistemology of the Forms, the immortality of the soul, and the access of the soul to the Forms. In other words, Plato consistently anchored rhetoric in his own developing epistemology. Plato's epistemology is, of course, a shifting issue. His attitudes toward ultimate reality, for example, changed during the course of his long career. His developing ideas about rhetoric changed as well. Plato provides, in *Phaedrus*, a summary of the potential of rhetoric:

> But perhaps rhetoric has been getting too roughly handled by us, and she might answer: What amazing nonsense you are talking! As if I forced any man to learn to speak in ignorance of the truth! Whatever my advice might be worth, I should have told him to arrive at the truth first, and then come

to me. At the same time I boldly assert that mere knowledge of the truth
will not give you the art of persuasion. (Jowett translation, p. 304)

Plato here, by personifying rhetoric, typically connects rhetoric to the
philosophical issues of knowledge and truth. A crucial aspect of his
philosophy was memory, which he inextricably connected to knowledge. Because human souls had to have existed before birth, they have
already acquired enormous knowledge by the time they exist in human
beings. Recollecting previously acquired knowledge constitutes learning. So achieving knowledge is to a large extent remembering what the
soul already knew. Memory, *mneme*, acts as a foundation of Platonic
epistemology. It connects past, present, and future through the eternal
life of the soul. Partly through the operation of memory, the soul
residing in a human being can move toward recalling the contact with
the Forms that it has had. In *Phaedrus, Phaedo,* and other dialogues, Plato
explains that a soul cannot exist in a human being unless it has had some
access to the Forms. So a precondition of being human is to have had
contact with the eternal Forms. Rhetoric can contribute to improving
memory (to improving the soul) or to impairing it (ignoring the reality of
the soul and its existence before and after human life). Memory
therefore is temporalized in a new way.

The essential role of memory in Plato's philosophy cannot be interpreted as mere rote remembering, as a simple summoning of past
events. It is not just a recalling, for example, of a portion of one's lived
human experience. Rather, memory is an inclusive system of mind and
soul that transcends the individual person's ability to encompass it and
that at the same time offers that individual a way to realize his or her
capacities more fully; that is, memory enables an individual to achieve
his or her *arete,* or unique excellence. It is closely related to modern
issues in psychology, as I explored in Chapter Four. Plato's appropriation of memory helped to establish this complex mental phenomenon as
one of the emerging canons of rhetoric which functioned, as did the
canons of invention, arrangement, style, and delivery, as an interactive
system for the understanding of written and spoken discourse and for
the operation of all discourse in social as well as in private situations.

Partly because Plato recognized the utilitarian malleability of rhetoric
as part of its power and its danger, he advocated, as Isocrates and
Gorgias had, an educational system that would productively harness
the power of rhetoric.

Chapter Four explored the completeness of the five classical parts of
rhetoric as a system and traced their appearance in Greek rhetoric before
they were canonized by the anonymous writer of the *Rhetorica Ad
Herennium* from about 86 to 82 B.C. The Greek parts of *heuresis, taxis,*

*lexis, mneme,* and *hypocrisis* can be used to extend the usefulness of Platonic rhetoric, that is, its practicality, and to show how it formed a radical system for producing and analyzing written and spoken discourse within various fluctuating Greek contexts. Plato advanced classical rhetoric; he helped to make it more sophisticated.

As with memory, delivery cannot be deleted from this particular classical system without destroying its effectiveness. The wholeness of the interactive five canons offers a means of accounting for encoder, decoder, code, and "reality" and the ways that these four dominant discourse issues impinge on one another. The reduction of the five canons to three (to invention, arrangement, and style)—which typifies Heritage School reception of classical rhetoric, as we have seen— divorces rhetoric from social context, from cultural power, and from the dailiness of ordinary language. The three-part system, which disguises itself as a complete system because it resembles the original five-part system, and whose assumptions and background are rarely examined, lead to a privileging of the text. Text dominance edges out emphasis on encoder, decoder, and "reality." It pretends that the culture from which the text emerged is irrelevant. This cultural and ideological denial is strong. The result is that the truncated canons implode into one another. The three-part canon constitutes a reconfiguration of classical rhetorical theory that bears only residual resemblance to the scope of the original theory as the ancient Greeks developed it. Dropping the last two canons can be regarded as an ideological act because the reduced canons operate on the tacit assumption that culture is unimportant or even absent. It denies the political implications of rhetoric not by overt condemnation but by glaring and unacknowledged omission. The three canons metamorphose into a mere taxonomy, into what is virtually a list. By "ideology" I mean here a shared system of belief that appears to be "normal" and "natural" and that therefore is never opened to probing. It is assumed to be a given. In the *nomos/physis* opposition that frequently preoccupied the sophists, this ideological stance would be categorized as *physis,* as endemic, innate, or "natural."

A major problem with the truncated canons and an overemphasis on the text lies in the fact that they do not have any aim. They lose meaning because they are prevented, by the deletion of memory and delivery, from referring to any life outside the text. They point back only to themselves. Rhetoric ordered according to the three-part, text-bound system of invention, arrangement, and style leads to blandness and perhaps boredom. To avoid these problems, rhetoric defined according to the truncated canons turns to the aesthetic, where the three canons can be productively studied. The analysis of invention, arrangement, and style of Milton in, say, *Lycidas* or in *Paradise Lost* yields enormous and gratifying (although not sufficient) interest. The cumulative beauty and *pathos*, for example in the patterns of vegetation and of water, make studying *Lycidas* according to the partial canons a meaningful reading experience.[22] One of the reasons for this gratification emerges from the fact that *Lycidas* is a completed work. Its encoding is completed, from the point of view of the writer. The literary artifact can be studied endlessly, using the truncated canons and innumerable other critical devices. However, when the truncated canons are applied to nonliterary texts, they do not flourish. Analyzing, for instance, a written speech, a newspaper story, or even a graffito, three important forms of writing, according to invention, arrangement, and style will yield a severely limited amount of knowledge and insight. The limitation is caused by setting aside cultural and social issues that help to create interest in graffiti and in newspaper stories. The limitation further resides in the fact that the "text" of the graffito and the newspaper story are spare compared to the "text" of, say, *Lycidas*. The interest in the literary text is so great that interpretation can focus endlessly on that text. The public statements of a written speech, a newspaper story, or a graffito, on the other hand, require psychological investigation of the kind incorporated in the fullness of the canon of memory; these problems are, as we have seen, involved in medium, or delivery. The five canons function partly to extend rhetoric to all discourse issues, not to the aesthetic ones alone, crucial though aesthetic issues are at various times.

The application of the truncated canons to literary discourse privileges the aesthetic properties of artistic writing over social, cultural, and value-system considerations. This reduction often, in fact, trivializes literature, an issue that has contributed to the decline of importance of literary studies in the twentieth century.[23] Aestheticism often leads to reverence, which in turn excludes the vast majority of written discourse (see David Bleich on literary studies and the reverential in *Subjective Criticism*, pp. 3–9). Aestheticism and reverence are very far away from the utilitarianism that defined Greek rhetoric, from the power deriving from the daily repetition and rehearsal of language.

Plato's rhetoric and Plato's literature cannot exist if the canon of memory is removed. In fact, Plato's work as a whole cannot exist if memory is made to disappear, as we saw in Chapter Four. It is one key to his epistemology. For Plato, memory includes subjectivity. All of Plato's writing makes use of subjectivity, in the sense that the processes

---

[22]See Wayne Shumaker's explication of plants and water imagery in *Lycidas* in "Flowerets and Sounding Seas."

[23]For a detailed analysis of this historical shift, see Applebee's *Tradition and Reform in the Teaching of English*, especially the chapter "Narrowed Goals" (pp. 139–184).

he discusses are not verifiable. For example, his discussion of knowledge in *Protagoras* is elaborate and complex but not empirically locatable. The Platonic Socrates' typical manipulation of the extended definitions depends as much on the amorphous and nonscientific use of *ethos* as it does on any other strategy. Studying Plato's work requires relying on an accumulation of images and associations. This process includes his rhetorical theory as well as his investigation of Forms and the nature of soul. One result of Plato's use of issues such as subjectivity is that none of the dialogues has a definite conclusion. No concrete, decisive formulation can be established by the reader. One cannot say, "A form is . . ." Rather, Plato's subjectivity demands that one remain tentative, amorphous, and say "A form is like, a form resembles," and so on. This strategy is poetic and associative, not merely logical and linear. Plato tends not to be empirical. Included among the concepts that cannot be pinned down in the dialogues or the letters is rhetoric. Readers are compelled to give up a desire for a definitive statement about what rhetoric is. Instead, readers have to work with Plato in associating rhetoric with cookery or cosmetics, as in *Gorgias,* or with love, as in *Phaedrus.* In other words, readers cannot formulize Plato's rhetoric into a three-part definition or a series of dicta, strategies that came to prominence in rhetoric with Aristotle and that have continued in some rhetorical traditions. Plato privileged subjectivity and the impressionistic over the objectivity of concrete definition. When objective, clear-cut dicta are derived from Plato's writing, by those whose interpretive styles have been formed exclusively in an objectivist mode, some simplistic results are a mindless dualism and the idea that Plato opposed all rhetoric. When these familiar formulas are applied to Plato's rhetoric, the advancement of Platonic interpretation tends to stop. In an oversimplified dualism, the important issues are placed in a largely inaccessible other world that does not affect the everyday world of the senses. This kind of dualism excludes in its very reductiveness the interaction between Plato's forms and the sensible world and the importance he placed on the latter. A blatant dualism denies the sensual aspects of existence. Similarly, the familiar stance that Plato despised all rhetoric depends on bypassing the fact that Plato consistently used (or showed) rhetoric and that *Phaedrus* presents an appealing, powerful, and useful rhetoric, one that, like love, is available to all human beings. Plato's philosophy generally, and his rhetoric specifically, are not conducive to the constraints of the formula. Formulizing Plato's epistemology is like formulizing a painting. The essence, acquired in the temporal experience of reading, or of accompanying Plato on a linguistic journey, is lost.

Just as memory is crucial to Plato's rhetoric, so is delivery, or *hypocrisis.* Delivery and memory join the more familiar canons of invention, arrangement, and style to form a complete discourse theory. Disregarding the last two canons is like disregarding Plato's rhetoric. Both interpretations share in an impulse to limit rhetoric and to deny its centrality in human action. In the contemporary reception of classical rhetoric, these two interpretations have tended to accompany each other. As we saw in Chapter Four, denying two-fifths of the classical canons and denying the existence of a positive Platonic rhetorical theory result from the same tacit motive of dismissing rhetoric as a means of cultural analysis. The canons of memory and delivery and Plato's work on rhetoric are deemed to be irrelevant from this point of view.

A key issue in according Plato's rhetoric the status of irrelevance and, indeed, in according all of classical rhetoric irrelevance, has been an erroneous division of the classical world as orally dominant and the modern world as literacy dominant. As Havelock, Ong, and Lentz have shown, no such clear distinction exists. This inaccurate rendering depends on two related assumptions: (1) that the fifth canon, delivery, refers only to gesture and physical projection; and (2) that classical rhetoric was mainly oral. Delivery contains the material necessary for theories of medium as Mahony and McLuhan have indicated. From this point of view, delivery signifies not merely gesture or the ability to present material directly, through speaking in face-to-face encounters; rather, delivery signifies spoken communication and all the other media as well. A modern rendering occurs in the theory of Susanne K. Langer, or in symbolic forms or symbol systems.[24] Symbolization, according to this theory, is an innate human act and is necessary for thought to take place. Symbolization does not derive from thought but takes place nearly automatically and allows thought to take place. Symbolization occurs in a number of ways, through writing, speaking, dancing, painting, and so forth. Speaking in classical Greece, then, provided one kind of symbolization that was central to and helped to define rhetoric. Another means of symbolization, another kind of *hypocrisis*, emerged with the invention of a workable, flexible Greek alphabet between 720 B.C. and 700 B.C. As this alphabet gradually moved from being a recording device (a keeper of accounts, for instance) to finding more and more uses, its power as a medium of communication grew immensely. After three hundred years of use, writing had come, by Plato's time in the fourth century B.C., to change the way that people think. It had gradually acquired the power that speaking had long enjoyed because it helped to shape the way that people thought.

---

[24]See Langer, *Mind: An Essay on Human Feeling*, Vol. I, and Cassirer, *The Philosophy of Symbolic Forms*, Vol. 1. See also James L. Collins and Bruce E. Miller's "Presentational Symbolism and the Production of Text" for an important application of Langer's theory.

## THE ORALITY-LITERACY HYPOTHESIS
## AND CLASSICAL RHETORIC

Havelock, in *Preface to Plato*, writes:

> All human civilizations rely on a sort of cultural 'book', that is, on the capacity to put information in storage in order to reuse it. Before Homer's day, the Greek cultural 'book' had been stored in the oral memory. . . . Between Homer and Plato, the method of storage began to alter, as the information became alphabetized, and correspondingly the eye supplanted the ear as the chief organ employed for this purpose. The complete results of literacy did not supervene in Greece until the ushering in of the Hellenistic age, when conceptual thought achieved as it were fluency and its vocabulary became more or less standardized. Plato, living in the midst of this revolution, announced it and became its prophet. (p. vii)

The orality-literacy hypothesis presented by Ong and Havelock in works such as Ong's *Orality and Literacy* accounts for many central interactions of speaking, writing, and thinking, and shows their mutual dependence. The theoretical implications of orality/literacy research by Ong and Havelock have been explored by Lentz, Enos, Swearingen, Connors, and others.[25] The orality-literacy thesis provides unique material for theoretical bases in rhetoric and composition studies, particularly the rhetoric of Plato. Ong and Havelock's presentation of orality and literacy work depends on a three-part division of the history of consciousness. The first part consists of primary orality, which was responsible for the construction of consciousness before the Greek alphabet was invented between 720 B.C. and 700 B.C. People in primary orality store cultural knowledge and educate their youth through the spoken performance of stories. This stage is perhaps most evident to us in the Homeric poems, which have been demonstrated as being arranged formulaically and thematically for semi-improvisational performance (Havelock, *Muse*, p. 11). Hearing has special importance in this phase.

The second stage of consciousness in the Ong-Havelock thesis consists of what is designated as "literacy." This stage begins with the invention of a flexible Greek alphabet, the first alphabet that had the ability to convey the substantial depth and resonance (Havelock, *Muse*, p. 8) previously available only in speaking. The invention of the Greek alphabet brought about a stage of protoliteracy when writing was

---

[25]See Lentz; Enos, *The Literate Mode of Cicero's Legal Rhetoric*; Swearingen, "The Rhetor as *Eiron*: Plato's Defense of Dialogue;" and Connors, "Greek Rhetoric and the Transition From Orality."

practiced by only a few skilled crafts people. By Plato's time in the fourth century B.C., writing had become interiorized (Havelock, *Preface*, p. 29) as a way of thinking, or as "consciousness." This change in thinking is referred to as change in consciousness by Ong (*Orality*, p. 78) and Havelock (*Muse*, p. 10). Literacy assumed dramatically new importance with the invention of the movable print press in the fifteenth century, as Marshall McLuhan has demonstrated in *The Gutenberg Galaxy*. The linearity of print and its ability to store cultural memory changed the way that people think, according to the thesis. Formal logic (deriving partly from the inexorable logic of lines of writing) contributed to the second stage of consciousness, as did changes in the nature of memory.

The third stage of consciousness in Ong and Havelock's thesis is secondary orality. This largely electronic stage began with the invention of the telegraph (Czitrom, p. 3), gained more importance with motion pictures, and advanced greatly with the proliferation of video. Secondary orality represents a "cultural recall" of primary orality because the emphasis on speaking and hearing takes on new meaning with the invention of electronic forms of communication.

The three stages of consciousness are not, according to Ong and Havelock, merely successive stages. They are recursive and mutually reinforcing as well. Secondary orality depends on primary orality and on literacy. The contemporary period relies on the complexity and the possibility of all three stages of the Ong-Havelock thesis. Ong's "presence of the word" refers to the life of the spoken word in group consciousness, of the written word, and of the electronically transmitted word (Ong, *Presence*, p. 4). The present interaction of all three kinds of consciousness is characterized by Havelock like this:

> The potential of the oral spell had been reasserted after a long sleep that had set in perhaps about the time McLuhan said it had, perhaps earlier, perhaps later. As we now probe orality in history we are probing its partial resurrection in ourselves. (*Muse*, p. 31)

This reassertion of the "oral spell" after "a long sleep" provides a condition for revised approaches to contemporary rhetoric and composition studies. The Ong-Havelock thesis can lead to a strengthening of literacy because it transcends the familiar binary opposition of writing and speaking as discrete verbal activities. This strengthening relies on taking advantage of the strongly literate aspects of our culture and the strongly oral aspects of our culture.

The possibility of integrating the Ong-Havelock thesis to rhetoric and composition studies rests on two assumptions about the nature of "ordinary language." The first assumption is that all people—if they speak—are already experts at manipulating spoken discourse (although not necessarily dominant-culture English). A familiar stance toward everyday language use is a forgetfulness of the power of language. This forgetfulness results partly from its near universality among people and the consequent response in all of us therefore to disregard its power. Because almost everyone shares in verbal power, we tend to lose awareness of how extraordinary it is. This existing language source provides opportunities in rhetoric and composition studies. The orality of human culture—our speaking/hearing selves—makes us all language experts of one sort or another. This speaking expertise, which is based on an emphasis on the ear, can be transferred to the written word, which is based on an emphasis on the eye. In other words, residual orality can help to define an essential and unique part of the nature of rhetoric and composition studies.

The second assumption I make here about integrating the Ong-Havelock thesis into current work is that all people who speak are members of discourse communities that have funds of repeatedly uttered stories, lessons, melodramas, parables, thrillers, farces, and so on. A member of a discourse community is an authority on these tales. He or she derives the authority first of all from lived experience. This experience is from one point of view unique and from another point of view shared by families and friends who are actors in the stories. We all derive authority from the spoken repetition of our discourse communities' stories. The fund of unique episodes that every person has (or that every life contains) presents material for writing. The uniqueness of this stance toward speaking and its transformation into writing lies in the fact that speakers and writers do not have exactly the same material. At the same time, a commonality of speaking and writing lies in the hearers' and readers' familiarity with the types of stories. The shared experience provides part of the phenomenon of what Kenneth Burke calls consubstantiality—or identification. Burke writes in *A Rhetoric of Motives*:

> A is not identical with his colleague, B. But insofar as their interests are joined, A is *identified* with B. Or he may *identify himself* with B even when their interests are not joined, if he assumes that they are, or is persuaded to believe so. Here are ambiguities of substance. In being identified with B, A is "substantially one" with a person other than himself. Yet at the same time he remains unique, an individual locus of motives. Thus he is both joined and separate, at once a distinct substance and consubstantial with another. (pp. 20–21)

Burke's A and B have come together mostly through language. Even as they are separate, the unique capacity of language enables A and B to come together—to become identified or consubstantial—at the same time. Because of their everyday uses, spoken and written language exert unusual power in consubstantiality. These two related kinds of language can be considered the center of power in consubstantiality. Burke phrases it this way: ". . . since our *Grammar of Motives* was constructed about 'substance' as key term, the related rhetoric selects its nearest equivalent in the areas of persuasion and dissuasion, communication and polemic" (p. 21). Burke's interpretation fits into the Ong-Havelock thesis on orality and literacy because it accounts for the quotidian uses of language.

Burke implies that all people possess the ability to become consubstantial with others. We can elaborate on this concept by saying that orality and literacy provide the primary means for enacting consubstantiality. The interplay of spoken stories and written stories provides new areas for composing research.

The orality/literacy hypothesis enables rhetoric and composition scholars many possibilities, including the exploiting of authority that all speakers or writers possess and that is tacitly acknowledged by their readers and hearers. The means of presentation available to speakers and writers forms one of the possibilities.

The first issue, the speaker-writer's automatically accorded authority, offers important possibilities for rhetoric and composition studies. The unique knowledge of the storyteller empowers speakers. Expertise and self confidence can follow from this authority. Because speaker-writers are accorded belief at least for awhile, there are no challenges to the substance of the autobiographical piece of writing. This acknowledgment of authority that all speakers and writers are accorded at least briefly will shift writer and reader expertise to frequently overlooked issues such as the malleability in the presentation of self, to readability and coherence, and even to the psychological aspects of memory as a part of speaking and writing. The familiar problem in writing classes of the absence of writerly authority diminishes in autobiographical writing in just the way that the problem diminishes in autobiographical speaking. The authority derives from the fact that no one can know more about the writer's material than the writer. In addition, the repetition of the speaker's and writer's narratives or ideas provides the student with the ability to transfer those stories to the written word. When the large—sometimes overwhelming—problem of authority is deemphasized, concentration on other writing issues leads to the development of writing strengths such as experimenting with presentations and increasing readability. This shift in the writer's preoccupation from establishing authority to other, equally compelling writing issues enables students to work on aspects of writing that often they have never reached in their previous writing instruction. The authority derives from the oral power—years of spoken repetition—of the stories and issues that students tell on paper.

In addition to increasing writerly authority, the traversing of the spoken word to the written word available in the Ong-Havelock thesis exploits existing writing ability in a second compelling way. The presentation of self in writing depends partly on the issues that the writer has repeatedly spoken to herself or himself or has heard spoken. Ong's orality-aurality emphasis finds a powerful existence in the teaching of writing. The connection between presenting a self in speaking and presenting a self in writing is much closer than many researchers have recognized. Connecting speaking and writing can illuminate the manipulation of *ethos*, arguably one of the most important issues in speaking and in writing but certainly a center of both spoken and written presentation.

*Ethos*, as was discussed in Chapter Two, is one of Aristotle's three interior persuaders presented in the *Rhetoric*.[26] *Ethos*, the general idea of a writer or a speaker's general character, is crafted both in speaking and in writing. *Pathos* is persuasion relying on an appeal to emotions, while *logos* is persuasion relying on an appeal to reason (Cooper translation, pp. 9–10). Aristotle goes so far as to say that *ethos* may be the most powerful of these persuaders (p. 9). The presentation of self—*ethos* acts up the conditions of belief in any spoken or written discourse.

*Ethos*, then, is a presentation of a self that engenders belief. Believability is the reason Aristotle applied the complex notion of *pistis* to *ethos*: persuasion of one's hearers or speakers depends on enabling the audience to interiorize the speaker/writer's material. This capability—manipulating presentation for specific purposes—is the cornerstone of both effective speaking and writing. *Ethos* determines the success of presentation to a great extent. If an encoder is not believed, then no other rhetorical issues make any difference, as the life of Cassandra illustrates.

Reliance on the orality/literacy thesis enables speakers and writers to use their language ability to make connections between ear dominance and eye dominance. They see how both the eye and the ear work, for example in drafting. Writing moves from resembling the spoken to enacting the written. For example, writers' first drafts often contain

---

[26]As argued in Chapter One, I find the familiar English translations of the *pisteis* as "artistic proofs" or "artificial proofs" to be very misleading. The word "proofs" bypasses the crucial Greek concept of belief that is present in *pisteis*. The translation "proofs," connects this concept more closely to the tradition of Anglo-American empiricism than to Aristotle's analysis of the means of persuasion.

residually oral material such as platitudes and dead metaphors (useful tools in spoken discourse) that can be recast in subsequent drafts.

The Ong-Havelock thesis enables encoders to see more clearly their individual relationships to primary orality, literacy, and secondary orality, all three of which exert great power in late twentieth-century culture. The thesis can help to situate writers in language history. They acquire permission to write with more authority and to experiment with presentations of self through working with *ethos*. Only recently, according to Ong, have we been able to become aware of the enormous changes brought on by changes in media dominance. Only since secondary orality began, about one hundred years ago, have we been able to see the power of literacy.[27] With this new and probably revolutionary perspective we are afforded many opportunities in the research and teaching of writing that we had not known about before the research on orality and literacy.[28]

The orality/literacy hypothesis presents a relatively new framework that depends on speaking and writing consciousness that all the members of our culture share. This framework depends on the recognition that advanced language ability is already present in all people who write. If rhetoric and composition researchers can exploit the theoretical possibilities of orality and literacy, then we can exploit the power of the spoken word more precisely to achieve more effective writing. The Ong-Havelock thesis enables us to find—to echo Aristotle—one of the most powerful means of persuasion in the particular case for bringing about more effective writing and more effective historicizing of rhetoric. (Cooper translation, p. 1). We can take advantage of the interaction and the mutual dependence of speaking and writing.

The orality-literacy thesis explains many of the apparently inexplicable aspects of fourth-century B.C. Greek rhetoric, writing, and culture. The pivotal writers Plato, Isocrates, and Gorgias responded deeply to the shifts in consciousness and understanding brought about by the

---

[27]The fact that the discipline of English came into being at the time electronic symbol systems were invented, especially film—is probably not a coincidence. The startling power of film brought about among its myriad effects a new interest in the study of English. See Czitrom, pp. 30–59; Innis, *Empire and Communications*, pp. 53–84; and McLuhan, *The Gutenberg Galaxy*, especially pp. 24–25, pp. 31–33, pp. 40–42, and pp. 128–129.

[28]The relationship of rhetoric's primary existence as a faculty and its necessary attachment to subject matters recognized by McKeon ("Rhetoric in the Middle Ages") resembles Plato's definition of rhetoric in *Phaedrus*:

> The theories implicated in the shifts of its [rhetoric's] subject matter will emerge, not merely as philosophic or sophistic disputes, but in concrete application, each at least defensible and each a challenge to the conception of intellectual history as the simple record of the development of a body of knowledge by more or less adequate investigations of a constant subject matter. (McKeon, p. 3)

technical revolution of a workable phonetic alphabet. Each of these thinkers reveals to us—as a result of the permanence of their written discourse—a different aspect of the revolution in thinking that the fourth century B.C. provided and that we continue to gain insight from. Traditionally, Plato's rhetoric has been made secondary and inferior to his philosophy. In Hegel's terms, rhetoric has played the role of slave to philosophy's master. More recently, Isocrates' "philosophy" and his remarkably complete system of education have fallen away from central interest in disciplines outside rhetoric. Gorgias, perhaps most seriously of all, has frequently been dismissed as a dazzling, mystical manipulator of language, whose "style" is frequently regarded as a decoration and therefore not to be given significant consideration.

The rehistoricizing of rhetoric and composition has gone a long way in revaluating these three thinkers. Disciplinary boundaries have provided serious problems as well as mutually beneficial help. In shifting from the empirical perspective of rhetorical history as a discernible, discoverable entity "out there," to a post-Kantian perspective that the "out there" material depends on fluctuating perceptions, the history of rhetoric has had to be *rewritten*.

# 6

Classical Rhetoric and
Contemporary Rhetoric
and Composition Studies:
Electrifying Classical Rhetoric

> [The media] make it possible for the first time to record historical
> material so that it can be reproduced at will. By making this material
> available for present-day purposes, they make it obvious to anyone
> using it that the writing of history is always manipulation. But the
> memory they hold in readiness is not the preserve of a scholarly
> caste. It is social. The banked information is accessible to anyone,
> and this accessibility is as instantaneous as its recording.
>
> Hans Magnus Enzensberger,
> "Constituents of a Theory of the Media"

The writing and speaking careers of Gorgias, Isocrates, and Plato have
become new sources for study with the gradually emerging awareness
of secondary orality. For some readers, it may seem inaccurate to say
that the three writers provide us with new sources, because Speech
Communication and English scholars, philologists, classicists, philosophers, and other writers have taught us so much about Gorgias,
Isocrates, and Plato. Nonetheless, new consciousness is forming on the
basis of secondary orality, as Ong states in *The Presence of the Word*. As
he writes in that book, classical culture in all its aspects must be
reconsidered in light of the emergence of secondary orality. We can now
begin to particularize this agenda by reconceptualizing Gorgias, Isoc-

143

rates, and Plato, whose writings and "traditions" must be re-created in the light of the new technology that we all live in, with, and through, whether we are aware of that newness or not. All three writers enabled writing—or literacy—to form. They wrote and spoke in a world of language fluctuation and so helped to create literacy. Their formations—including abstraction, written dialogue, and prose crafted on a page rather than ordered in the memory—remain very much with us.

The work of classical writers—as with writers from other centuries—has significance for readers on the basis of the readers' apprehension of the texts and contexts. In other words, readers create meanings. When we give up the definiteness of texts that the Heritage School writers and other positivists rely on, we can see that ancient writers exist largely according to the ways readers decode them now. We are not able to read, for instance, Isocrates' *Evagoras*, the third of the Cyprian "orations," without the effects imposed by secondary orality (*Isocrates*, Volume III).

Gorgias's own writing and the writing out of his oral presentations (writing that enables speaking) helped to define the nature of Attic prose. Commentators on Gorgias from the ancient period to the present describe his oral presentations as "dazzling," "riveting," and "extraordinary." The strong language that is used to describe Gorgias's work is due partly to the uniqueness of Gorgias's prose as it emerged in that time. Contemporary response to Gorgias is conditioned by the fact that his treatment of spoken and written language was so new, so untried. Gorgias's application of poetic language (to a great extent Homeric poetry) to prose accounts for part of the strong reception of his work not only among his contemporaries but among later commentators who formed their own interpretations of the earlier responses. So a tradition of response grew up around Gorgias and remains intact. The outrageousness attributed to Gorgias's prose, with the elaborate figures and the engaging images, no longer shocks. We have all read this kind of prose before, so we are conditioned, 2400 years later, to read it with new constraints. In *Classical Rhetoric and Its Christian and Secular Tradition from Ancient to Modern Times*, George Kennedy acknowledges some twentieth-century responses to Gorgias's work when he cites Jacqueline de Romilly's interpretation of Gorgias as magician, Enos's re-examination of Gorgias, and Mario Untersteiner's rhetorical stances toward Gorgias's prose (pp. 30, 248). While Kennedy designates the latter two as "philosophical," they provide new epistemological bases for reading Gorgias at the present time. John Poulakos, in "Gorgias' *Encomium to Helen* and the Defense of Rhetoric," discusses the over-literal readings of many traditional interpretations of one Gorgianic piece and so helps to condition readers in new ways to the effects of this powerful early prose writer.

Much less off-putting to traditional readers have been the writings of

Isocrates, who created a different, more respectable, image of himself in the generation following that of Gorgias. (No one would think of calling Isocrates "gauche," a word that has been attached to Gorgias[1]). Isocrates devoted himself to written discourse and to his school. Isocrates' work helped partly to merge speaking and writing by creating fictions of speeches in his writing, as he does in *Antidosis*. The standard explanation that Isocrates was too shy to present his work orally has become an inadequate explanation. From our vantage point in rapidly changing secondary orality, we can see that Isocrates, like his peer Plato, realized exactly what the most powerful discourse was: writing. His dodging of public speaking reminds one of the argument of physical weakness used by writers such as Charles Darwin and Florence Nightingale. All three of these writers believed that they had more important missions than to speak in public (that is, to perform) and in private (another kind of speaking performance) and all three appear to have arranged explanations of physical impairment to keep live audiences away from them. This distancing tactic allows people the solitariness that writing requires. Isocrates appears to have understood the writer's need to be left alone to compose.

Like Isocrates, Plato committed himself as thoroughly as Isocrates to the written word as well as to the spoken word. As Chapter Four partly investigated, Plato mourned the inevitable losses that literacy was bringing. The nature of memory (construed here as psychology) had to change as abstraction emerged from the world of writing.

Plato as a writer looks so much like Isocrates and Gorgias that we can declare, as Jasper Neel has done in a different context, that Plato is a Sophist. He used, as Neel has shown in *Plato, Derrida, and Writing*, all the same devices in his writing, including elaborate images and figures (what writing could be more "dazzling" than the horses and charioteer in *Phaedrus*, horses that at times sprout wings whose emergence hurts, horses that lunge in various directions in competition with each other). Moreover, Plato relied on a pedagogical structure very similar to that of Isocrates. Both Isocrates' school and Plato's even longer-lasting Academy established one version of educational practice that continues in various guises to this day. Isocrates' school has been called "the first European university."[2] The name of Plato's school, the Academy, has been and continues to be synonymous with educational institutions, including vocational schools.

Many writers and readers will be unhappy to see Gorgias, Isocrates, and Plato placed on the same plane as I am doing here for the rhetorical

---

[1]*Classical Rhetoric and Its Christian and Secular Tradition from Ancient to Modern Times*, p. 30.

[2]See H. Ll. Hudson-Williams, *Three Systems of Education: Some Reflections on the Implications of Plato's Phaedrus*, p. 4.

moment. More writers and readers will be unhappier still to see Plato put on the same level as Gorgias and Isocrates. This placement appears to contradict all the known "facts" about Plato; it interrupts the common sense of many interpreters, who take it as a given that Plato is superior in knowledge, in text, and therefore as a person. Nonetheless, while it is easy to grant that Plato exerted more influence over the centuries than did Isocrates or Gorgias, it is helpful in making the Sophists' writing and teaching understandable to us to put Plato on the same plane as Gorgias and Isocrates for the interpretive moment or longer. Plato has not been made superior to all his peers because his work was inherently superior; he has been made superior because his work was appropriated in various strands of thought.

Plato railed against the old-fashioned treatment of language as it appeared in the out-of-step Homeric poems, texts that dominated fourth-century Greek thought and educational practice to a degree we tend to forget. The domination of interesting but out-of-date texts in fourth-century Athens' education resembles the domination of interesting but out-of-date texts in the last generation of English curricula in the United States. Havelock demonstrates in *Preface to Plato* and elsewhere that Plato's agenda consisted partly of transferring the power of the spoken and written-down Homeric poems to a language that was more abstract, to a language that was less antiquated. The words that appear in a Homeric dictionary differ from the words that appear in a dictionary that includes Attic prose.[3] More words, and more abstract words, occur in the fourth century. This difference in vocabulary reflects the linguistic reality that Plato faced: the Greek world had changed as a result of writing. It had changed not only on the outside (communication, or exterior discourse) but on the inside as well (expression to self, or interior discourse). Consciousness itself began to take on the constraints and possibilities presented by the written word. Plato wanted to change what we would now call the canon. Plato resembles Isocrates in that he exploited writing fully. Both Isocrates and Plato realized that they needed to be writers and that encoding with the technology of stylus and papyrus presented a force that could not be ignored or relegated to the status of an addition or a decoration.

## THE INTERIORIZING OF DISCOURSE TECHNOLOGIES

Writers now can analogize the emergence of secondary orality/electronic discourse by analyzing the writing and the speaking of these three of

---

[3]See, for example, *A Lexicon of the Homeric Dialect*, by Richard John Cunliffe. See also Havelock, *Preface to Plato*, pp. 278–290.

many creators of literacy, in the sense of the changes in consciousness brought about by the interiorizing of written discourse, from ancient Greece. Lodged as we are one hundred years into secondary orality, or since the advent of effective motion picture technology, we are in a position to reinterpret these three ancient writers in ways that take into consideration radical changes in communication (including interior discourse, or the part of thinking that is in one's primary language or languages). Marshall McLuhan explored these changes in *The Gutenberg Galaxy* (see, for example, pp. 24–26 and pp. 241–243).

Many critics will find the analogy between ancient discourse and modern discourse incorrect or even inferior. Three of the various stances that fit this reception of classical writing include:

1. The critical stance that assumes crossing historical eras and disciplines leads to an absence of rigor. This reception may be called the field-coverage stance because it constructs knowledge as a totality, as a definite thing that can be known without considering perceptual issues. It follows from this stance that everything known—that is, everything written—must be "covered" in order for one to join the critical conversation. Anything less than the totality of field coverage, according to this stance, will not be adequate to the task of analogizing ancient discourse and technology issues with modern discourse and technology issues.

2. The critical stance that contends that literacy as it emerged in the eighth to fourth centuries B.C. appears to be too far apart in time, cultures, and social constraints to be analogized to the twentieth and twenty-first centuries.

3. The critical stance that assumes that the study of visual texts will not develop rigor in the people who study it because the visual texts are necessarily (inherently) inferior to written texts.

The critical stance that depends on a field-coverage paradigm remains the structuring device of most of the disciplines within the humanities. Every discipline has enjoyed a proliferation of knowledge, or even facts. This widely recognized increase in the amount of raw material available for analysis has resulted in the flourishing of subdisciplines, or specialties. In order for a critic to succeed in a given field, she or he must master all the material within that field. Since no person can master all aspects of a discipline, the field-coverage paradigm has turned to the mastering of one segment of the discipline. So, for instance, in the discipline of English one may specialize in a historical era such as sixteenth-century literature or Victorian literature, or even one writer within those areas;

one can be, for instance, a Spenserian or a Dickensian, words that sound natural and "true" to people in the discipline of English but peculiar to the ears of many non-English-specialist people. In the discipline of Speech Communication, one may specialize in, for instance, mass communication or rhetoric and public address. With these smaller boundaries, the student who studies a smaller area is better able to master the material. However, even with more closely demarcated areas, the written critical response to Dickens, or Shakespeare, has become too vast even for an expert to "keep up." In these areas that are so densely populated by critics, virtually no one can master the material that is available and that continues to be produced. The same situation exists in medicine, law, most of the academic areas, and other clusters of study.

The tacit field-coverage paradigm produces undergraduate curricula that reflect the teachers' areas of mastery and not so-called general education courses. This paradigm succeeds insofar as successful teaching occurs when the teachers are enthused by and committed to their material and communicate this enthusiastic, committed inquiry to the students who in turn establish their own relationships with the material. In this kind of teaching (applied for the moment to higher education), characterized by student-teacher inquiry and dialectic, advanced undergraduate courses and graduate courses are regarded as locations for university teachers to exercise their greatest talents, to enable students to learn with the most powerful material the teachers possess. This version of teaching needs to be encouraged, to be nurtured. It would entail the promotion of "the virus of learning," as George Steiner has characterized the most important part of teacher-student transactions.

However, one problem that tends to emerge from this pedagogical structure is a possible gap between the teacher's specialty and the current capacities of many of the students. We know from educational theorists such as Jerome Bruner that learners at every stage must have material to attach learning to. A conceptual apparatus, as it were, needs to be considered and analyzed by any teacher and then extended. Specialization in the traditional sense may offer a twenty-ish student very little because he or she does not have a conceptual universe to connect the specialized material to. In analyzing the audience that is their students, teachers need to understand what conceptualizations their students already have before they can begin to engage them.

This problem continues beyond the walls of the classroom. The frequent rejection of poststructuralist theories has derived partly from the fact that teachers and other thinkers have not had a conceptual basis on which to attach the new theories. The complex vocabulary of these theories, for example, the specialized language of deconstruction or of psychoanalytic theory, and the conceptualizations that they represent, have led frequently to a rejection of the theories. When people have no conceptual framework for material, they tend to dismiss it. Thinkers outside of school as well as in-school thinkers must have ways to synthesize new material. If no synthesis seems possible, then the thinker tends not to bother. Similarly, if the new material appears threatening, a wholesale rejection frequently results.

The field-coverage paradigm exacerbates the problem of acquiring new kinds of learning by teachers (developing awareness of the "how," rather than relying on the "what"). In addition, it increases territoriality within disciplines. While this form of competition can lead to intellectual energy and vitality, it frequently leads to closure and loss as well. New ideas that could help reconceptualize a field are left out because they do not "fit" the field-coverage paradigm. The test of whether something fits a speciality derives power from the tacit assumptions that govern that field of study. The familiar demarcation of writing and literature in the discipline of English offers us one continuing example of territoriality and its consequences. Another example of field-coverage as tacit paradigm occurs in I.J. Gelb's *A Study of Writing*. In the preface Gelb writes:

> Much of the theoretical reconstruction of writing as presented in this study may sound heretical to some scholars, especially to those philologists who, being imbued with sacred traditions in their narrow fields of specialization, feel reticent about accepting conclusions drawn from a comprehensive view of writing. Indicative of this attitude is the request of one of my colleagues not to quote his name in acknowledgement for help I had received from him in matters pertaining to Chinese. (p. vi)

Gelb, who wrote the preface in 1951 at the University of Chicago, provides a useful example of intellectual territoriality and one kind of response to specialization. Gelb's anonymous scholar responds in a way that is ultimately anti-intellectual: conforming to the exclusionist demands of his specialty, and fearing damage to his scholarly *ethos*, the anonymous scholar prevents his or her abilities and those of his or her colleagues from being shared. As a result, knowlege is contained in a holding pen, a marked-off territory where only particular people are allowed to enter. The sharing of ideas with people outside the territory is regarded as unrigorous. In other words, these people do not communicate very much with those who stand outside the prescribed territory.

The field-coverage paradigm continues to dominate many disciplines. The territoriality that often characterizes a field is reflected, not surprisingly, in curricula that divide and subdivide a field. Since the proliferation of knowledge in every field has meant that the only field coverage possible is that of a very small area, some college and university professors find themselves unable to become enthusiastic about courses that do not play on that particular knowledge. Learners need to make the connections and take the risks of stepping over the line marked off as outside the territory. It is imperative that university professors continue to conduct intensive study. Their students, as well, need to be trained to engage in intensive study, investigation, and inquiry. Without this intensity, the stretching of the intellect cannot happen. In addition to intensive, specialized study, students and their teachers need to be able to make connections to other issues, or, to change images, to see the historical ruptures and discontinuities that Foucault discusses in *The Archaeology of Knowledge* and other places.

The second stance that opposes the analogizing of classical communication technologies to modern communication technologies concerns the time and space issues. Critics who resist analogizing from classical discourse to modern discourse generally are conditioned by formalist training. Privileging a text over writer, cultures, and readers means that the only connection that could be made between ancient and modern texts would be a text-centered one. Consequently, this interpretive stance would insist on privileging aesthetic attributes in comparing ancient and modern texts. However, aesthetics are not enough, particularly in the realm of rhetoric, which by definition adheres itself to public spheres as well as to private ones. The textual isolation brought about by formalist reading training makes many readers uncomfortable with social/cultural applications. These readers often respond with a vague sense that something is wrong in breaking the boundaries provided by chronology.

The argument against analogizing modern discourse and technology issues with ancient ones relies on a third critical stance as well as the two just explored. This argument centers on another version of the argument of rigorousness. This belief resides on an either spoken or unspoken belief that visual texts are inherently inferior to written texts. This belief, which has gone through many permutations since the invention of the camera and the resulting discussions about the nature of "realism," permeates the academy in the United States.

Many people now will routinely acknowledge the idea that film and video are "artistic" media. However, their own responses to these media often indicate that the newer symbol systems are not in fact taken as seriously as symbol systems such as print or painting or music. The most compelling evidence for this marginalization of newer discourse technologies is their nonintegration in general education requirements. They are regarded as peripheral concerns, unrelated to the study of print texts. When courses do appear in the electronic media, they tend to be segregated or marginalized. Their placement in the curriculum announces their secondary status. The written text of the canon reigns supreme. When educational resources become scarce, as they do from time to time and from region to region, the study of electronic media is one of the first kinds of training to be dropped. The conditioning that most people have toward electronic texts leads to statements (either explicit or, more frequently, implicit) that print texts are by nature superior. The situation can be characterized as a class system in texts: Great-Book texts are the aristocrats; some best-seller titles (for example, the books of James Michener) and European art films (the films, for instance, of Ingmar Bergman), contribute to the large middle class of texts; and television and United States "popular" films comprise the proletarian class.

Perhaps the largest class of all in the textual class system is the student-writing group of texts. It comprises the underclass, that huge pool of texts that we all realize exists and that are produced in huge quantities every year by students working their ways through educational systems. Many people working in the academy prefer not to have contact with this kind of text production or even to be aware of it. This hierarchy dominates the way most readers are trained to interpret written texts as well as texts from other symbol systems. The reintegration of student writing as a center of concern in higher education that the renaissance of rhetoric and composition studies brought has meant that student writing is regarded in some quarters as worthy of attention. Nonetheless, it remains as a group in the underclass. Many instructors are distressed when they have to come into contact with it for an extended period.

An additional and larger obstruction has occurred in promoting visual literacy. Film and video texts have frequently been taught as if they were print texts. Plot issues, for example, that might dominate the novel, are transferred to the visual realm. Hollywood Aristotelianism, as it has been called, derives from print culture. The grammar of film and the grammar of video have not been integrated into enough film pedagogy. Consequently, film and video courses appear to be pale versions of great print texts and so remain all the more susceptible to marginalization or deletion.

When one first studies the intermingling in the orality/literacy/ secondary orality hypothesis, a natural resistance can occur because it may seem rather far-fetched, or too neat. This concern is an important one. Sweeping claims can frequently lead to the settling of unsettleable problems and the closure of inquiry and dialectic. The analogy in this context acts as a tentative beginning for the analysis of burgeoning literacy and burgeoning secondary orality. The pressures and possibilities of fourth-century B.C. print literacy and of modern electronic discourse systems remain radically different in many ways. People's perceptions have changed radically. Nonetheless, a peculiar characteristic remains common: the dominance of oral discourse has become more important since film and video have become dominant symbol systems than at any time since the ancient period. Modern revolutions in ways of thinking have taken place and they resemble the revolutions in thinking of the fourth century B.C. These revolutions occur with great pain and difficulty and have made a lot of people angry, including Plato to a limited extent in the ancient era, and literacy hounds such as Allan Bloom to a great extent in the present era.

## SYNTHESIZING SECONDARY ORALITY AND LITERACY

Several alternatives exist for the synthesizing of literacy and secondary orality in the modern era and for recognizing their ruptures and silences as well.

Recognizing the changes in the nature of audiences can lead to a better understanding of discourse technologies and their effects on writerly and readerly consciousness. In the realm of primary orality, when Homeric poets, for example, spoke poems to a community, or when an Acoma tribal leader spoke the Origin Myth of Acoma to the group, one of the Pueblo tribes, the audience consisted of many people. The poet or leader was in charge of the group and spoke for the group as well as to it. In other words, performance was central to primary orality and to its residual existence in modern cultures. Literacy—both in manuscript cultures and in print cultures—required removal from the group, as Ong has pointed out. Writing generally required a certain amount of isolation, or at least a turning inward that is very much the inverse of the turning outward that performance requires. In the shifts that have occurred with the accretion of primary orality, literacy, and secondary orality, the constitution of audiences has changed. Oratory has always dealt partly with large audiences. Electronic discourse mostly speaks to large audiences. But as Plato's Socrates is made to say in *Phaedrus*, rhetoric "has to do with all audiences, great as well as small;" the private discourse of the household is as much the province of rhetoric as the discourse of the legislative assembly. It appears that Plato understood the constraints of literacy—including its requirement of more isolation from groups—than he is generally given credit for.

Secondary orality has brought about the condition of redefining a central characteristic of primary orality and a central characteristic of literacy. In the former case, performance has reemerged in a powerful way as people communicate on film or videotape with actual or perceived simultaneity of performance and reception. In the latter case, the isolation brought about by writing and reading has reemerged as people decode the texts of electronic discourse either alone or with a small group. Disembodied communication (literacy) has been reembodied through visual mechanisms such as video monitors and film screens. This technology gives the fifth canon of delivery (medium) the urgency of simultaneous communication. The lag time of print seems to disappear. I write "seems to" because electronic discourse in the majority of its manifestations appears to be "live" but in fact is stored on film or tape. The immediacy of this appearance, the attractiveness of the liveness, is part of the performative power of the symbol systems of secondary orality. In other words, the lag time that modern writers and readers associate with print and regard as "normal" exists in many of the forms of secondary orality as well. Something is lost, but something is gained as well.

Performance in the electronic symbol systems means that the fourth and fifth canons come to life again after centuries of atrophy and in turn help to reconstitute the familiar first three canons of invention, arrangement, and style. When classical rhetoric was appropriated as lists of schemes and tropes (and as it still is by the listing that comprises Group $\mu$'s *A General Rhetoric* and that of various other writers on classical rhetoric, including those of the Heritage School), the last two canons become dormant. This dormancy also accounted for part of the boredom and triviality associated with classical rhetoric as well as with other rhetorical eras. Invention, arrangement, and style implode when they are separated from the cultural and psychological issues that memory and delivery necessarily include.

Deciding on a medium in which to encode, or determining how to use the fifth canon, has become a major issue for many encoders in art, business, entertainment, and, to a lesser extent, in academics. In addition, the widespread use of telephones provides one obvious example of simultaneous, disembodied communication; it is in fact so familiar that it appears to be nearly a natural part of life. In a less obvious way, the facsimile machine has provided live, simultaneous, disembodied discourse in a way that includes the first demand of literacy: documents exist as part of and as a result of the instantaneous communication. The nature of performance has undergone radical change.

One change lies in the fact that performance has assumed more importance in the era of secondary orality than it has for many centuries. Susan C. Jarratt, in "The First Sophists and the Uses of History," classifies nineteenth and twentieth-century responses to the Sophists in three ways, the pragmatic, the analytic, and the performative (pp. 70–73). In addition, Jasper Neel, particularly in the chapter "Weak Discourse and Strong Discourse" in *Plato, Derrida, and Writing,* declares himself a Sophist; he can be said to be identifying with the performance that was so important to the Sophists. Neel writes:

> For Isocrates, as well as for his teacher Gorgias and his predecessor Protagoras, rhetoric and writing belong at the center of the curriculum because rhetoric and writing are the ways to make choices in a world of probability. Sophistical rhetoric, therefore, is both a study of how to make choices and a study of how choices form character and make good citizens. (p. 211)

Rhetoric for the Sophists included performance in speaking and performance in writing. Neel's emphasis here on the "how" that preoccupied the Sophists Gorgias and Isocrates points to the performative nature of sophistic thinking in writing and speaking. Depending on the decision an encoder makes about the fifth canon (that is, which medium or symbol system will be used), a different emphasis on a way of knowing will occur. But electronic discourse will contribute to the way of knowing even if one writes. Regardless of which medium is chosen, primary orality, literacy, and secondary orality will exist in each one; they will inform one another, infuse one another, and create one another. They are not mere additions, or accumulations; they are changes in consciousness, that is, in the ways one conceptualizes.

We do not have a choice about removing video from our lives and our individual or group consciousnesses. Even if an individual decides to remove all video monitors from his or her environments, that person will remain significantly formed by the small screen. Written discourse and electronic discourse do not compete as much as they change and reinforce each other, even if the encoder appears to be working only in one symbol system.

The implications for pedagogy of these performance issues are far reaching. The institution of the teaching of writing remains in a very tentative phase now, partly because the merging of primary orality, literacy, and secondary orality is in a tenuous – and very exciting – place.

## MAKING DISCOURSE ACTIVE

Hans Magnus Enzensberger's theory of electronic discourse necessarily includes reference to written discourse. In "Constituents of a Theory of the Media," Enzensberger writes:

> The new media are orientated towards action, not contemplation; towards the present, not tradition. . . . The media produce no objects that can be hoarded and auctioned. They do away completely with "intellectual property" and liquidate the "heritage," that is to say, the class-specific handing-on of nonmaterial capital. (p. 106)

The activity that inheres in electronic discourse provides one of its great strengths because it can help to create dialectic, or a productive, interactive clash of legitimate views, in its decoders. The activity that comprises dialectic is one of the promises electronic discourse offers us. Ong makes this point in "McLuhan as Teacher: The Future Is a Thing of the Past." He writes:

> All a teacher can ever do is get other people to think. Without a teacher, learners may be impoverished, unable to find much to learn. The teacher sets things up, whether by enlivening familiar matter or by providing new things for the learners to think about. But, even with the most brilliant teacher, if the learners are to do any learning, they are the ones who have to do it. The pipeline information-transfer model does not really work for the teacher-learner relationship, for it presents learners as passive recipients. Learners are doers, not recipients. (p. 129)

Activity in the mind must be present for learning to take place. Both these writers recognize the fundamental issue of the power of activity in creating or transferring knowledge, or the enabling of the learner to extend his or her already present abilities.

Michael C. Flanigan explores the primacy of activity in "Composition Models: Dynamic and Static Imitations." He discusses the way professional writing can be used to promote thinking in student writers to enable them to become more effective writers. He also describes the more familiar role of professional models in writing classes: the static model that students are assigned to read and mysteriously absorb and then mysteriously imitate.

All these critics realize that, in making decoding active (whether as readers or as spectators of visual media), change must occur. In other words, the decoder will undergo an activity that leads to reconceptualization. We can call the change new encoding. The popular concepts of critical writing and critical thinking appear to be related to the concept of active, new encoding on the part of the decoder.

When students are made aware of the varying constraints imposed by each symbol system (for example, the grammar of film as opposed to the grammar of writing in dominant-culture English), they are able to engage the symbol system in active ways. Raising an awareness of the fifth canon of delivery, or medium, empowers students in at least two ways:

(1) It makes them (and us, their teachers) conscious of the technology that will to a large extent determine the result of their decoding (that is, the meaning); and (2) Knowledge of what a medium consists of and where it came from shows students more of the possibilities of all media and connects students' usually isolated relationships to the media.

Conventionally, expertise in encoding with a video camera is isolated from the experience of encoding with a pen or a word processor or any other media. When encoders increase their consciousness of medium, the fifth canon, it can help them to transcend the frequently antagonistic relationship between language theory and language practice. Knowing that one is choosing a medium for expression empowers a writer, who will consider the constraints that each medium imposes as well as the possibilities it offers. Within one medium—for instance, in the medium of writing—students who study this reasserted canon can think about the kind of text production they want to engage in. Handwriting, typewriting, and word processing offer three possible technologies for written texts. Each one has particular powers as well as limitations. The recent rehistoricizing of classical rhetoric allows us to see the connections between the fifth canon (*hypocrisis, pronuntiatio,* or *actio,* delivery or medium) as it gathered power in the fourth century B.C. and the fifth canon as it exists differently but also similarly in the twentieth century.

One can extrapolate from Enzensberger's preoccupation with writing, film, video, and so on, that making students active encoders is a dangerous activity. If students achieve adequate consciousness of the ways they have been conditioned to respond and if they empower themselves through writing and the dialectic of inquiry, then the status quo might be in danger. If we empower too many students, they might want to change substantially the general culture we all partake of and help to create.

The potentially dangerous activity of writing is bypassed by constructing many—perhaps most—writing classes as passive reading classes (as opposed to active reading classes), a point that process compositionists such as Peter Elbow and James Moffett have been making forcefully and persuasively for a generation. Writing textbooks appear in most writing classes partly because they are comforting to the teachers and partly because they allow passive reading, as opposed to critical reading, to dominate the class. They reassure the apprentice teacher of writing by providing a map of uncharted territory, and they reassure many experienced writing teachers who are overwhelmed by the results of student writing (so unordered, so unlike a book that is neat in typeface and margins). Reading a "perfectly" produced textbook can be a tidy, organized, lovely, and passive experience. Looking at writing before it reaches this lovely state requires developing alternative sensibilities. It requires looking at tentativeness, messy lines, and blips of invention that appear to go nowhere. In other words, compelling the students and the teacher to write the course text as the class emerges throughout the semester creates a mess and a mass of disorganized documents that appear to contradict the "rules" of literacy, including order and neatness. Keeping track of drafts and distributing student writing intimidates many writing teachers, both apprentice teachers and experienced ones.

An even more substantial fear exists in the presence of the activity that comprises dialectic: print culture leads us to believe that whatever is typeset possesses authority. Moerover, the romantic tradition of English studies discussed in Chapter Two makes belletristic writing of the kind reproduced in most textbooks appear to be inherently superior. Both issues—the beauty of the professionally printed page and the attitude of reverence toward sanctified writers—leads to deemphasizing student activity in the form of writing. It reinforces the class structure of texts discussed above: the underclass of student texts cannot remain the center of attention very long.

Enzensberger's formulation of "contemplation" versus "action" summarizes one of the major conflicts between fourth-century B.C. language and twentieth-century A.D. language. In each era, a new form of activity challenged the contemplativeness of the status quo and the many comforts it invariably offers. Plato's complaints against writing resemble the complaints of many people in higher education against training students in the electronic media.

People in the late twentieth and early twenty-first centuries need to be aware of technology and consciousness, so that they can participate in the encoding (and so find one way of achieving dialectic) and so that they can understand the modes of persuasion and manipulation that immerse everyone. Becoming aware of one's place in print culture empowers student writers and the instructor writers. Taking print culture for granted enables the still-powerful formalist devaluation of culture and context to remain unexamined.

Classical rhetoric as it has been reappropriated by the writers in the Dialectical School can strengthen student writing ability by revealing the interconnections of print culture to electronic culture. Making language pedagogy active rather than passive can be done in an endless number of ways. One of them is through a study of technologies.

## THE NEW RHETORIC IS THE OLD RHETORIC

Electronic discourse and the changes in consciousness resulting from it have made classical rhetoric a compelling issue again. The triviality and boredom associated with much of classical rhetoric (traits it continues to possess for many decoders), can be regarded as pressures resulting from the domination of print literacy. The cultural situation of print domination probably required that two of the primary functions of rhetoric—memory and delivery—move underground to the realm of the trivial, to the realm of tropes-for-tropes' sake.

It is not easy to determine that there was any kind of "loss" when classical rhetoric was appropriated in silly ways (Ramus naturally comes to mind as an example of this phenomenon). The response of many writers on classical rhetoric that a "loss" has been sustained indicates a bypassing of the nature of cultural/contextual flux of consciousness. The imposing and sensitive reading of a writer such as Brian Vickers in the 1988 *In Defence of Rhetoric* presupposes that classical rhetoric has been attacked and needs a defense of the kind that supplies the title of his book. The critical stance of the defense appears as well in Vickers' use of the word "alien" in his discussions of classical rhetoric. This reception is not only understandable, but from many points of view is also very sensible. Nonetheless, an alternative reception of classical rhetoric resists the closure of alienation and embraces the possibility of adaptability. Rhetoric adapts so well that it is alien to virtually nothing. However, as was discussed in Chapter One, this adaptability makes it the chameleon of disciplines. If rhetoric can adapt to any kind of language and symbol system, then what is it? Where is its substance? Because it is partly a faculty, it can be applied to anything.

The adaptability of rhetoric—its power and its danger—leads inevitably to the construction and communication of value systems. Rhetoric as a faculty and a systematic form of study has been in its entire history, beginning in the fifth century B.C. and leading to the present moment, appropriated by people for negative purposes. This complaint formed the center of Plato's and Aristotle's long-lasting attacks against the Sophists. These patriarchs of western philosophy (which came to appropriate—one could say colonize—the field of ethics), Plato and Aristotle, disagreed on many issues, but they in a sense collaborated in their rigorous denunciation of the Sophists. The totalizing effect of their stance silenced the Sophists virtually until the nineteenth century, as various recent commentators have demonstrated. In the political realm, dictators have always adapted rhetoric to their ends. But then so too have beneficent rulers and those in ruling systems. So what can be done with a faculty or an ability that can go out of control so readily?

Rhetoric, more than any other field, points to the need for examinations of value systems. It points, in fact, to the need for the analysis of many kinds of value systems. Couched in different terms, it requires us to study ideology, or the interconnecting system of values and beliefs that informs attitudes and behaviors. Most significantly, rhetoric can teach people to become aware of these systems that are usually tacit and assumed to be factual, or based on reality, partly because they feel so "normal," so "natural." This enterprise leads to the emphasis on rhetorical consciousness.

## RHETORIC, CONSCIOUSNESS, AND "THE CONSCIOUSNESS INDUSTRY"

Print texts possess power that readers tend to take for granted. Print literacy has conditioned us to view published texts as more authoritative than manuscript texts or nonprint texts produced on videotape, film, or other means. Electronic texts have come to enjoy the same authoritativeness. (This is one reason that live television has become rare: its authoritativeness is jeopardized by mistakes or by unprogrammed material that enters the visual field.) The authoritativeness of printed texts leads to a greater emphasis on the text and, in turn, its life as a finished object. The completed nature of print texts appears to be natural or even inevitable.

If we move the focus from the text and its apparent objectivity and refocus on which institutions control the distribution of the printed or electronic text, then we confront Enzensberger's point: a consciousness industry possesses enormous control over the population. Enzensberger writes in "The Industrialization of the Mind:"

> while radio, cinema, television, recording, advertising, and public relations, new techniques of manipulation and propaganda, are being keenly discussed, each on its own terms, the mind industry, taken as a whole, is disregarded. Newsprint and publishing, its oldest and in many respects still its most interesting branch, hardly comes up for serious comment any longer, presumably because it lacks the appeal of technological novelty. (p. 6)

These institutions help comprise the fifth canon of rhetoric, delivery (medium). So great is the distribution power of the mind industry that the fifth canon, it can be maintained, is now the most powerful canon of the five. The fifth canon has become the consciousness industry. And the fifth canon remains the function of rhetoric most frequently ignored by writing instructors and their institutions.

Rhetoric, particularly when the fifth canon is fully considered, helps to create the consciousness industry. Rhetoric as both a faculty and a field of study provides not only the means of analysis for all these symbol systems but the means of producing new kinds of material as well. No other system for the production and reception of texts in all symbol systems possesses the completeness of rhetoric and its definitive connection to systems of education and to cultures.

Rhetoric, including the composition of texts in all media, has the capacity to make people conscious of the unprecedented power of print and electronic texts as systems of communication or of indoctrination. Along with the raising of fifth-canon consciousness, rhetoric provides one means for people to enact their own encoding. It enables writing, filming, taping, and so on. Part of the potential dialectic that inheres in all media occurs when decoders become encoders in a particular medium. For example, when a reader turns to writing, the nature of writing texts changes for him or her. The same situation holds true for filming, taping, playing the piano, and so on.

Because of the power of encoding of all kinds, rhetoric as it applies to the various symbol systems needs especially to be studied by novices as well as by more experienced encoders. In addition to being studied by critics (a modern version of a privileged, rather small group) rhetoric in literacy and in secondary orality must become part of the agenda of general education. Studying the technology of literacy and secondary orality has become a necessity for even a minimally educated population. Ink and paper, the word processor and printer, the film camera, the video camera, the frames of big and small screens, all must be studied for an understanding of cultural dynamics. Remaining unconscious of the media of literacy and secondary orality means that cultures will have functionally illiterate populations.

Functional illiteracy in this context means that the power of print and visual texts will remain centered in privileged groups; it also means that the status quo will appear to sustain itself. Appropriate training in print and visual literacy—when students encode as well as decode— would make students less passive. It would promote the interactive thinking that is dialectic. However, the institutionalization of visual literacy is not action enough. Educational institutions themselves must give up their marginality. The passivity of most educational practice (the student as empty vessel waiting to be filled by the knowledge of teacher and print text) is supplemented by an implied moral superiority that frequently accompanies the disciplines ordered under the rubric of the humanities. An unapparent transaction takes place: The humanities are given tacit moral superiority, in exchange for being relatively useless. Anthony Grafton and Lisa Jardine have traced some of the historical ramifications of this phenomenon in *From Humanism to the Humanities.*

## CLASSICAL RHETORIC, CONTEMPORARY RHETORIC,
## AND THE POWER IN THE ORDINARINESS OF LANGUAGE

The visual illiteracy of modern cultures, along with their sustained unconsciousness of delivery, or medium, means that the ability to understand systems of communication (including various forms of manipulation and control) remains at an elementary level. Only when the ordinariness of language is recognized—in exterior discourse as well as in the interior discourse that partly constitutes thinking—can extraordinary uses—artistic or literary discourse—be understood. The everyday uses of language are in constant flux, like Heraclitus's river and the person putting a foot in the river. Less noticeably, the uses of ordinary language are in flux as well. While a true rhetoric may exist for some people, that trueness is largely unlocatable. Fluid discourse—rhetoric and the mutual discovery and challenge of dialectic—remains the source of power in classical rhetoric. In this fluidity and dialectic, one may discover (as Plato believed possible at various points in his career as a writer) ultimate realities.

The fact that a primary reception of classical rhetoric has been made utterly definite (that is, static) in Heritage School positivistic presentations illustrates the moribund state not only of Cartesian dualism but of discourse education that remains marginalized, ghettoized, and useless. Walter Benjamin, in "The Work of Art in the Age of Mechanical Reproduction," explores the idea that electronic media enable oral discourse to gain power that it had not had in pre-electronic eras: permanence. Films, videos, and computer disks can maintain texts as readily as writing can. In primary orality, the dynamism of the word is powerful but transitory. In secondary orality, the dynamic of the spoken word is not only powerful, it is lasting. We have returned to a state of interdependence of oral and written discourse. With the technology of secondary orality, the spoken word and the written word are empowering each other in ways that previously were not possible. This situation makes classical rhetoric, which accounts for encoders, decoders, and cultures as well as texts, a newly powerful area. After residing in the nether world of tropes and figures for many centuries, classical rhetoric is newly resuscitated by the interdynamics of literacy and secondary orality. Benjamin writes:

> Around 1900 technical reproduction had reached a standard that not only permitted it to reproduce all transmitted works of art and thus to cause the most profound change in their impact upon the public; it also had captured a place of its own among the artistic processes. For the study of

> this standard nothing is more revealing than the nature of the repercus-
> sions that these two different manifestations—the reproduction of works
> of art and the art of the film—have had on art in its traditional form.
> (p. 220)

The fifth canon of delivery or medium as it has come to exist in various
electronic forms in the twentieth century influences all forms of art, as
Benjamin was one of the first to recognize. Art's reproducibility can
empower people who may not have had access to the power of
encoding. The means of producing discourse in several symbol systems
is available to a large population. In order for people to become
persuaded of the empowerment that is possible for them through
encoding, they must see the relationship between their own ordinary
language—including interior discourse—and that of artistic discourse.
This issue provides a powerful means of persuasion for writing instructors. Connecting a student's interior discourse—something that is lived
and felt—to a class essay or to a play by Shakespeare acts as an effective
means of empowering students. This connection treats conceptualizations, or "how" questions, not "content" or "what" questions. In
addition, this connection enables students to comprehend the interconnections of all language use and its existence as a communal activity
rather than as the merely private, hermetic possession that many people
assume it to be.

Plato and Isocrates appear in their writing to have understood the
primary relationship between inner speech (and its relationship to the
soul) and outer speech. Plato's rhetoric and dialectic, difficult though
they are to define, connect to both kinds of speech in a person engaged
in a search, or a process, that is not readily identifiable. Rhetoric and
dialectic are communal as well as singular activities. Their push and pull
require conversation (in any medium) with another person but, like
rhetoric, it requires interior change as well. Virginia N. Steinhoff has
written about these relational activities:

> the Platonic stance toward rhetorical arts and instruction is synthetic and
> artful, shaped from unexpected material into new forms that are, at best,
> suggestions of things not seen. The Socratic role requires, in addition, a
> kind of playfulness and suspension of goal-directed behavior that is
> unlikely to sit well with responsible institutions of higher learning or
> teachers anxious about productivity in the classroom, specifically about
> written products—papers, essays, themes, theses, scholarly articles, and
> so on. (p. 39)

These outward manifestations, or artifacts of the movement between
interior discourse and exterior discourse, have been privileged over the

syntheses Steinhoff alludes to. But the signature of Platonic rhetoric as well as of Isocratean rhetoric is the subjectivity of thinking rather than the objectivity of texts.

Plato obviously and Isocrates less obviously impelled their readers to use their own subjective selves to make contact with versions of reality and therefore to improve perceptive reality. While Isocrates remained more committed to ordinary communication, he nevertheless resembles Plato in his commitment to interior discourse. The impressionism that accompanies rhetoric and encoding in all symbol systems constitutes part of its definition. Positivists of the Heritage School and other groups do not take well to impressionism and subjectivity. It appears to interrupt the definiteness that tends to be reassuring. Writing that is relegated to the status of a mere "skill" partakes of this definiteness. As we have seen, however, writing as a skill-bound activity, as the mastering of the production of definite objects that reflect more or less definite interior realities, is boring for encoders and for decoders alike.

Secondary orality and its brief century of life have changed the nature of rhetoric, including that of classical rhetoric. In addition, the ways people perceive have changed radically. The changes brought about in audience as well as in interior discourse resemble (even as they in other ways do not resemble) the changes in epistemology that Plato, Isocrates, Gorgias, and other writers and performers experienced with the spreading of literacy as a dominant form of consciousness in the fourth century B.C. There is no point in worshipping these early writers, as has been done perenially. The hierarchy created by the worshipper and the supposedly divine being means that a huge gap of utter inequality exists. This space may be appropriate in religious practice but hinders discourse practice and pedagogy.

The study of secondary orality as a continuing dynamic will not progress if analogizing to the possibilities and constraints of fourth-century B.C. discourse leads to more of the tired, old fetishizing of classical rhetoric texts and the inevitable and tired, old response of rejecting those texts for being fetishized. Instead, the study of secondary orality can bring about a democracy of texts, in which student texts are produced and studied with the rigor and care that Great-Book texts (of whatever discipline) are studied. In addition, the privileging of one medium over the other media that the fifth canon offers us means that the power of delivery will never be realized. Instead, the status quo will remain.

It has been the task of many language educators to remain unconscious of the fifth canon, to act as if only one or two systems of delivery exist. This ingrained rhetorical unconsciousness is accompanied by a tacit assumption that good speaking and good writing are somehow innate. In other words, they act as if (that is, their performances as educators state that) good speaking and writing are not at all connected to technology but instead are basically natural traits. Those students unfortuante enough, according to these promoters of the rhetorical unconscious, not to have received this language goodness at home (the children of the underprivileged) must be trained in it. These spokes-people for the status quo tend to see good writing and speaking as the result of good breeding. If one is unfortunate enough to be ill-bred, then schools should train the student to acquire the discourse habits of good breeding. In this way the status quo can go on and on, with its native born and with its recruits reinforcing the power structure that feels familiar. The Allan Blooms, the William Bennetts, and the other literacy hounds have taken up the task of rushing toward the past as a reinforcment of the way things are rather than as reconstituting the past according to modern demands. Embracing the whatness of a definite history, with definite categories that feel natural and normal and require no questioning, these new literacy masters are among the first to recoil from the study of visual texts or the study of the revolutions in symbol systems that have been one of the major aspects of intellectual advance-ment in the twentieth century. All the canons of classical rhetoric have been reconstituted and revivified by secondary orality. If we continue to lapse into rhetorical unconsciousness, the status quo of the uselessness of the "humanities" will continue. The commonplace that the discipline of classics committed suicide in the United States is a lesson that the literacy masters need to consider. It is a lesson that the promoters of the Heritage School need to consider. Any work in the historicizing of classical rhetoric needs to take account of this phenomenon. Will other forms of discourse study follow the path of the classics in the United States? Or will the false issues of breeding, correctness, and unacknowl-edged elitism lead to the continued domination of the print and the electronic media by business people and statisticians who record "taste" (desire)? Will academics continue to create the artifacts of the humanities and hoard them among themselves?

The unusual adaptability of classical rhetoric and its preoccupation with producing discourse and not merely analyzing it after someone has produced it, makes it one of the most powerful discourse systems that we have. The fact that it has been appropriated by elitists from many centuries and traditions who invest particular ancient texts and writers with magical properties is no reason to dispense with it. In fact, its adaptability and usefulness make it an extraordinarily useful way of studying texts and their contexts. Classical rhetoric is too important to be left to the Heritage School. Instead, we need to continue the reappropriation shown us by dialectical critics of various stances (some of which are in opposition to one another) and to rewrite and reread classical rhetoric with the emerging critical sensibilities that have so enlivened and politicized discourse studies in the last generation. A new agenda lies before us, and part of that newness is as old as Isocrates.

# GLOSSARY
# OF KEYWORDS

These concepts from classical and contemporary rhetoric and composition theory are offered to further dialogue and not to restrict possibility. Moving toward a shared and renewed vocabulary can promote the rehistoricizing of rhetoric and composition, including its place in writing pedagogy. I borrow the concept of keywords from Raymond Williams' book *Keywords: A Vocabulary of Culture and Society*. These tentative explanations are of course reductive, incomplete, and open to revision. They are meant to increase ambiguity rather than to suppress it. In the case of Greek loan words, the suggested translations indicate categories of thought rather than one-to-one substitution. Accent marks are left out here and throughout the book to encourage wider use of the keywords in English.

**Arete.** Function, excellence. The movement toward the best expression of a person's or a thing's unique capacity.

**Arrangement.** The second of the five canons, or functions, of classical rhetoric. The form, order, or structure of a discourse event.

**Classical Rhetoric.** A group of writings that begin with the references to Corax and Tisias in the fifth century B.C. (the first known systematic treatment of rhetoric) and span about 700 years until Quintilian and later Roman rhetoricians. The writings, writers, and contexts of this broad and arbitrary, category have been received in varying ways according to traditions of reception.

**Composition.** One kind of rhetoric that focuses on writing, or the production of texts.

**Decoding.** The interpretation of any text in any medium (for example, writing, speaking, filming, videotaping, and playing musical instruments).

**Delivery.** The fifth canon, or function, of classical rhetoric. In ancient times, this canon indicated gesture, movement, and other physical issues in oral presentations. With the burgeoning power of literacy and later of secondary orality, it came to signify medium, or symbol system. The ability to perform in any medium.

**Dialectic.** In rhetoric, a productive clash of initially opposing verbal forces that results in the furthering of insight by all involved. A mutual inquiry that depends on active engagement by all participants. Individual writers, both ancient and modern, provide more technical meanings of the term.

**Dialectical Critics.** A wide-ranging group of contemporary interpreters of classical rhetoric who present classical rhetoric as problems rather than as commodities. In divergent ways, they reject formalist reading that privileges texts over other discourse issues. These writers, who can differ markedly, tend toward inquiry in the connectedness of classical rhetoric rather than discovering a definite rhetorical "reality."

**Electronic Discourse.** Texts (written, visual, musical, etc.) that are produced with electricity. The first electronic medium was the telegraph. Eventually, technology such as film, video, and computers made this form of discourse revolutionize communication and change consciousness. With some exceptions (such as the use of microphones for assemblies), electronic discourse provides disembodied, instantaneous communication.

**Encoding.** The production of a text in any medium, or symbol system, including writing, speaking, playing an instrument, shooting film, etc.

**Ethos.** The most important of Aristotle's three interior persuaders. The general idea of a writer's or a speaker's (or any encoder's) character.

**Exterior Persuaders.** Part of Aristotle's **pisteis.** Usually translated into English as "inartistic proofs." Changing people according to nonbelief issues such as torturing, swearing, going to court, and so on.

**Five Canons.** A critical system that takes account of the production of discourse as well as the reception of discourse. Also called the functions, or parts (**erga**) of rhetoric, they consist of invention, arrangement, style, memory, and delivery/medium. The canons change and undergo differing relationships with one another in different epochs and acquire different meanings according to the kinds of discourse that dominate a given culture.

**Heritage School.** Interpreters who share a critical stance that regards classical rhetoric as a series of objective writings. The positivistic attitude sets forth an external reality of retrievable, definite texts, regardless of perception and its fluctuations.

**Ideology.** A shared system of belief that appears to be "normal" and "natural" and that therefore is not ordinarily open to probing.

**Interior Persuaders.** Three kinds of **pisteis** that Aristotle analyzes. Usually translated into English as "artistic proofs." **Ethos, pathos,** and **logos.**

**Invention.** The first of the five canons of classical rhetoric. The generation, or creation, of ideas for a given discourse.

**Kairos.** The opportune moment. The time that a particular point can be conveyed. Evaluating the appropriate, or the most effective time, to persuade people of something.

**Keyword.** A term that contains a cluster of related meanings and resonance. Their complexity in ancient Greek is best maintained by making them loan words. These concepts contain their own dialectics.

**Literacy.** A general consciousness in a culture that bases its thought processes on writing in addition to oral dynamics. The wide dissemination of writing through print accelerated this kind of consciousness.

**Logos.** One of Aristotle's three interior persuaders (artistic proofs). Persuasion that appeals to reason. A concept that figured in the work of the Presocratics, the Sophists, Isocrates, and Plato as well. Its undulations of meaning include word, thought, story, speech, and deliberation.

**Memory.** The fourth of the five canons of classical rhetoric. The ability to recall issues, ideas, concepts, feelings, etc. This canon includes psychology and interior discourse (talking to oneself). The ability to form and reform constructions.

**Nomos/Physis.** Intertwined concepts that recur in classical rhetoric. **Nomos** signifies law, convention, more, that which is human made, habit, while **physis** indicates nature, or that which contains essence or reality.

**Orality.** Language communicated through sounds produced by the human voice.

**Pistis.** Plural, **Pisteis.** The means of persuasion and the conditions for bringing about belief.

**Primary Orality.** A condition of culture in which communication, the transmission of values, and the structures of thought are brought about by spoken discourse. Writing and its effects are unknown in cultures such as these. The Homeric Greeks provide one example of a culture formed by primary orality.

**Style.** The third canon of classical rhetoric. A way of presenting any type of discourse. A mode of displaying a text from any medium.

**Reception.** The response of decoders either as a group or individually to one text from any medium or groupings of texts. Reception takes place largely according to the conditioning of readers.

**Rhetoric.** A faculty for determining what kind of persuasion a situation requires. A 2500-year-old system for the production and the reception of discourse.

**Rhetorical Stance.** Related to **ethos,** this term indicates a point of view taken for the writing, speaking or other encoding of a particular text. An encoder can shift rhetorical stance according to persuasive needs.

**Rhetorical Unconscious.** Borrowed from Fredric Jameson's concept of the "political unconscious," this term indicates the decontextualizing of some versions of rhetoric without an awareness that this procedure is taking place. A collapsing of rhetorical distinctions.

**Secondary Orality.** A developing kind of consciousness brought about by electronic discourse and dependent on primary orality and literacy. A way of thinking that increases its power as electronic transmission of ideas takes on increasing importance.

**Topoi.** The places one can look for lines of persuasion to bring about belief in a particular discourse situation.

**Writing.** A technology that occurs in manuscript, print, or computer. One type of encoding that places thought in linear form.

# References

Abrams, M. H. *The Mirror and the Lamp*. New York: Norton, 1958.

Adams, Hazard (Ed.). *Critical Theory Since Plato*. San Diego: Harcourt Brace Jovanovich, 1971.

Allen, R. E. *Dialogues of Plato*. New Haven: Yale University Press, 1984.

Anderson, John R. *Cognitive Psychology and Its Implications*. San Francisco: W.H. Freeman, 1980.

Applebee, Arthur N. *Tradition and Reform in the Teaching of English* Urbana, IL: National Council of Teachers of English, 1974.

Aristotle. *The "Art" of Rhetoric*. Trans. J.H. Freese. Cambridge, MA: Harvard University Press, 1926.

_____ . *The Complete Works of Aristotle*. Ed. Jonathan Barnes. 2 vols. Princeton: Princeton University Press, 1984.

_____ . *The Rhetoric of Aristotle*. Trans. Lane Cooper. Englewood Cliffs, NJ: Prentice-Hall, 1932.

Arnold, Matthew. "The Study of Poetry." In *Essays in Criticism: Second Series*. New York: Macmillan, 1913.

Axelrod, Rise B., & Cooper, Charles R. *The St. Martin's Guide to Writing*. New York: St. Martin's, 1985.

Barnes, Jonathan. *Early Greek Philosophy*. Harmondsworth, England: Penguin Books, 1987.

Beardslee, J.W., Jr. *The Use of Physis in Fifth Century Greek Literature*. Chicago: University of Chicago Press, 1918.

Benjamin, Walter. "The Work of Art in the Age of Mechanical Reproduction." In *Illuminations*. Trans Harry Zohn. New York: Schocken Books, 1969.

Berlin, James A. *Rhetoric and Reality: Writing Instruction in American Colleges, 1900–1985*. Carbondale, IL: Southern Illinois University Press, 1987.

_____ . *Writing Instruction in Nineteenth-Century American Colleges*. Carbondale, IL: Southern Illinois University Press, 1984.

Berthoff, Ann E. *Forming/Thinking/Writing: The Composing Imagination*. Upper Montclair, NJ: Boynton/Cook, 1980.

Bessinger, Jess B. "Oral to Written: Some Implications of the Anglo-Saxon Transition." *Explorations*. No. 8 (1957), pp. 11–15.

Bizzell, Patricia, & Herzberg, Bruce. *The Bedford Bibliography for Teachers of Writing*. 2nd ed. Boston: St. Martin's Press, 1987.

_____ . "A Response to Kathleen E. Welch." *Rhetoric Review*. Vol. 6, No. 2 (Spring 1988), p. 246.

Black, Edwin. "Plato's View of Rhetoric." In Keith V. Erickson (Ed.), *Plato: True and Sophistic Rhetoric*. Amsterdam: Rodopi, 1976, pp. 171–191.

Bleich, David. *Readings and Feelings: An Introduction to Subjective Criticism*. Urbana, IL: National Council of Teachers of English, 1975.

_____ . *Subjective Criticism*. Baltimore: Johns Hopkins University Press, 1978.

Bloom, Allan. *The Closing of the American Mind*. New York: Simon, 1987.

Braddock, Richard, Lloyd-Jones, Richard, and Schoer, Lowell. *Research in Written Composition*. Urbana, IL: National Council of Teachers of English, 1963.

Britton, James. "What's the Use? A Schematic Account of Language Functions." In *Language Perspectives: Papers from the Educational Review*. Ed. Barrie Wade. London: Heinemann Educational Books, 1982, pp. 110–124.

Bruner, Jerome S. *The Process of Education*. Cambridge, MA: Harvard University Press, 1966.

Burke, Kenneth. *A Grammar of Motives*. Berkeley: University of California Press, 1969.

_____ . *A Rhetoric of Motives*. Berkeley: University of California Press, 1969.

Burnet, John. "Law and Nature in Greek Ethics." *Essays and Addresses*. London: Chatto & Windus, 1930.

_____ . *Early Greek Philosophy*. London: Adam & Charles Black, 1892.

Cassirer, Ernst. *The Philosophy of Symbolic Forms*. Vol I. Trans. Ralph Manheim. New Haven: Yale University Press, 1953.

Cherniss, Harold. *Aristotle's Criticism of Presocratic Philosophy*. Baltimore: Johns Hopkins University Press, 1935.

Christensen, Charles H. "Publisher's Note." *The Bedford Bibliography for Teachers of Writing*, 2nd ed.

Cicero. "Brutus." In *Cicero on Oratory and Orators*.

_____ . *Cicero on Oratory and Orators*. Trans. J.S. Watson. Carbondale, IL: Southern Illinois University Press, 1970.

_____ . *De Oratore; or, On the Character of the Orator*. In *Cicero on Oratory and Orators*.

_____ . [*On Invention.*] *De Inventione, De Optimo Genere Oratorum, Topica*. Trans. H.M. Hubbell. Cambridge, MA: Harvard University Press, 1949, pp. 1–163.

Coles, William E., Jr. *Teaching Composing*. Rochelle Park, NJ: Hayden Book Co., 1974.

Collins, James L., & Miller, Bruce E. "Presentational Symbolism and the Production of Text." *Written Communication*. Vol. 3, No. 1 (January 1986), pp. 91–104.

Comte, Auguste. *Auguste Comte and Positivism: The Essential Writings*, Ed.

Gertrud Lenzer. Chicago: University of Chicago Press, 1983.

Connors, Robert J. "Greek Rhetoric and the Transition from Orality." *Philosophy and Rhetoric*. Vol. 19 (1986), pp. 38–61.

Connors, Robert J., Ede, Lisa S., & Lunsford, Andrea A., Eds. *Essays on Classical Rhetoric and Modern Discourse*. Carbondale, IL: Southern Illinois University Press, 1984.

Connors, Robert J., Ede, Lisa S., & Lunsford, Andrea A. "The Revival of Rhetoric in America." In *Essays on Classical Rhetoric and Modern Discourse*, pp. 1–15.

Cooper, Lane, trans. *The Rhetoric of Aristotle*.

Corbett, Edward P.J. *Classical Rhetoric for the Modern Student*. 3rd ed. New York: Oxford University Press, 1990. Originally published 1965.

———. "The *Topoi* Revisited." In *Rhetoric and Praxis: The Contribution of Classical Rhetoric to Practical Reasoning*. Ed. Jean Dietz Moss. Washington, D.C.: Catholic University of America Press, 1986, pp. 43–57.

Cornford, Francis MacDonald, trans. *The Republic of Plato*. London: Oxford University Press, 1945.

Crowley, Sharon. "The Current-Traditional Theory of Style: An Informal History." *Rhetoric Society Quarterly*. Vol. 16, No. 4 (Fall 1986), pp. 233–250.

Culler, Jonathan. *Ferdinand de Saussure*. Harmondsworth, England: Penguin Books, 1977.

Cunliffe, Richard John. *A Lexicon of the Homeric Dialect*. Norman: University of Oklahoma Press, 1963.

Czitrom, Daniel J. *Media and the American Mind. From Morse to McLuhan*. Chapel Hill: University of North Carolina Press, 1982.

D'Angelo, Frank J. *A Conceptual Theory of Rhetoric*. Cambridge, MA: Winthrop, 1975.

Derrida, Jacques. *Dissemination*. Trans. Barbara Johnson. Chicago: University of Chicago Press, 1981.

Descartes, René. *Descartes: Selected Philosophical Writings*. Trans. John Cottingham, Robert Stoothoff, Dugald Murdoch. Cambridge, England: Cambridge University Press, 1988.

Dodds, E.R. (Ed.). *Plato: A Revised Text with Introduction and Commentary*. Oxford: Clarendon Press, 1959.

Eagleton, Terry. *Literary Theory: An Introduction*. Minneapolis: University of Minnesota Press, 1983.

———. *Walter Benjamin: Or Towards a Revolutionary Criticism*. London: Verso, 1981.

Ehninger, Douglas. "On Systems of Rhetoric." *Philosophy and Rhetoric*, Vol. I (1968), pp. 131–144.

Ehrenzweig, Anton. *The Hidden Order of Art: A Study in the Psychology of Artistic Imagination*. Berkeley: University of California Press, 1971.

Elbow, Peter. *Writing without Teachers*. New York: Oxford University Press, 1973.

Enos, Richard Leo. "The Classical Period." In Winifred Bryan Horner, Ed. *The Present State of Scholarship in Historical and Contemporary Rhetoric*. Columbia:

University of Missouri Press, 1983, pp. 10–39.

_____ . "The Composing Process of the Sophist: New Directions (and Cautions) for Composition Research." Unpublished manuscript.

_____ . "The Art of Rhetoric at the Amphiareion of Oropos: A Study of Epigraphical Evidence as Written Communication." *Written Communication.* Vol. 3, No. 1 (January 1986), pp. 3–14.

_____ . "The Hellenic Rhapsode." *Western Journal of Speech Communication.* Vol. 42, No. 2, pp. 134–143.

_____ . *The Literate Mode of Cicero's Legal Rhetoric.* Carbondale, IL: Southern Illinois University Press, 1988.

Enzensberger, Hans Magnus. "Constituents of a Theory of the Media." In *The Consciousness Industry: On Literature, Politics, and the Media.* New York: Seabury Press, 1974, pp. 95–128.

_____ . "The Industrialization of the Mind." In *The Consciousness Industry: On Literature, Politics, and the Media.* New York: Seabury Press, pp. 3–15.

Erickson, Keith V. "The Lost Rhetorics of Aristotle." *Communication Monographs,* Vol. 43, pp. 229–237.

_____ (Ed.). *Plato: True and Sophistic Rhetoric.* Amsterdam: Rodopi, 1976.

Febvre, Lucien, & Martin, Henri-Jean. *The Coming of the Book: The Impact of Printing, 1450–1800.* Trans. David Gerard. London: Verso, 1984.

Fish, Stanley. *Is There a Text in This Class?* Cambridge, MA: Harvard University Press, 1980.

Flanigan, Michael C. "Composition Models: Dynamic and Static Imitations." *Theory into Practice.* Vol. 19, No. 3 (Summer 1980), pp. 211–219.

Freedman, Aviva, & Pringle, Ian (Eds.). *Reinventing the Rhetorical Tradition.* Conway, AR: L&S Books, 1980.

Freeman, Kathleen. *Ancilla to the Pre-Socratic Philosophers: A Companion to Diels, Fragmente der Vorsokratiker.* 2nd ed. Cambridge, MA: Harvard University Press, 1959.

Foucault, Michel. *The Archaeology of Knowledge.* Trans. A.M. Sheridan Smith. New York: Pantheon Books, 1972.

_____ . *The Order of Things: An Archaeology of the Human Sciences.* No translator cited. New York: Vintage, 1973.

Gadamer, Hans-Georg. *Truth and Method.* New York: Seabury Press, 1975.

Gelb, I.J. *A Study of Writing.* Chicago: University of Chicago Press, 1952.

Gorgias. *Encomium on Helen.* In Freeman, pp. 131–133.

Gorrell, Robert M., Bizzell, Patricia, & Herzberg, Bruce. *The Bedford Bibliography for Teachers of Writing.* Boston: St. Martin's Press, 1984.

Grafton, Anthony, & Jardine, Lisa. *From Humanism to the Humanities: Education and the Liberal Arts in Fifteenth- and Sixteenth-Century Europe.* Cambridge, MA: Harvard University Press, 1986.

Graff, Gerald. *Professing Literature: An Institutional History.* Chicago: University of Chicago Press, 1987.

Graham, Joseph F. (Ed.). *Difference in Translation.* Ithaca: Cornell University Press, 1985.

Grene, Marjorie. *A Portrait of Aristotle.* London: Faber and Faber, 1963.

Grimaldi, William M.A. *Aristotle, Rhetoric I: A Commentary*. New York: Fordham University Press, 1980.

_____ . *Studies in the Philosophy of Aristotle's Rhetoric*. Wiesbaden: Franz Steiner Verlag, 1972.

Group μ (Dubois, J., Edeline, F., Klinkenberg, J.-M., Minguet, P., Pire, F., Trinon, H.). *A General Rhetoric*. Trans. Paul B. Burrell and Edgar M. Slotkin. Baltimore: Johns Hopkins University Press, 1981.

Guthrie, W.K.C. *The Greek Philosophers from Thales to Aristotle*. New York: Harper & Row, 1960.

_____ . *The Sophists*. Cambridge: Cambridge University Press, 1969.

Havelock, Eric A. "The Alphabetization of Homer." In *Communication Arts in the Ancient World*. Ed. Eric A. Havelock and Jackson P. Hershbell. New York: Hastings House, 1978, pp. 3–21.

_____ . *The Muse Learns to Write: Reflections on Orality and Literacy from Antiquity to the Present*. New Haven: Yale University Press, 1986.

_____ . *Preface to Plato*. Cambridge, MA: Harvard University Press, 1963.

Hayes, John R. *Cognitive Psychology: Thinking and Creating*. Homewood, IL: Dorsey Press, 1978.

Hinks, D.A.G. "Tisias and Corax and the Invention of Rhetoric." *Classical Quarterly*. Vol. 34 (1940), pp. 61–69.

Hirsch, E.D., Jr. *Cultural Literacy: What Every American Needs to Know*. Boston: Houghton Mifflin, 1987.

Holland, Norman. *Five Readers Reading*. New Haven: Yale University Press, 1975.

Homer. *The Iliad*. Two vols. Trans. A.T. Murray. Loeb Classical Library. Cambridge, MA: Harvard University Press, Vol. I, 1924, Vol. II, 1925.

_____ . *The Odyssey*. Two vols. Trans. A.T. Murray. Loeb Classical Library. Cambridge, MA: Harvard University Press, 1919.

Horner, Winifred Bryan. *The Present State of Scholarship in Historical and Contemporary Rhetoric*. Columbia, MO: University of Missouri Press, 1983.

_____ . *Rhetoric in the Classical Tradition*. Boston: St. Martin's Press, 1988.

Howell, Wilbur S. *Logic and Rhetoric in England, 1500–1700*. Princeton, N.J.: Princeton University Press, 1956.

Hudson-Williams, H. Ll. *Three Systems of Education: Some Reflections on the Implications of Plato's Phaedrus*. Oxford: Oxford University Press, 1954.

Innis, Harold. *Empire and Communications*. Toronto: University of Toronto Press, 1972.

Iser, Wolfgang. *The Act of Reading: A Theory of Aesthetic Response*. Baltimore: Johns Hopkins University Press, 1979.

Isocrates. *Isocrates*. Vols. I & II trans. George Norlin. Vol. III trans. La Rue Van Hook. Loeb Classical Library. Cambridge, MA: Harvard University Press, Vol. I, 1928, Vol. II, 1929, Vol. III, 1945.

Jaeger, Werner. *Paideia: The Ideals of Greek Culture*. Trans. Gilbert Highet. 3 vols. Oxford: Oxford University Press, 1939–45.

Jameson, Fredric. *The Political Unconscious: Narrative as a Socially Symbolic Act*. Ithaca, NY: Cornell University Press, 1981.

Jarratt, Susan C. "The First Sophists and the Uses of History." *Rhetoric Review.* Vol. 6, No. 1, pp. 67–78.

———. "Toward a Sophistic Historiography." *Pre/Text.* Vol. 8, Nos. 1–2, pp. 9–26.

Johnson, Barbara. "Translator's Introduction," *Dissemination,* Jacques Derrida. Chicago: University of Chicago Press, 1981.

Johnson, Nan. "Ethos and the Aims of Rhetoric." In *Essays on Classical Rhetoric and Modern Discourse,* ed. Connors, Lunsford, & Ede, pp. 98–114.

Kaufer, David S. "The Influence of Plato's Developing Psychology on His Views of Rhetoric." *Quarterly Journal of Speech,* Vol. 64, pp. 63–78.

Kennedy, George A. *The Art of Persuasion in Greece.* Princeton, NJ: Princeton University Press, 1963.

———. *Classical Rhetoric and its Christian and Secular Tradition from Ancient to Modern Times.* Chapel Hill, NC: University of North Carolina Press, 1980.

Kerford, G.B. *The Sophistic Movement.* Cambridge: Cambridge University Press, 1981.

Keuls, Eva C. *The Reign of the Phallus: Sexual Politics in Ancient Athens.* New York: Harper & Row, 1985.

Kinneavy, James L. "Restoring the Humanities: The Return of Rhetoric from Exile." In *The Rhetorical Tradition and Modern Writing,* Ed. James J. Murphy. New York: Modern Language Association, 1982, pp. 19–28.

———. *A Theory of Discourse: The Aims of Discourse.* New York: Norton, 1971.

Kirk, G.S., Raven, J.E., & Schofield, M. *The Presocratic Philosophers: A Critical History with a Selection of Texts.* 2nd ed. Cambridge: Cambridge University Press, 1983.

Knoblauch, C.H., & Brannon, Lil. *Rhetorical Traditions and the Teaching of Writing.* Upper Montclair, NJ: Boynton/Cook, 1984.

Langer, Susanne K. *Mind: An Essay on Human Feeling.* Vol. I. Baltimore: Johns Hopkins University Press, 1967.

———. *Philosophy in a New Key: A Study in the Symbolism of Reason, Rite, and Art.* 3rd ed. Cambridge, MA: Harvard University Press, 1980.

Lentz, Tony M. *Orality and Literacy in Hellenic Greece.* Carbondale, IL: Southern Illinois University Press, 1989.

Liddell, H.G., & Scott, R. *A Greek-English Lexicon.* 9th ed. Oxford: Clarendon Press, 1980.

Lord, Albert B. *The Singer of Tales.* New York: Atheneum, 1976.

Lovejoy, A.O. et al. *A Documentary History of Primitivism and Related Ideas.* Vol. I. Baltimore: Johns Hopkins University Press, 1935.

———. "The Meaning of *Physis.*" *Philosophical Review,* 1909.

Lunsford, Andrea A., & Ede, Lisa S. "On Distinctions between Classical and Modern Rhetoric." *Essays on Classical Rhetoric and Modern Discourse.* Carbondale, IL: Southern Illinois University Press, 1984, pp. 37–49.

Mackin, John H. *Classical Rhetoric for Modern Discourse: An Art of Invention, Arrangement, and Style for Readers, Speakers, and Writers.* New York: Free Press, 1969.

Macrorie, Ken. *Uptaught.* New York: Hayden Book Co., 1970.

Mahony, Patrick. "Marshall McLuhan in the Light of Classical Rhetoric." *College*

*Composition and Communication.* Vol. 20, pp. 12–17.

Marrou, H.I. *A History of Education in Antiquity.* Trans. George Lamb. Madison, WI: University of Wisconsin Press, 1982.

McKeon, Richard (Ed.). *Introduction to Aristotle.* New York: Random House, 1947.

_____ . "Rhetoric in the Middle Ages." *Speculum.* Vol. 17 (January 1942), pp. 1–32.

McLuhan, Marshall. *The Gutenberg Galaxy: The Making of Typographic Man.* Toronto: University of Toronto Press, 1962.

_____ . *Understanding Media: The Extensions of Man.* New York: New American Library, 1964.

Matthews, Robert J. "What Did Archimedes Mean by *Chrysos?*" *Difference in Translation.* Ed. Joseph F. Graham. Ithaca, NY: Cornell University Press, 1985, pp. 149–164.

Moffett, James. *Teaching the Universe of Discourse.* Boston: Houghton Mifflin, 1968.

Mohrmann, G.P., Stewart, Charles J., & Ochs, Donovan J. (Eds.). *Explorations in Rhetorical Criticism.* University Park, PA: Pennsylvania State University Press, 1973.

Montale, Eugenio. *The Second Life of Art: Selected Essays of Eugenio Montale.* Trans. and Ed. Jonathan Galassi. New York: Ecco, 1982.

Moss, Jean Dietz. "Prolegomenon: The Revival of Practical Reasoning." In *Rhetoric and Praxis,* Ed. Jean Dietz Moss, pp. 1–21.

Moss, Jean Dietz (Ed.). *Rhetoric and Praxis: The Contribution of Classical Rhetoric to Practical Reasoning.* Washington, D C: Catholic University of America Press, 1986.

Murphy, James J. (Ed.). *The Rhetorical Tradition and Modern Writing.* New York: Modern Language Association, 1982.

_____ (Ed.). *A Synoptic History of Classical Rhetoric.* New York: Random House, 1972.

Myres, J.L. *The Political Ideas of the Greeks.* London: Edward Arnold & Co., 1927.

Nadeau, Ray. "Delivery in Ancient Times: Homer to Quintilian." *Quarterly Journal of Speech.* Vol 50 (1964), pp. 53–60.

Neel, Jasper. *Plato, Derrida, and Writing.* Carbondale, IL: Southern Illinois University Press, 1988.

Nussbaum, Martha. "Talking It Through." *Times Literary Supplement.* August 7, 1987, p. 850.

Ochs, Donovan J. "Cicero's *Topica:* A Process View of Invention." In *Explorations in Rhetoric: Studies in Honor of Douglas Ehninger.* Ed. Ray E. McKerrow. Glenview, IL: Scott, Foresman, 1982, pp. 107–118.

Ohmann, Richard. *English in America: A Radical View of the Profession.* New York: Oxford University Press, 1976.

Ong, Walter J. "McLuhan as Teacher: The Future Is a Thing of the Past." In *Journal of Communication,* Vol. 31, pp. 129–135.

_____ . *Orality and Literacy: The Technologizing of the Word.* London: Methuen, 1982.

_____ . *The Presence of the Word: Some Prolegomena for Cultural and Religious*

*History.* 2nd ed. Minneapolis, MN: University of Minnesota Press, 1981.

_____ . *Ramus, Method, and the Decay of Dialogue: From the Art of Discourse to the Art of Reason.* Cambridge, MA: Harvard University Press, 1958.

_____ . *Rhetoric, Romance, and Technology.* Ithaca, NY: Cornell University Press, 1971.

"Origin Myth of Acoma." In *American Indian Literature.* Ed. Alan R. Velie. Norman, OK: University of Oklahoma Press, 1979, pp. 12–28.

*Oxford Classical Dictionary.* Ed. N.G.L. Hammond & H. H. Scullard. 2nd ed. Oxford: Clarendon Press, 1970.

Parry, Milman. *The Making of Homeric Verse: The Collected Papers of Milman Parry,* Ed. Adam Parry. Oxford: Clarendon Press, 1971.

Pater, Walter. *Plato and Platonism: A Series of Lectures.* London: Macmillan, 1910.

Plato. *Gorgias,* Trans. W.C. Helmbold. Indianapolis: Bobbs-Merrill, 1976.

_____ . *Ion.* In *The Dialogues of Plato.* Vol. I. Trans. Benjamin Jowett. New York: Random House, 1937, pp. 285–297.

_____ . *Letter VII.* In *Phaedrus and Letters VII and VIII.* Trans. Walter Hamilton. Harmondsworth, England: Penguin Books, 1973, pp. 111–150.

_____ . *Phaedo.* In *Plato.* Vol. I. Loeb Classical Library. Trans. Harold North Fowler. Cambridge, MA: Harvard University Press, 1982, pp. 195–403.

_____ . *Phaedrus.* Trans. W.C. Helmbold and W.G. Rabinowitz. Indianapolis, IN: Bobbs-Merrill, 1956.

_____ . *Protagoras.* In *Protagoras and Meno.* Trans. W.K.C. Guthrie. Harmondsworth, England: Penguin Books, 1956, pp. 38–100.

_____ . *The Republic of Plato.* Trans. Francis MacDonald Cornford. London: Oxford University Press, 1941.

_____ . *Symposium.* In *The Dialogues of Plato.* Trans. Benjamin Jowett. New York: Random House, 1937, pp. 301–345.

Plochmann, George Kimball, & Robinson, Franklin E. *A Friendly Companion to Plato's Gorgias.* Carbondale, IL: Southern Illinois University Press, 1988.

Polanyi, Michael. *Knowing and Being.* Chicago: University of Chicago Press, 1969.

Pomeroy, Sarah B. *Goddesses, Whores, Wives, and Slaves: Women in Classical Antiquity.* New York: Schocken Books, 1975.

Poulakos, John. "Argument, Practicality, and Eloquence in Isocrates' *Helen.*" *Rhetorica.* Vol. 4, No. 1 (Winter 1986), pp. 1–19.

_____ . "Gorgias's *Encomium to Helen* and the Defense of Rhetoric." *Rhetorica.* Vol. 1, No. 2 (Autumn 1983), pp. 1–16.

Quandahl, Ellen. "Aristotle's *Rhetoric:* Reinterpreting Invention." *Rhetoric Review.* Vol. 4, No. 2 (January 1986), pp. 128–137.

Quintilian. *On the Teaching of Speaking and Writing.* Ed. James J. Murphy. Trans. John Selby Watson. Carbondale, IL: Southern Illinois University Press, 1987.

Ransom, John Crowe. "Criticism as Pure Speculation." *Criticism: The Major Statements.* Ed. Charles Kaplan. 2nd ed. New York: St. Martin's Press, 1986, pp. 450–460.

*Rhetorica Ad Herennium.* Trans. Harry Kaplan. Cambridge, MA: Harvard University Press, 1954.

de Romilly, Jacqueline. *Rhetoric and Magic in Ancient Greece.* Cambridge, MA: Harvard University Press, 1975.

Rose, Mike. "Sophisticated, Ineffective Books: The Dismantling of Process in Composition Texts." *College Composition and Communication.* 32 (1981), pp. 65–73.

Runes, Dagobert D. *Dictionary of Philosophy.* Totowa, NJ: Littlefield, Adams, 1975.

de Saussure, Ferdinand. *Course in General Linguistics.* Ed. Charles Bally & Albert Sechehaye. Trans. Wade Baskin. New York: McGraw-Hill, 1966.

Scaglione, Aldo. *The Classical Theory of Composition from Its Origins to the Present: A Historical Survey.* Chapel Hill, NC: University of North Carolina Press, 1972.

Schilb, John. "Differences, Displacements, and Disruptions: Toward Revisionary Histories of Rhetoric." *Pre/Text.* Vol. 8, Nos. 1–2 (1987), pp. 29–44.

_____ . "The History of Rhetoric and the Rhetoric of History." *Pre/Text.* Vol. 7, Nos. 1 & 2 (1986), pp. 11 35.

Shumaker, Wayne. "Flowerets and Sounding Seas: A Study in the Affective Structure of *Lycidas.*" *Publications of the Modern Language Association,* Vol. 66, 1951.

Sophocles. *The Tragedies of Sophocles.* Trans. Edward P. Coleridge. London: G. Bell & Sons, 1910.

Steiner, George. *After Babel: Aspects of Language and Translation.* London: Oxford University Press, 1975.

_____ . *Language and Silence: Essays on Language, Literature, and the Inhuman.* New York: Atheneum, 1970.

Steinhoff, Virginia N. "The *Phaedrus* Idyll as Ethical Play: The Platonic Stance." In *The Rhetorical Tradition and Modern Writing,* Ed. James J. Murphy. New York: Modern Language Association, 1982, pp. 31 45.

"Students' Right to Their Own Language." *College Composition and Communication.* Vol. 25 (1974), pp. 1–32.

Swearingen, C. Jan. "Oral Hermeneutics During the Transition to Literacy: The Contemporary Debate." *Cultural Anthropology.* Vol. 2, No. 1 (June 1986), pp. 138–156.

_____ . "The Rhetor as *Eiron:* Plato's Defense of Dialogue." *Pre/Text.* Vol. 3 (1982), pp. 289–336.

Tate, Allen. "Literature as Knowledge." *Critical Theory Since Plato.* Ed. Hazard Adams. San Diego: Harcourt, 1971, pp. 928–41.

Tate, Gary, and Chapman, David W. "A Survey of Doctoral Programs in Rhetoric and Composition." *Rhetoric Review.* Vol. 5, No. 2 (Spring 1987), pp. 124–134.

Untersteiner, Mario. *The Sophists.* Trans. Kathleen Freeman. New York: Philosophical Library, 1954.

Vickers, Brian. *In Defence of Rhetoric.* New York: Oxford University Press, 1988.

Vitanza, Victor J. "Critical Sub/Versions of the History of Philosophical Rhetoric." *Rhetoric Review.* Vol. 6, No. 1 (Fall 1987), pp. 41–66.

_____ . "'Notes' Towards Historiographies of Rhetorics; or, Rhetorics of the Histories of Rhetorics: Traditional, Revisionary, and Sub/Versive." *Pre/Text.*

Vol. 8 (1987), Nos. 1 & 2, pp. 63–125.

Vygotsky, L. S. *Thought and Language*. Ed. and Trans. Eugenia Hanfmann and Gertude Vakar. Cambridge, MA: MIT Press, 1962.

Waller, Gary F. "A Powerful Silence: 'Theory' in the English Major." *ADE Bulletin*, No. 85, 1986, pp. 31–35.

Weaver, Richard M. *The Ethics of Rhetoric*. Chicago: Henry Regnery, 1953.

_____ . *Language Is Sermonic*. Baton Rouge, LA: Louisiana State University Press, 1970.

Welch, Kathleen E. "Ideology and Freshman Textbook Production: The Place of Theory in Writing Pedagogy." *College Composition and Communication*. Vol. 38, No. 3 (October 1987), pp. 269–282.

Williams, Raymond. *Keywords: A Vocabulary of Culture and Society*. 2nd ed. New York: Oxford University Press, 1983.

Winterowd, W. Ross. "Composition Textbooks: Publisher-Author Relationships." *College Composition and Communication*. Vol. 40, No. 2 (May 1989), pp. 139–151.

Yates, Frances A. *The Art of Memory*. Chicago: University of Chicago Press, 1966.

Young, Richard E., Becker, Alton L., & Pike, Kenneth L. *Rhetoric: Discovery and Change*. New York: Harcourt, Brace & World, 1970.

# Index